*Patrick J. Hurley and*
*American Foreign Policy*

# Patrick J. Hurley and American Foreign Policy

RUSSELL D. BUHITE

Cornell University Press

ITHACA AND LONDON

First published 1973 by Cornell University Press.
Published in the United Kingdom by Cornell University Press Ltd., 2–4 Brook Street, London W1Y 1AA.

International Standard Book Number 0-8014-0751-6
Library of Congress Catalog Card Number 72-10917

Printed in the United States of America by Vail-Ballou Press, Inc.

*Librarians: Library of Congress cataloging information appears on the last page of the book.*

For Mary

# Contents

# Illustrations

(All photographs are from the Western History Collections, University of Oklahoma Library, Norman, Oklahoma.)

*following page 176*

1. Secretary and Mrs. Hurley, New York, December 13, 1930
2. Meeting to consider Philippine independence, September 1, 1931
3. Prime Minister Peter Fraser, General Hurley, and Secretary of State Cordell Hull, Washington, D.C., August 1942
4. General Joseph W. Stilwell and General Hurley, Chungking, November 12, 1943
5. General Chu Teh, General Hurley, and Mao Tse-tung, Yenan, November 7, 1944
6. T. V. Soong, General Albert C. Wedemeyer, Generalissimo Chiang Kai-shek, and General Hurley, November 1944
7. Mao's chief of staff, Mao Tse-tung, Lin Tsu-han, General Hurley, General Chu Teh, Chou En-lai, and Col. David Barrett, Yenan, November 7, 1944
8. General Hurley, Chungking, 1945

# Preface

Doing biography is never an easy task. Dealing with Patrick J. Hurley's life is in some respects especially difficult because he does not fit neatly into any category. He was not an "old guard" Republican, though he often seemed conservative enough and was not uncomfortable with that wing of the party. He was neither a Populist nor a Progressive, though he reflected elements of both. He cannot be considered a prototypical southwestern entrepreneur or businessman, though he never submerged his heritage. He cannot be dismissed as a snake-oil salesman, though he possessed some of the traits. A pragmatist and poorly educated in a formal sense, he seldom mused about the nature of man nor does he appear to have done much philosophical questioning; and while it is possible to draw some conclusions about his views, he never evolved any really organized political theory. His thoughts about United States foreign policy were, moreover, essentially ad hoc.

Most of all Hurley was a kind of careerist, an opportunist, and an accommodator of people in high position, especially of presidents. While he served his country ably in various capacities, some of them requiring considerable sacrifice on his part, his life and work may best be understood in terms of the promotion, for some explicable and some inexplicable reasons, of Hurley—his wealth, influence, and prestige. His life has historical significance, in my judgment, primarily because of his involvement in American foreign policy. I have therefore linked the story of Hurley to some vitally important episodes in two decades of United States foreign policy in an attempt to shed more light on both his life and American policy.

While Hurley was Secretary of War, Philippine independence became a compelling issue for the Hoover administration. Because the Philippines were under the purview of the War Department and because his close relationship with President Hoover impelled the President to heed his advice, he played a prominent role in shaping policy on this critical question.

Later in the decade, as a private emissary for oilman Harry Sinclair, Hurley negotiated a settlement with the Cárdenas government of Mexico providing payment for Sinclair's property expropriated by the Mexicans. The agreement broke an impasse in the expropriation controversy and led to a general settlement with the oil companies on the eve of American entry into World War II. The issue also brought Hurley into closer communication with the State Department and President Roosevelt.

During World War II, President Roosevelt, who became as contemptuous of State Department procedures as he was impatient with Secretary Hull, frequently by-passed the Department by using personal envoys to conduct American diplomacy. Attracted by Hurley's personality and acting upon the recommendations of advisers, the President entrusted him with several assignments. Roosevelt sent him first to the South Pacific to organize a supply mission to General MacArthur in the Philippines, then briefly to New Zealand as minister. Later he sent Hurley as his personal representative on "fact finding" missions to the Middle East and the Soviet Union, and in 1943 encouraged Hurley to play a role in shaping American policy toward Iran. In 1944, in the most significant of these wartime assignments, he dispatched Hurley as his special envoy to China to compose relations between General Joseph Stilwell and Chiang Kai-shek and help adjust other Sino-American differences. Hurley, his status eventually changed to ambassador, also worked from November 1944 until his departure for Washington in September 1945 for a resolution of China's internal conflict between the Kuomintang and

the Communists. These were matters of considerable consequence which placed Hurley, if not always in the center, at least
on the periphery of some of the major decisions of his generation.

This book was inspired by the lack of an objective and schol-
arly study of Hurley. In 1932, Parker La Moore, a journalist
friend of Hurley's, published a brief glamorizing biography entitled "*Pat*" *Hurley: The Story of an American* in the hope of
furthering Hurley's political career. In 1956, Don Lohbeck, also
a journalist, published a more nearly complete but "authorized"
biography. Lohbeck, prior to undertaking his work, had been
editor of Gerald L. K. Smith's monthly magazine, *The Cross and
the Flag*, and had sought to establish a right-wing nationalist
political party to be led by General MacArthur and Senators John
Bricker and William Knowland. His views, especially his reputed
anti-Semitism, seemed so extreme that when he approached Hurley about undertaking his biography, Hurley had serious reservations. After some serious thought and consultations with friends,
however, Hurley granted his consent. What emerged is not, to
say the least, an unbiased account.

Anyone undertaking a study of this nature naturally contracts
a multitude of debts along the way. My own work has been generously assisted by so many people that it is possible to name
only a few. I owe my thanks to all the archivists, curators, search-
ers, and librarians who have given so unselfishly of their time,
and to the many people—those who knew him in official capacities as well as those who were friends or acquaintances—who
answered my questions about Hurley. I owe special debts to Jack
Haley of the Manuscripts Division, University of Oklahoma, for
his many kindnesses and more specifically his help with the Hurley Papers; to Gilbert C. Fite for his many constructive criticisms
of the manuscript; to Arrell M. Gibson, Louise Welsh, and Donald
Berthrong, who talked with me about Oklahoma history and led
me to books on the subject; to Paul A. Varg, who shared with
me his knowledge of and interest in the China question and
whose comments on various aspects of the work were extremely

helpful; to Maryon Kaplan, who typed the manuscript; and finally, to my wife, Mary Buhite, for reasons that I could only inadequately describe.

I wish to acknowledge grants from the American Philosophical Society, the Kittredge Foundation, the Research Associates of the University of Denver, and the Faculty Research Committee at the University of Oklahoma which facilitated my research and writing. I also want to thank the editor of the *Pacific Historical Review* for permission to use material previously published in that journal, and the Western History Collections, University of Oklahoma Library, for the photographs appearing in this volume.

RUSSELL D. BUHITE

*Norman, Oklahoma*

Patrick J. Hurley and
American Foreign Policy

# I

# Formative Years

That part of the country known today as Oklahoma was, for much of the nineteenth century, Indian territory into which the United States pushed thousands of native Americans whose fertile lands in the southeastern and gulf states it appropriated for its citizens. Here the Five Civilized Tribes joined countless other Indian groups, ostensibly to live their lives forever unmolested by greedy white settlers. Over the course of time, the United States government divided this territory into separate parts or nations in which the major tribal groups established their own governments, developed education, and set up their own social and legal institutions and economies: the Cherokees in the northeast; the Creeks in the central region; the Chickasaws in the south central; the Seminoles in the east central; and the Choctaws in the southeast.

White explorers had previously entered the territory and, though the region in the mid-nineteenth century was dominated by Indians, various other whites soon began to appear; there were soldiers, and missionaries, traders and farmers, renegades and cowboys; most of them living in the various tribal nations upon the sufferance of the Indians. As might be expected, economic development in the Indian nations attracted the most white settlers, with ranching in the Chickasaw Nation, farming in the Cherokee Nation, and railroad building and coal mining in the Choctaw Nation responsible for much of the immigration.

Although it did not attract widespread attention at first, some of the explorers in the area of the Choctaw Nation found surface deposits of coal which they used as a fuel for blacksmithing and heating. Later, in the 1870's, as the newly completed Missouri, Kansas, and Texas railroad sought ways to promote its business, increased interest was focused on coal; the railroad realized the dearth of manufacturing and agriculture along its line, needed the revenue available in shipping the black mineral, and began entering into lease arrangements with the Indian owners of the land. In 1875, a four-foot vein of bituminous coal was discovered near the McAlester station; and the M.K.T. promptly entered into a lease arrangement to mine it. Since the land actually belonged to the Choctaws, the railroad was compelled at the same time to pay a royalty to the Choctaw council.

Similar arrangements were worked out with the Indians in other areas of the Choctaw Nation, and before long coal shafts dotted the countryside along the M.K.T. line. Like the mining areas of the East the region soon attracted thousands of immigrants, many of them Italians and eastern Europeans as well as some Irish who brought their families to Indian territory to make a new life for themselves; they helped build such new towns as McAlester, Hartshorne, Coalgate, Krebs, and Lehigh, communities in which one still finds more significant European cultural impact than anywhere else in Oklahoma. In most respects these towns, which varied in size in the nineteenth century from several hundred to several thousand, were of the same genre as their eastern counterparts: dust and grime and filth were everywhere; the miners lived in rectangular-shaped, black, weather-boarded, company-owned shacks, unvarying in appearance or comfort except when some enterprising occupant whitewashed his fence or privy; waste, human and animal, was dumped into open sewers along the edges of the dirt streets which curved their way through the community; outhouses compounded outhouses adding their stench to the open sewers, and in the sizzlingly hot summers attracted millions upon millions of disease-carrying flies and other insects; company stores offering limited fare and charging exorbitant prices fleeced the miners who had nowhere else to buy. The company accounted only to God and to the Indians who, as long as the royalties flowed in, allowed both miners and company to function on their land. Life, if one survived, was dull, drab, and incredibly hard. One of the most unsightly of these mining towns in the Choctaw Nation was Lehigh, a small community served by a branch line of the M.K.T. and located about four miles from metropolitan Atoka.

Among the immigrant families moving into the coal-mining section of Indian territory was that of Pierce O'Neil Hurley, a pugnacious, fiery-tempered and nearly destitute Irishman who had cast his lot first in Texas before entering the Choctaw Nation. Pierce Hurley was born in 1835 in Barristown near Waterford, Ireland, the first son of Robert Hurley and Nancy Power Hurley who made their living by farming. As the oldest child, Pierce inherited the farm upon his parents' death and, had circumstances allowed, probably would have lived out his own life tilling his soil in Ireland. But lack of fortune with his crops and his own involvement in the Irish Republican movement forced him to sell the farm and ultimately to flee his homeland. Pierce left Ireland in the late 1870's, came to the United States, landing in Galveston, Texas, and for a while wandered about as a farm or ranch hand, just barely eeking out a living.

He had earlier met Mary Kelly, married her, and begun raising a family. Mary, a quiet, gentle lady, much younger and much different in disposition from her husband, was born in 1854 in Bishop's Court near Waterford, Ireland, the daughter of Patrick Christopher and Abigail Welch Kelly, devout and prosperous farmers who apparently valued Christian education. Upon her parents' death (her mother died when she was born, her father, when she was eight) young Mary was placed in school with the Ursuline Order where she received formal education until she was about eighteen. Shortly thereafter she married Pierce Hurley and followed him to the United States.

Using some money left from the sale of his farm in Ireland and what little he had saved, Pierce in 1880 took his bride and family (two young children) to Luling, Texas, where he purchased a house and some land and attempted to raise cotton. But, owing to his own ineptitude in handling the new crop, the difficulty he encountered with the Texas climate, and the loss of his house by fire, his venture ended in utter failure. Embittered at his experience in Texas, which had been frustrating from the start, Pierce decided in 1882 to take his family, now including three children, north into Indian territory.

Arriving near Lehigh in what is now Coal County, where Pierce hoped to do some tenant farming and eventually perhaps get some land of his own, the family began casting about for a place to live. By good fortune they learned about an unoccupied house on land owned by Benjamin F. Smallwood, later a chief of the Choctaws, who, with help from numerous tenants, raised cattle and farmed a 500-acre spread in addition to looking after the extensive tribal interests. Smallwood agreed to take on another tenant, and the Hurley family moved into a little log house on the prairie. Here, some six months later, on January 8, 1883, Mary Hurley gave birth to the one member of the brood who was to become nationally prominent, a son, Patrick Jay Hurley.

Young Patrick, or "Paddy" as his mother called him, thrived in the country atmosphere, as did the other Hurley children. Their house was small but relatively comfortable, the open fields offered an appealing place to play, and the livestock on the Smallwood land proved an added attraction to the youngsters. Moreover, "Ben" Smallwood was a beneficent landlord who paid attention to his tenants and who was attracted to the Hurley children, especially to young "Paddy" whom he came to adore as one of his own. But Pierce Hurley seemed destined to fail, and three successive years of relatively sparse rainfall, which made sharecropping extremely unprofitable, combined with a second disastrous fire, sent him looking for another job. He went to the coal community of Lehigh where he got a job with the Atoka Coal Company as a coal digger at $2.50 a day, and then took his family to the little mining village of Phillips about two miles from Lehigh. Here the family moved into an ugly, run-down, four-room shack near shaft number six. The house, which the Hurleys were forced to share with another family, was clearly an unsatisfactory accommodation after the relatively comfortable place on the Smallwood ranch and a deplorable situation in which to raise children. Later, however, the family was able to move into a different house in Phillips where there was a small apple orchard and sufficient space to permit the planting of vegetables and the keeping of a couple of cows and some chickens to assist in putting food on the table. Pierce gave the new place some character by whitewashing the outbuildings and the rocks in the yard, and Mrs. Hurley, while she lived, made the house as comfortable for the family as one would expect under the circumstances.

Young Patrick experienced a relatively happy childhood in this home, though he always had to work around the house to help keep the family going. Yet there was time for play, and for horseback riding with the other boys in the neighborhood, and for visits to the Smallwood ranch. Smallwood has to be considered the first major influence outside his immediate family on the young Hurley. A generous man, then in his late fifties, with a grown family of his own, he doted on the young boy, gave him presents, and took him to his home as frequently as possible; more importantly, his communication with the youngster was like that of a grandfather with a cherished grandson, and a closeness developed between them which was never duplicated in young Hurley's relationship with his own father. It was apparently through Smallwood that Hurley first learned about books, for, pedestrian as the materials in the Smallwood collection were, the chief's library was one of the few in the whole Choctaw Nation. There is little evidence that the Smallwood library stimulated a great hunger for knowledge in young Hurley, but the fact that the chief read to him often and allowed him access to his books was a significant step in his education.

As young Patrick grew, the opportunity for play diminished, and the burden of helping to support the family increased, for his father, as in his previous jobs, found it impossible to make enough money to meet his familial responsibilities. Consequently, in 1894, when Patrick was eleven years old, Pierce, like many a father in mining towns across the nation, took his son and got him a job in the mines. He was hired as a trapper boy in mine number six in Phillips, where his job was to work one of the traps in a system designed to keep fresh air in the mine; for this he received $.75 per day for a nine-and-one-half-hour day. Frontier communities were comprised of a rough lot of men, and mining towns contained some of the roughest, so young Hurley quickly began to lose whatever boyhood innocence remained as he associated with the hard bitten miners; like other boys of the period forced out of the nest by the material needs of their families, he grew up rapidly; after 1894 he was largely self-supporting; after 1896 he would assume considerable responsibility for supporting his family.

In February of 1896, when Patrick was thirteen years old, his mother died shortly after giving birth to her ninth child. To any boy the loss of a mother is a tremendous shock; to the young Hurley, who had no firm relationship with his blustering, ill-tempered father and who depended upon the gentle guidance of his mother, it caused deep trauma. He never got over it, and throughout his life Mrs. Hurley's teachings and love, magnified by her sudden death, remained his most precious memories of his family. Mrs. Hurley, a tall angular woman, possessed what her neighbors referred to as a mark of refinement; she was pretty in a rough way, though worn by childbearing and toil as the wife of a miner and farmer. She was a devout Catholic and sought to impart to her children the teaching of her faith. Devoted to her children, she kept a clean house, provided ample meals and clothing when money was available to do so, and began the process of educating her brood; she attempted to gather them around her daily to read to them from the Bible or from other books or magazines she had acquired and would have them read passages back to her and recite important verses. In this way she taught her children how to read; through constant effort she also taught them to write, for, having received some education herself she knew of its tremendous importance. It seems everyone who knew her considered her a kind, gentle, intelligent, loving mother, a remarkable and refined woman several cuts above the average miner's wife.

In contrast was Hurley's father. It would be a mistake to describe him as a ne'er-do-well, but it would be just as great a mistake to say that he was an adequate father. Small and benign in appearance with a white beard, he was in the words of one of his daughters, a "brilliant, moody, sensitive, irritable, erratic man with a violent and explosive temper." [1] He was at the same time easily brought to tears by anything beautiful or pathetic; in some ways he was as unstable as his wife was sturdy. He was only a nominal Catholic, never able to accept the teachings of the church, and was a kind of born rebel who liked to argue, "cuss," and fight and was not discriminating as to his opponent. Compounding Pierce Hurley's instability and adding a corroding bitterness was his inner knowledge that he was a failure; though a hardworking man, he was the one who lost the family home in Ireland after generations had held it; he "lost his shirt" as a farmer in Texas; he could not succeed on the Smallwood ranch; in the mines, try as he would, he could hardly make enough to keep his family. He hated the mines and disliked leaving the farm to go there and had never been by choice a pioneer; he disliked unsettled places and longed for the ancient city of Waterford in his native Ireland—he proudly unfurled his Irish flags on every Irish holiday.

No evidence exists that he was abusive to his family, but he did not pay much attention to the children, except to whale them when they misbehaved or when his sour disposition moved

[1] Mrs. Alice Mackey to Grant Foreman, Oct. 9, 1942, Hurley Papers, Manuscripts Division, Bizzell Library, University of Oklahoma, Norman, Oklahoma. Unless otherwise noted, this is the source of the references that follow. This sketch of Hurley's background and his family is based mainly on letters and interviews contained in the Grant Foreman materials, Boxes 9, 10, and 11, of the Hurley collection.

him to do so. He spent a good part of his spare time with the other miners and, while he was not an alcoholic, occupied many an evening getting drunk with them on "Choctaw beer," a drink made of barley, hops, tobacco, and fishberries, and "raising hell" at the expense of his family who needed the money for other things. Patrick had very little love for his father and never sought to emulate him, though it seems apparent that he did inherit some of the father's traits: his sensitivity, his unwillingness to avoid a scrap regardless of the consequences, and his extreme explosiveness of temper.

After the death of his mother, Patrick continued his work in the mines because his father needed the contribution he made to the family's income. His job changed to that of mule skinner in which he hauled coal cars out of the mine and looked after the mules; he received an increase in pay to about $2.00 per day. But intermittent strikes, especially the long and violent one of 1898, began to impress him with the need to do something else for a living and to get some kind of an education to enable him to do so. Meanwhile he had begun elementary school in the class-room of one Thomas Golightly, a Scotsman and laborer turned schoolmaster, who had opened a night school for the miners in Phillips. Though he had never previously attended school, the teenage boy impressed Golightly with his diligence in problem solving and his intelligent questions: "He was a very earnest, persistent student, and if there were matters or subjects, which he did not fully understand, by the time I was through answering his questions, he knew about as much as I did about them." [2] Golightly encouraged young Hurley to continue his studies, forc-ing the boy to re-examine his life and his goals, and Hurley al-ways looked upon his association with the Scottish schoolmaster as a turning point in his career.

By 1898 the strapping fifteen-year-old Irishman began to dream of striking out for himself in some less harsh environment. The

[2] T. E. Golightly to Foreman, June 24, 1941.

immediate cause of his decision to move, however, was his father's marriage. Pierce Hurley's new wife was a woman he contacted through a matrimonial agency and one described by the neighbors as a shrewish "hell cat" who made life unbearable for Patrick and the other Hurley children; with ambivalent feelings toward his father and a stepmother whom he could not abide, Patrick wished to get away.[3] His decision was only one step in the tragic collapse of the Hurley family. His older brother left home, living for a time in Texas, after which he changed his name, became a prospector, and disappeared, not to be seen again by Patrick for 45 years. His oldest sister entered a convent; one of his younger sisters, Monica, was killed when she attempted to pull a loaded shotgun off a bed in the home; the youngest child had died shortly after Mrs. Hurley; later Patrick's favorite brother Johnie, whom he adored, fled from home after a beating by his father who had grown angry because the boy was late getting home from play. The boy went to see Patrick, who was then in Muskogee and who convinced him to return home. On the way, he attempted to jump a freight train at McAlester, was thrown under the wheels and killed. Years later Hurley wrote his sister: "I know you remember how I loved Johnie. I have never gotten over it."[4]

With the beginning of the Spanish-American war in 1898, young Hurley decided to do his patriotic duty and seek fame and fortune as a soldier. When Theodore Roosevelt issued his call for his "Rough Rider" unit, he went to Houston to enlist. Since he was only fifteen years old he was not eligible for service and ultimately was caught in his attempt to falsify his age. He then returned to eastern Oklahoma to the Creek Nation and found a job as a hand on the ranch of one Homer Spaulding, his first employment outside the mines. Later he worked feeding cattle on a ranch along the Arkansas River and still later on a farm in the area. He was always fond of describing himself as a

[3] Interview of Terence O'Hara by Foreman, Feb. 14, 1942.
[4] Hurley to Mackey, Oct., 1918.

cowboy and took pride in his experience. Some measure of his seriousness and sense of responsibility during these years is evident in the fact that he drew upon his limited earnings to contribute to his family.

While working on the farm he met a young mixed-blood Cherokee his own age named Thomas Madden with whom he became close friends and with whose family he frequently visited. Young Madden was a student at Indian University, a Baptist school for Indians, later to become Bacone College, located at Muskogee. He convinced Hurley that he should try for admission to the school and appealed to the president, Dr. J. H. Scott, to accept Hurley into the program and help him find a job. Indian University in 1900 was at best no more than an academy in which young Indians were given a very crude equivalent of a secondary education and, though one could go on to get a B.A. degree, to call the school a university was a considerable misapplication of the term; the institution had few teachers of any distinction and almost no library. Even so, Hurley's qualifications were so meager as to make his success there highly questionable; at age seventeen he had never attended day school, and the short period in Golightly's class was his only formal schooling. Nor had he done any significant independent reading.

His prior education consisted of the lessons he learned at his mother's knee and the earthy philosophy and language he picked up from miners and cowboys. Moreover, Hurley's Irish Catholic background did not accord with the normal admission requirements at Indian University. Nevertheless, he was accepted, partly because of Madden's pleas, but more importantly because of the recommendation of a Baptist missionary to the Choctaws, J. S. Murrow, who knew Hurley when he was a young boy visiting the Smallwood ranch and who was a close friend of the president of the school.

Extremely grateful, young Hurley sought to make the most of his chance at an education, which was one way, he had begun to realize, to escape the drabness and dreariness of the coal fields.

To support himself, he took jobs driving the school hack between the campus and town, feeding the institution's livestock, and on weekends and summers working in a drugstore in Muskogee. He also threw himself into his studies as few of his colleagues did at the school; he worked as one who knew the alternatives and was so far behind; and, as a result of his efforts, he managed to finish his high school studies in one year. He then went on to the college section of the school, completing his B.A. in 1905. He continued to work hard; he unquestionably made great strides intellectually, and he graduated near the head of his class.

But the shortcomings of an education at Indian University as compared to other more established institutions were all too apparent. He was forced to read his textbooks, to recite some poetry and quotations from the Bible, the Declaration of Independence, and Lincoln's Gettysburg Address, and to do his exercises in algebra; this for Hurley required much time and effort, but he was not challenged to read widely nor was he culturally broadened by the academic life at the school. He read some American history and considered it his favorite subject, but again, aside from his textbooks, the opportunities for any advanced study were limited. Hurley himself said later in what must be interpreted as part apologia for Indian University that he considered himself fortunate to have attended a school that possessed few books for it gave him the opportunity to digest what he did read and to avoid cluttering his mind.[5]

The playing fields of Oklahoma, like those of Eton for many English boys, accorded better with Hurley's capabilities and interests than did the classroom. He did not neglect the latter, but it was in the social setting that the young Irishman threw off the hardship of his early youth and joined in the extravaganza of young Americans on the make. Hurley was a minor sensation, and his successes and sudden climb from penury and drabness probably led him quite intuitively in later years to play the game

[5] Hurley statement in Memoirs begun with Lee Bowen, Bowen MSS.

in accordance with the outgoing and aspiring who measured success in terms of wealth and acceptance by the business community.

The former miner and cowboy adjusted readily to the more carefree aspects of small college life. Tall at six feet two inches, and handsome with a shock of rich auburn hair and bright smile, he became one of the most popular boys in the school. He sang in the choir, helped edit the school paper, and participated in a number of plays. But it was in athletics that he excelled. He was captain of the football team, and was quite good, though the Indian University team did not have especially outstanding opponents. He also played baseball, which was his best sport, and like many American boys dreamed of a professional career.

The years that Hurley spent at Indian University were critical in his life. He received at least a rough education on which foundation his native intelligence could build; it was an education that opened doors to future business success and implanted in him faith in hard work, shrewdness, and acumen, although largely devoid of deeper philosophical questioning, exposure to other values, other ways of thought, or the rise and fall of societies. It was well attuned to success in Tulsa but scarcely contributed to facing the obstinacy with which political groupings would fight for survival in Chungking.

While life at Indian University bred in him little philosophical understanding and small appreciation of literature or the arts, it did then spark him to acquire knowledge in some highly practical subjects. He thus went on to achieve a comprehension of economics and business and of politics that can only be described as sophisticated; in addition he became a highly successful lawyer, with an acute awareness of the statutes pertaining to the oil industry.

It was also during this period that he seems to have confirmed his religious beliefs. As a teenager he developed serious questions about the religion of his family; he wanted to be a good Catholic mainly because of his memory of his devout mother, but he could

not, though he did not officially break with the church. His association with the Baptists at Indian University, however, pulled
him further from Catholicism and made him much more the
independent spirit. As a result, he never joined a church nor accepted any particular creed, though he did believe in a higher
being and got down on his knees and prayed every night of his
life before retiring. Hurley's religion was a constant worry to his
sister Nan, and she frequently wrote and spoke with him admonishing him for his unorthodox beliefs. After one such admonition
he wrote another sister, Alice, saying, "my memories of our dear
mother and her beautiful devotion to the Catholic Church have
sealed my lips on any opinions I may have which are in conflict
with the teachings of the Roman Church. But, Alice, I've got 'em
and they are part of me and I would have to be a hypocrite if I
appeared to be a good Catholic; I am not going to be that. I am
going to stay on good terms with myself even if I have to be
looked upon as a black sheep." [6]

Upon graduating from Indian University, Hurley took a job
at Muskogee as a clerk in the Indian Service, where his main
tasks were to copy deeds and to issue orders to Indian police for
removing white squatters from Indian land allotments. During
the 1880's and 1890's more white settlers moved into Indian territory, and prospective homesteaders looked longingly toward it
with a view to locating there. Pressures by these citizens and by
the railroads who wished to see the area developed further economically resulted in dividing what is now Oklahoma into Oklahoma territory (in the west and central region) and a more restricted Indian territory in the east. In 1889, after making several
deals with the Indians, the U.S. government opened up the
Oklahoma territory for homesteaders. Meanwhile, immigration
to Indian territory intensified as well, until by 1905 whites out-
numbered Indians by about seven to one even in that region.
Through much of the eighties and nineties all land of the Five

[6] To Mackey, May 13, 1926.

Civilized Tribes remained in the hands of each tribe; there was no private ownership. And all political authority rested with the Indians. However, a series of federal laws constituting encroachments on Indian prerogatives began to change this situation, with the Curtis Act of 1898, sponsored by Congressman Charles Curtis of Kansas, giving whites the right to vote, establishing public schools, and eliminating the tribal courts. As pressures for statehood built up in Oklahoma territory and after various plans were considered, the government finally determined that both the Oklahoma and Indian territories would be brought into the Union under one banner. But Congress then had to deal with the question of the tribal lands, which meant changing the system to provide for private ownership; this the U.S. government began doing, after securing the reluctant agreement of the Indians, by parceling out private allotments of various sizes to individual Indians. Hurley, as clerk in the Muskogee office, was commissioned to write directives for evicting whites so the Indians could assume private control.

Leaders of the Five Civilized Tribes disliked the change from tribal ownership of land; they were similarly distressed at the prospect of statehood which would mean fusion with Oklahoma territory. Consequently, in 1905 they held a convention at Muskogee and drew up a constitution for a separate Indian state named Sequoyah. This move did not ultimately deter the drive toward statehood but did reinforce the position of Indian territory when Congress established the procedure for creating the new state. Hurley's position in the Indian Service allowed him to become acquainted with Indian problems, while the beginning struggles regarding statehood—which he witnessed but had no part in— gave him a valuable lesson in political science.

During his tenure in the Indian Service, Hurley spent much of his spare time reading law under the direction of James H. Huckleberry, a member of a local law firm in Muskogee, who opened up his office to him and loaned him his books. His interest stimulated by this experience, Hurley decided that he wanted to become a lawyer; he approached his supervisor about a transfer to Washington where he might work and at the same time acquire some formal legal training. When his request was rejected, he set out on his own for the nation's capital. Arriving in Washington in 1907, Hurley, practically penniless, had two priorities: to find a job to support himself and to get admitted to one of the city's law schools. The latter proved difficult, for his previous education was deficient in many respects; he was summarily rejected by both Georgetown and George Washington Universities before finally securing a place in the night classes at the National University Law School. Meanwhile, he drove a cab and held various other jobs to scrape enough money together to complete his degree. In 1908 he was awarded a Bachelor of Laws degree. During this brief stay in Washington, Hurley seems to have been too busy to pay much attention to national affairs or to assimilate the mood of the city, for there is no record of his comment on any important issues. Yet he did get around some and in particular enjoyed his first experience at the theater that year.

Prior to going to the capital he had consulted John R. Thomas, Judge of the United States Court at Muskogee regarding the best place in Oklahoma to begin practicing law once he achieved his degree. The judge advised Tulsa because of the oil discovered in the region in 1901. In 1907, the year Hurley went to Washington, Indian territory and Oklahoma territory were fused together and brought into the Union as the new state of Oklahoma. Heeding Judge Thomas' advice and aware of the various opportunities available in the oil district in a new state, Hurley, upon receiving his LL.B., returned to Oklahoma and settled in Tulsa, a city then of about 7,000 people. He quickly passed his bar examination and joined a law firm—that of Gregg, Gormley, and Hurley.

Hurley thus began the business ascent that was to result in his becoming a millionaire by the time he entered President Hoover's cabinet in 1929. As he established himself in the legal profession, his fees increased until by 1910–1911 he was earning a very generous annual income; and with the dissolution of the firm of

Gregg, Gormley, and Hurley in 1909, he developed what was to become the largest independent practice in Tulsa; he handled mainly litigations regarding land titles and oil rights. Much of the money he received in fees, on a few occasions as much as $40,000 to $50,000 a case, he invested in real estate, which, as the city grew, tripled and quadrupled in value. He also invested modestly in oil, but, during this period of his life as later, such investments were meager compared to what he put into land and real properties.

With the growth of his law practice came increased fame. Oil producers quickly came to know him as an expert on Indian land titles and access rights. He pushed himself into a prominent position in the community by joining civic organizations and associating with the other rising business lights of the area, oilmen like W. G. Skelly and Waite and Frank Phillips. Bright, extremely gregarious, even brash, and perhaps just as important, tall, erect, and handsome, he was no shrinking violet; he in fact cut a wide swath through the city socially as well as economically and politically. In 1910, he helped organize the Tulsa Bar Association and became its president; the same year he received the Republican nomination for the State Senate in the Tulsa and Washington County district.

Why Hurley became a Republican is impossible to assess adequately; however, it seems that his admiration for Theodore Roosevelt, the appeal of the President's charisma and his masculine vigor, as well as the fact that, when Hurley first became conscious of national politics during his year in Washington, the Republicans were in power, in part accounted for his party affiliation. In any event, in the contest of 1910 which was to be his last until he entered the New Mexico Senate race after World War II, he ran a very close second to a strong opponent. The Democratic opponent was Judge A. F. Vandeventer, a former resident of Arkansas, one-time state legislator and candidate for governor there, and more recently a member of the first Oklahoma legislature. Hurley carried Washington County, which was Republican, and the city of Tulsa, where he lived, but he lost the rural Democratic precincts in Tulsa County, and ultimately fell nine votes short of victory. In the losing effort, however, he gained in stature for he acquired many friends, and, in carrying on a running debate with this opponent, he demonstrated his speaking abilities and advanced himself as a future political power in the state.

The following year, 1911, brought a new turn in Hurley's career. One of his boyhood friends, Victor Locke, Jr., was named by President Taft as principal chief of the Choctaws, a position that mainly involved executing deeds and fulfilling other duties assigned by the federal government. One of Locke's early actions as chief was to contact his old chum, requesting that he accept the position of national attorney for the tribe. Aware that the job would take him back to Washington and anxious once more to be associated with Locke, Hurley accepted; with the approval of the President on November 28, 1911, he became national attorney for the Choctaws. His salary was $5,000 per year, less than half what was paid to his predecessor Ormsby McHarg of New York, former Assistant Secretary of Commerce and Labor under Roosevelt, whose salary the Indians reduced to force him out because he neglected his job. This position, the principal duties of which were to look after the Indians' interests in dealing with the government, was most significant in bringing the young lawyer in close contact with important governmental figures, including the Secretary of the Interior and the Oklahoma delegation as well as Senators and Representatives from other states. Though the salary was low compared to what he earned in his practice in Tulsa, he considered the appointment a stroke of good fortune. Years later he wrote: "Dick Locke and the Choctaws gave me my first opportunity for public service. I will never cease to be grateful to them." [7]

At the local level Hurley's job involved a variety of duties ranging from consideration of wills to mineral leases to Indian

[7] To Mackey, Mar. 14, 1935.

schools. In dealing with Congress he was concerned largely with appropriations and litigations regarding Indian lands. His first important assignment was to help defeat exorbitant claims against the tribe by J. Frank McMurray, a former attorney for the Indians under Locke's predecessor as chief. McMurray had written contracts with individual Indians which would have given him as much as 10 percent of the sale price of Choctaw land and other property considered surplus because unallotted under the original land distribution.

When the federal government prepared the territory for statehood, specified amounts of land in the Choctaw Nation and elsewhere in Indian territory were allotted to each individual Indian on the basis of private ownership. But there was still much land and mineral property left over which was to be sold by the tribe, as it was communal property. McMurray proposed to negotiate the sale of this property on favorable terms, get a profit for the Indians with whom he had contracted, and for himself. As Hurley put it: "If Mr. McMurray were successful in having these contracts approved he would be entitled to collect under them at least $3,500,000 for doing that which the United States government is treaty bound to do for the Indians and the doing of which Mr. McMurray and his associates could not in any manner expedite."[8] Hurley, who had moved to Washington shortly after his appointment, joined Locke and the Oklahoma congressional delegation in blocking the claims. Senator Thomas Gore of Oklahoma led the fight against McMurray, temporarily checked his claims, and then introduced an amendment to the Indian Appropriation Bill of 1913, drafted by Hurley, which stated that no contract made with an individual Indian was valid where such a contract related to *tribal* funds or property, unless consent was obtained previously from the U.S. government.[9] When some Senators, including Senator Albert B. Fall of New Mexico, a friend of McMurray's, attempted to block the amendment by withhold-

[8] To Warren Moorhead, Apr. 10, 1913.
[9] Hurley to Moorhead, July 10, 1913.

ing approval of the appropriations act until McMurray's claims were validated, Gore again went to work. Hurley testified in behalf of the amendment and against the contracts before the Committee on Indian Affairs, and with this help Gore succeeded in gaining sufficient support to defeat the contracts and secure passage of the appropriations bill with the amendment.[10]

The other important Indian matter with which Hurley dealt was the claim advanced by Mississippi Choctaws to lands owned by the Choctaw Nation in Oklahoma. After the signing of the treaty of 1830 the majority of the Choctaw Indians living in Mississippi moved to Indian territory, but a number remained behind. Many of their descendants eventually migrated to the Choctaw Nation, but even as late as the 1890's some Choctaws, both full bloods and mixed bloods, still resided in Mississippi. When the federal government began enrolling the Indians in Indian territory for the purpose of allotting land just prior to statehood, the Dawes Commission in 1899 made a ruling in regard to these Mississippi Indians; it stated that few if any of them had a right to enrollment as citizens of the Choctaw Nation. However, after 1899, the Choctaws and Chickasaws agreed to enroll gratuitously all members of their tribes still in Mississippi if they would establish a residence in either the Choctaw or Chickasaw Nation. Some 1,634 Choctaws thereafter received allotments under these terms. Subsequently in April of 1906, the U.S. government enacted a law stating that as of March 4, 1907, the rolls of both the Choctaw and Chickasaw Nations would be closed; no further enrollment was to take place. Pursuant to a treaty of 1902 with the U.S. government the remaining Indian lands after the rolls were closed were to be sold by the government and the proceeds divided per capita among the enrolled members of the tribes.

Complicating the execution of this provision after 1907 was the fact that numerous Indians in Mississippi, as well as lawyers

[10] Semiannual Report by Hurley, national attorney for the Choctaw Nation, to Victor Locke, Jr., May 28, 1913.

working with them on a commission basis and two of the state's leading political figures, Senator John Sharp Williams and Congressman Pat Harrison, demanded the reopening of the rolls. Harrison introduced a bill in the House calling for the enrollment of 20,000 Mississippi Choctaws; then Williams and Harrison thwarted any attempt to begin per capita disbursements to the Choctaws until their demands were met. Obviously, the Mississippi Indians—some of whom could establish only a tenuous relationship to the Choctaws—and their lawyers, stood to profit a good deal if the rolls were reopened. And the motive of the lawyers was obvious: Mr. Albert J. Lee, one of the attorneys wrote a friend: "Mr. Webster Ballinger and I represent some 13,000 persons who claim a right in the tribal property in Oklahoma. . . . We represent these people under contract providing for a contingent fee of from 12-1/2 to 40% of the value of each share. . . . You will observe that my individual share of said fee will amount to $850,911.00 based on the cases I consider certain . . . ; if we succeed in enrolling the doubtful cases my share would be $2,065,911." [11] Hurley, this time with the assistance of Senator Robert L. Owen of Oklahoma, fought the reopening; he stated before a House committee that he found it remarkable that such a small band of Choctaws left in Mississippi "could have descended 20,000 claimants." He later alleged that it was "the agent and the runners who are employed by the attorneys" who incited the Mississippi Choctaws; it was not their own idea.[12]

[11] To Harry Masterson, Oct. 17, 1912. During the course of the discussion of the claims of the Mississippi Choctaws, Hurley heard that a syndicate had been organized and capitalized to get a provision through Congress to reopen the rolls. "I have not enough information to make a charge of the nature suggested and be able to establish the charge after it became public." But he requested that Secretary of the Interior Franklin Lane "detail an inspector to investigate this matter and the facts relative thereto" (Hurley to Franklin Lane, June 12, 1913). Later Hurley himself and others found plenty of information; such a syndicate was organized out of Houston, Texas (Charles Moling to W. L. Dechant, June 12, 1911).

[12] Extract from U.S. House of Representatives, *Hearings before the Subcommittee on Indian Affairs*, Aug. 11, 1914, 63rd Cong. 2nd Sess., 1915, p. 139. Hereafter cited as *House Indian Hearings*.

In letter after letter to various congressional delegations he argued that he had repeatedly shown "that the Mississippi Choctaws have no legal, equitable, or moral right to share in the property of the Choctaw Nation." [13] Moreover, "there have been partial crop failures in Oklahoma for the past four years"; the distribution of money to the Choctaws must not be held up by those seeking to reopen the rolls.

Hurley also informed the congressional committee that those lawyers and representatives from Mississippi who posed as their friends were not really friends of the Choctaws at all. "The Mississippi Choctaws have been reduced to a state that is almost peonage. . . . They are now a stolid people, who gaze at the ground with the emptiness of age in their faces. That is what these friends of the Mississippi Choctaws have done for the Choctaws in Mississippi. These are the friends who are appearing here and asking you to send the money belonging to the Oklahoma Choctaws to Mississippi for the Mississippi Choctaws. For whom do they want this money. For the man to whom they have denied in practice the right of citizenship which they gave him under the laws." [14]

Hurley's pleas proved fruitful, as the committee recommended against reopening the rolls largely on the basis he cited. Then in February of 1915 in the Senate, Robert LaFollette of Wisconsin and Henry Lane, acting largely upon the urging of Ballinger, threatened to throw a monkey wrench into the machinery. They urged reopening on the claim that, because of the pressure of time, the Interior Department failed to consider properly individual cases which were entitled to enrollment prior to March 4, 1907. In preparing to thwart this tack, Senator Owen requested a memorandum from Hurley to use as ammunition.[15] Hurley proceeded then to write such a memo, the substance of which he also included in a letter to LaFollette indicating that in the previous session of Congress such individuals who were equitably

13 *Ibid.*, pp. 137–138.
14 *Ibid.*, pp. 54–55.
15 James Beller to Hurley, Feb. 24, 1915.

entitled to enrollment but not provided for because of the time factor were indeed enrolled.[16] Using Hurley's arguments, the statement of the House committee, and the report of the Secretary of the Interior, Franklin Lane, as well as further testimony by the young attorney, Senator Owen successfully blocked the move to reopen in the Senate and thus won the battle; some $5,000,000 was subsequently distributed to the Oklahoma Choctaws with additional funds going to the Chickasaws as well. Hurley informed his sister: "I think I made the greatest argument of my life yesterday before the committee on Indian Affairs of the senate. We won and now we are certain that the 'Chocks' and the 'Chicks' will get eight millions this year."[17]

In defending the interests of the Choctaws, Hurley, in view of his limited education, displayed a remarkable knowledge of the history of Indian removal and government treaties. Perhaps the more outstanding was his facility at debate that required a dexterity in the use of language and extreme rapidity of response. When one reads the published hearings before the House subcommittee it is apparent that he frequently bested his opponents in heated exchange both as to amount of relevant information presented and the logic of his position; he came off especially well in a lengthy confrontation with Webster Ballinger, the lawyer who sought to promote the interests of the Mississippi group. More than this, he demonstrated a confidence unusual in a thirty-one-year-old attorney—he often admonished Ballinger and others not to interrupt him, and to "pay attention" to his testimony.[18]

Although he liked the position and wanted to continue in it, he also displayed frustration and anger with his constituents who seemed to him at times unaware of his efforts in their behalf. On April 21, 1915, a group of mixed-blood Choctaws held a meeting at Durant and passed resolutions calling for the removal of Victor Locke as principal chief and of Hurley as national attorney

[16] To Robert LaFollette, Feb. 27, 1915.
[17] To Mackey, Mar. 1, 1916.
[18] See *House Indian Hearings.*

and his replacement with someone of Indian blood. However, the action was quickly repudiated by a full-bloods meeting at Kanima, Oklahoma. Had it not been, Hurley said, he would "tell the Choctaw people what David Crockett told the people in his district in Tennessee just before he started to Texas."[19]

From 1911 to 1917, Hurley divided his time between Washington and Oklahoma. When he was not occupied with Indian affairs, he attended lectures at George Washington University Law School. He also joined the Sigma Chi fraternity, because, as he put it, "it had tradition, a sweetheart and a song"; and he loved the fraternity life for the same reason many scorned it: it was a way of prolonging adolescence—an adolescence which he had not experienced as a boy because he was forced to work in the mines to help support his family. In the fall of 1912 Hurley, then in Oklahoma, wrote a friend that he was anxious to get back to Washington; he enjoyed the city immensely, and he had heard from the Sigma Chi house "and they are having great times. They tell me that one of the big dances is scheduled to take place on December 4th. I would like to be around when said dance is pulled off."[20]

His stay in the nation's capital covered the remaining years of the Taft and part of the Wilson administration, and his political ideas were set during this period. It is difficult precisely to categorize Hurley politically, for he did not read much nor did he write any organized expositions of his theories. However, he was by now a regular Republican, and, insofar as he had a philosophy, was not uncomfortable in the Taft wing of the party; he voted for Taft in 1912. Yet he remained an ardent admirer of Theodore Roosevelt; and his views were tinctured by the progressivism manifested in Roosevelt's New Nationalism and Wilson's New Freedom. Wilson reappointed him national attorney for the Choctaws, and, though he never voted for Wilson, he also had great respect for him and for his legislative program. Polit-

[19] To Redford Bond, Apr. 24, 1915.
[20] To H. A. Meyer, Nov. 18, 1912.

ically, then, Hurley must be seen as a staunch Republican, in part a product of Washington in the era of progressive reform, a man whose views were further tempered by the politics in his native Oklahoma in early statehood.

During the first decade of its statehood, political life in Oklahoma comprised a curious mixture of liberalism, populism or farm-laborism, socialism, conservatism, enlightenment, and bigotry. The constitutional convention was perhaps illustrative of future developments: the colorful "Alfalfa Bill" Murray, later to be governor, presided over an assorted collection of predominantly rural delegates who began each session singing "Nearer My God to Thee," and who passed ringing resolutions in favor of such items as the initiative and referendum, the direct primary, an eight-hour day for miners, prohibition of alcoholic beverages, and "Jim Crow" laws.

Later the first legislature continued the trend. It enacted into law an extensive labor code, precursor of reforms under Wilson and Franklin D. Roosevelt, providing a mine safety code, a child labor law, a health and sanitation code, a factory inspection law, and employer's liability. It also passed legislation outlawing the Yellow Dog contract and establishing Labor Day as a state holiday.

Dominated as it was by the farmer-labor bloc with its intense feeling about the monied interests, the legislature also created a corporation commission to regulate "corporate greed," though this agency later functioned better in theory than in practice. Railroads were prevented from charging passengers more than two cents per mile, and lobbyists were compelled to register with the state. The legislature passed a bank guaranty law which forced participating banks to submit to a one-percent tax on daily balances to collect money which was then placed in a fund underwriting deposits. It likewise passed revenue bills which taxed the property of coal-mine owners, oil interests, railroads, and later, incomes—on a graduated basis.

At the same time, however, Jim Crow laws were created, formalizing the separation of the races. To prevent or restrict Negro voting, the "Grandfather Clause" was approved in a state referendum in the summer of 1910, while the state passed a large quota of blue laws regulating "immoral" behavior like horse racing and prize fighting.

Of the two major political parties, the Democrats were dominant in the state. The governors were all Democrats, as were an overwhelming majority in the legislature; with a few exceptions, the congressional delegations were unanimously Democratic. Yet there was a vocal Republican minority party tied to the railroads and to the growing oil industry. At the same time there was considerable Socialist strength in the state; in the election of 1914, the Socialist gubernatorial candidate received about 52,000 votes out of approximately 248,000 votes cast.

Although he associated closely with conservative Republicans both in his own state and nationally, Hurley reflected a quasi-Populist-Progressive position all his life. He believed in state legislation as a necessary way to avoid corporate abuse and special privilege and was never as suspicious as many of his later conservative associates were of the extension of federal power in the name of reform. The United States Constitution, he once stated, "not only established the equality of the people before the law, it guaranteed *equality of opportunity*. It gave each individual the assurance that he could aspire to and obtain that place in the community to which his character and ability entitled him." [21] Regarding the Federal Reserve Act, which he strongly favored, he wrote: "the use of the banking and currency power is not an invasion of States rights," and he opined, in 1933, that "the field still open for expansion of Federal Authority in national economics within the limits of the Constitution is even greater than all the field now occupied." [22] Later he bitterly informed President Hoover: "The masters of great fortunes . . . financed the Roosevelt campaign against you. Your demand that wages be sustained in

[21] Address at William and Mary, May 1, 1933.
[22] *Ibid.*

the beginning of the depression displeased wealth. Do not be mistaken about this. The wealthy people of this nation were against you because of your efforts in behalf of the workers." [23] Once, in a speech to a Republican group in Detroit, he stated: "Interest rates have been and are too high. . . . A study of the history of money from the days of Solon to the present should convince anyone that the fate of those who charge too high a rate for money is always . . . the same fate as that of the unfortunate borrower. . . . What I have said of interest rates is true also of exorbitant business profits. The reduction of interest and profits should go into wages." [24] "I despise the so-called power of money," he wrote a friend in 1933, "I have learned to dislike the devious ways of great fortunes. I dislike the sofa smokers and the lounge lizards who live by the sweat of an ancestor's brow." [25]

Speaking of the depression, he said it "indicated to us the necessity of improving our economic system by providing for a greater and more equitable distribution of wealth." But, he continued, "the period through which we are passing does not repudiate our economic system. . . . Where adjustments in that system may be indicated, they can be made by carefully conceived legislation." [26] Though he often spoke politically to the contrary, he supported part of the New Deal domestic program. As a candidate for the United States Senate in New Mexico following World War II, he vigorously urged conservation of the country's natural resources and developed a plan for better supply and use of water in the state. He also bragged about his union membership—he joined the United Mine workers as a youth in the Choctaw Nation —and argued that one of the important elements of Americanism was "regulated free enterprise."

While he did thus develop a set of beliefs—albeit ill-organized

[23] To Herbert Hoover, Aug. 25, 1933, Hoover Papers, Hoover Presidential Library, West Branch, Iowa.
[24] Address, Detroit, Feb. 28, 1935.
[25] To Victor Locke, Jr., Aug. 3, 1933.
[26] Address at Independence Hall in Philadelphia, July 4, 1931.

—to Hurley personal relationships in politics as in other endeavors were more important. He was attracted by people (like Theodore Roosevelt who early became his political hero) and, when he voted, often was more concerned about the man than his program. Partly, this came from his experience in Oklahoma, a new state where it was not unusual for a large portion of the population to know personally many of the prominent political figures; as a youth still in his twenties Hurley himself became acquainted with many of the state's leaders. Much of his success in life may be attributed to the close personal relationships he established— first with Victor Locke, then with Harry Sinclair, Herbert Hoover, Douglas MacArthur, and Franklin Roosevelt to name the most prominent. In his association with foreign statesmen later in his career he seems to have believed that handshakes, smiles, anecdote swapping and other forms of personal camaraderie would sweep away divisive and long-standing issues; in this sense he resembled Franklin Roosevelt.

Similarly, it is not inaccurate to say that Hurley cultivated people. Effusive, handsome, witty, full of stories about Oklahoma and the West—traits which conveyed a sense of warmth and trustfulness—he made a superb first impression. He also employed a casual familiarity, which, though offensive to some, inspired a friendly response from most, even in his youth; later in his career many were obviously flattered to get such attention, especially after Hurley gained national prominence. He was an inveterate first-namer. Dougles MacArthur, pompous and unaccustomed to such informality was "Doug" or "Douglas," and was frequently addressed by Hurley as "Dear Douglas"; it was often "Dear Cordell" with Cordell Hull; "Dear Jim" with Byrnes; "Dear Ed" with Stettinius; and "Andy" with Andrew Mellon. Hurley it would appear, often acted like the stereotypical southwestern small-town Rotarian.

This is not to say, however, that he necessarily lacked compassion or sincerity. He had a number of durable friendships. And he always remembered those who had helped or befriended him in his youth. He had deep affection for Victor Locke and wrote him regularly until his death. Years after he left Phillips he remained close to one of his early friends, a man named Terence O'Hara, with whom he worked in the mines; Hurley corresponded with him frequently and sent him a regular monthly check. When his duties would permit—while in Tulsa and later as Secretary of War —he visited in the O'Hara home and on several occasions sat up all night reminiscing and drinking Choctaw beer with O'Hara and several other friends. "Hurley," said O'Hara, "was at home in the poorest house and equally in the richest residence." [27] When another of his boyhood friends, Roy Caldwell, grew ill and lay near death in a Dallas hospital, he dropped his appointments in Washington and flew to Dallas to visit him before he died. His former boss in the number six mine, John McLaughlin, he helped support for years, and when he died he was buried in a suit Hurley had sent him. "You were my friend," he once wrote McLaughlin, "when I was a young and lonely youngster who needed the friendship of older people. I remember . . . the many kind considerations shown me in those days. I remember how you used to take me hunting with you." [28] He worked hard finding jobs for his friends when in a position of power and influence, often after they no longer deserved his attention. Of one he wrote: "For a long time . . . I have thought that Jack was worth worrying about. I have placed him three different times in his short life on what I believed to be the highway to success and honor. He does not stay put." [29]

From age thirteen Hurley worked to support his family; he was extremely generous in helping his father whom he moved to Tulsa with him after he established his law practice. His favorite sister, Alice, with whom he was probably closer than any other member of his family, he virtually adopted; he bought her clothes, saw to it that she completed her secondary schooling, paid her way

[27] Foreman interview with O'Hara, Feb. 14, 1942.
[28] To John McLaughlin, Apr. 9, 1934.
[29] To Victor Locke Jr., July 2, 1932.

through college, and remained very solicitous in the early years of her marriage. As their letters indicate, he remained the doting brother throughout his life.

Their correspondence, which began while Hurley was Choctaw attorney and increased in volume during World War I, is warm, full of humor, love, and a measure of braggadocio, and adds insight into his character and personality. Interestingly, however, until 1917 he appears to have given little attention to foreign affairs; except for brief comment on Wilson's Mexican policy which he "deplored," the letters to his sister and his friends contain almost no mention of American policy; his legal activities consumed his time to the extent that he seemed actually unaware and unperturbed about the war in Europe—until the imminence of American involvement. Then with the deterioration and ultimate break in United States-German relations he became acutely aware; he helped draft a Tulsa war resolution, resigned his position with the Choctaw Nation, and after some difficult maneuvering, became a soldier.

# II

## Soldier, Businessman, and Politician

Although Hurley yearned eagerly to contribute to America's effort in World War I through service at the front, his military ambition far exceeded his experience. His previous "soldiering" consisted only of brief stints in the Indian Territorial Militia and the Oklahoma National Guard, in which organizations he received little formal training.

The Territorial Militia, established in 1903 by Clarence Douglas, editor of the *Muskogee Phoenix,* was essentially only a quasi-military outfit mustered to protect the interests of white men from Negro and Indian depredations in an area nominally controlled by the Indians but rapidly being settled by whites. Douglas organized a company of seventy men in Muskogee and encouraged other communities to do the same. The result, after the forming of these various armies, was the creation of a regiment with units spread across the territory. With little or no equipment and only such uniforms as could be rehabilitated from the Spanish-American War, the group was ragtag at best; its arms consisted of privately owned firearms, and often the Muskogee unit drilled with broomsticks. The militia also operated without the sanction of either the War Department or the Interior Department, with the latter particularly critical of the military group. In 1904, Hurley, then in Muskogee and a student at Indian University, joined Douglas' company and before long became a lieutenant and then captain in the organization.[1]

[1] Based on interview by Grant Foreman of Col. Clarence B. Douglas, July 24, 1941, Grant Foreman materials, Hurley Papers. Unless otherwise noted,

With statehood, the Indian Territorial Militia ceased to exist. In any event, after his graduation and subsequent departure for Washington, Hurley dropped out, not returning to a military organization until 1914 when he joined the Oklahoma National Guard as a captain. Then in 1916, he was briefly called to active duty and sent along with some 150,000 other guardsmen, to the Mexican border as part of Wilson's effort to capture Pancho Villa and impress Mexico with a show of force; General Pershing pursued Villa into Mexico, while the guardsmen secured the border. Hurley did not like Wilson's Mexican policy and felt some resentment at the disruption in his affairs caused by the assignment. He was too busy making money and looking after Choctaw interests to concern himself with military matters.

However, in April of 1917, after the declaration of War on Germany, Hurley resigned as Choctaw attorney and returned to Oklahoma where he drafted a war resolution for the city of Tulsa. The resolution recited the reasons for the birth of the United States and the principles associated with its existence. It then went on to point out that one of the principles for which America previously had fought was freedom of the seas. In the present European war President Wilson had shown great forbearance in the face of humiliations, loss of life, and other indignities inflicted by Germany prior to breaking relations. It was now time for action, and the citizens of Tulsa were ready to cooperate in whatever action the President and Congress deemed necessary.[2]

He also sought to recruit troops for the Oklahoma National Guard. He was not successful in his efforts to raise cavalry units because of the governor's opposition, but he did recruit an aviation company and an engineers' company, though he obviously could not lead them because he had no technical training. Consequently, he joined the regular army, taking a commission as a major. In

---

the Hurley Papers are the source of the letters noted in the references that follow.

[2] Hurley to Mrs. Alice Mackey, Apr. 4, 1917.

August of 1917 he was promptly remanded to the Judge Advocate General's Office where he worked with problems associated with the Selective Service law and where, he feared, he might be stuck for the duration of the war.

The Judge Advocate General's Office was the bane of his existence. "I want to get to the field," he daily reminded his superiors. "Maybe," he said, he would "dislike the trenches," but he didn't care; he wanted "to hear the big guns rattle." [3] Through the summer and early fall he persisted in his requests for reassignment, while he perfunctorily performed additional duties in the military clemency division of the office. He finally got what he wanted; he received a transfer to artillery and prepared to go to France.

Arriving in France in April 1918, Hurley trained briefly at the artillery school at Besançon, and then joined the staff of General Ernest Hines, Commanding General of Artillery of the First Army. This still did not satisfy him, and he constantly requested a transfer to the front; he wanted, he said, to be out "where the glory gleams brightest . . . far out on the roaring red fighting line." [4] He never got to where the glory gleamed brightly, though he was close to where some fierce fighting occurred: his unit was in reserve during the Aisne-Marne operation, where in his words he "went through three weeks of 'hell' and didn't even get a scratch." It was a bad fight but, "when our big guns hit the Boche line that line melted before them like snow under a July sun." [5] The offensive convinced him that "the Kaiser is going to be whipped and we are going to round up the entire Hohenzollern outfit and give Germany a chance to be free." [6] Later, in September, he carried orders for the beginning artillery barrage at St. Mihiel as adjutant for the commander of the First Army Artillery. These days were "the most exciting as well as the most interesting" of his life. The

[3] To Mackey, Aug. 20, 1917.
[4] To Mackey, Aug. 18, 1918.
[5] To Mackey, Aug. 5, 1918.
[6] *Ibid.*

results indicated that "the Boche are about full of the war. They know they are whipped. . . ." [7]

In November, now a lieutenant colonel, he got a chance to participate in some action and, interestingly, had some second thoughts: "It looks as though we are to have peace. I hope it will come before many more of us have to pay 'the last full measure of devotion' if it is coming at all. I wouldn't like to be killed in action on the last day of the war . . . I don't feel good tonight and that probably accounts for the feeling I have . . . to be real frank, it's just plain scared." [8] Yet on November 10 and 11 near Louppy he again carried orders and made a reconnaissance, this time through dangerous territory under fire and as a result was decorated for gallantry; for his efforts on the last day of the war he was granted a silver star.

The war provided Hurley the time of his life. It brought out his nationalism and generated drama and excitement unsurpassed in his previous experience. Seeing the American flag in France he wrote: "It is beautiful and tender as a flower to those who love it . . . it seems beautifully to represent the home and the glory and aspirations and the power of a hundred and ten million Americans. . . . I have lived all my life for this opportunity to do something *real* for my country." [9] Most of all, he hoped there would be no premature end to the war, no end until Germany had been dealt with satisfactorily and until the United States had undergone a transformation of spirit. "I am praying every day that the war will not be stopped until the Boche are whipped so they will stay whipped, and until our own dear country has acquired a soul. She is in a fair way to get a soul, but it hasn't gone far enough yet. She hasn't had a real soul since the days of Lincoln. This war if it lasts long enough will make strong, God loving men out of hundreds of thousands of cigarette smoking, cocktail drinking, tango trolling, fish walking, lounge lizards. It will teach our girls that there

[7] To Mackey, Sept. 13, 1918.
[8] To Mackey, Nov. 1, 1918.
[9] To Mackey, Aug. 18, 1918.

are ideals higher than those they learn at pink teas and street carnivals." [10]

If Hurley's World War I view regarding the side virtues of war were Rooseveltian in spirit, his comment about his heroes in history also reveals a kind of romantic militarism. Bonaparte, Washington, Sheridan, Henry, Lee, and Roosevelt were all great men, but Marion—"I never hear that name that my blood doesn't run a little faster, my back become a little straighter, and my chin a little higher. I think of the Hills and Forests of the Carolinas, the bloody fights at Moultrie and Ft. Sullivan, of Nelson's Ferry and Parker Ferry, of the handsome figure of the leader in every one of these fights, and I can almost hear his name above the din of battle. It is a name that represents all the chivalry, all the valor, all the kindness of spirit, all the patriotism and all the glory of American manhood. I feel like taking my hat in hand when I hear the name of Francis Marion." [11] He urged his sister, if she had a son, to name him "Marion."

Hurley also enjoyed the camaraderie imposed by the war, and he made the most of his first trip to Europe. His letters reveal a spirit of fun, humor, and adventure more like that of a boy scout at camp than of a soldier in grim battle. He wrote his sister that he was spending some time in Paris, which for a while was the most dangerous place he had been. He told of his buddies and the times they had, mentioning on one occasion that they had just finished singing a song they had worked on. "It is a wonderful song," he said, "full of pathos, valor and prunes"; he went on to recite a version of the familiar "Sweet Marie." Of the German planes which occasionally drove them to their trenches he said their "hum has Hun in it. It reminds me of the rattle of a rattlesnake." [12] Another time he told his sister that he had sat down to write her but got sick on his army food. "I had a lot of nice things I wanted to write you but trying to say nice things when you have the belly-

10 To Mackey, Oct. 21, 1918.
11 To Mackey, Mar. 5, 1918.
12 To Mackey, Oct. 22, 1918.

ache is like trying to drive a mule and be a Christian at the same time." [13]

He also had a woman friend while in France, the twenty-four-year-old Comtesse de Flammercourt who lived near Chateau-Thierry with her husband. He visited her often, and they frequently went horseback riding together, she on Hurley's horse "Choctaw Belle." The comtesse gave him "souvenirs" and showed him some old castles, property of her family. Hurley, tongue in cheek, reported that he told her his family house "was very old looking but had a new lean-to built to it in the latter part of the nineteenth century. I told her I came from a fighting family and that old home of ours way out in the Choctaw Nation is the scene of many a well fought battle. I told her my dear old dad was usually successful in these battles, and nearly always took the object of his attack by storm." [14] When the war was over Hurley left this "Peggy of the Artillery," as he called her, spent more time in Paris, and visited in London and in Ireland before returning to the United States.

Actually, six months passed following the armistice before Hurley departed from Europe. Assigned Judge Advocate of the Sixth Army Corps, he was dispatched along with his unit to Luxembourg, where he assisted in negotiating an agreement with that government. When the war ended, the Third Army, which was to occupy the American area of German territory, had advanced across Luxembourg on its way to Germany. While passing through, its representatives had made an agreement with the Grand Duchy for the use of Luxembourg territory, and for supplies and billets for its troops. The Third Army departed and was replaced by the Sixth, which was to facilitate communication with, and provide supplies for, the Third Army across Luxembourg. When the Sixth Army arrived, its command found some dissatisfaction with the previous agreement and feared that it would be interpreted as having been exacted from Luxembourg

13 To Mackey, n.d.
14 To Mackey, Aug. 9, 1918.

under duress. Rather than unilaterally to violate the small Duchy's neutrality or have it so appear, the Sixth Army command decided to negotiate a new agreement to permit American use of her territory and transportation facilities. Hurley was given the job. The task required neither skill nor strenuous effort, since the Grand Duchy was anxious to accommodate, and the conferences in which he took part dealt largely with tedious detail regarding U.S. payment for the use of Luxembourg equipment and accommodations. The agreement stated that the United States reaffirmed its recognition of the Duchy's neutrality and then specified that the United States would pay for the use of roads, railroads, rolling stock, and anything else used in traversing its territory.[15] This assignment completed, he prepared to return home.

When he arrived back in the United States in May 1919, Hurley immediately contacted his sister and his family (he bemoaned the fact that he did not have family waiting for him when he arrived in Richmond with a contingent of troops) and resumed his courtship of Ruth Wilson, daughter of Admiral Henry B. Wilson, whom he hoped to marry. Of his previous love life little of certainty can be established. As a youth in the Choctaw Nation he dated a young Indian girl named Willie York of Atoka, and local rumors had it that they were engaged to be married.[16] For whatever reason, however, they drifted apart; she married a local boy with whom she lived happily ever after, as Hurley put it, in "the forks of the creek." Later in school and as a young lawyer he had romantic attachments, and then there was the young "Peggy of the Artillery" with whom it is difficult to define his specific relationship. In any event, for marriage he was waiting until "the right girl came along"; Ruth Wilson was the "right" girl.

Daughter of the Commander of the Atlantic Fleet and from a family of considerable means, beautiful, charming, and gracious, Ruth Wilson caught young Hurley's eye at a Ride and Hunt Club

[15] See Report of the Judge Advocate, Sixth Army Corps, Hurley Papers.

[16] Interview by Grant Foreman of Victor Locke, Jr., June 30, 1941, Grant Foreman materials, *ibid.*

ball in Washington prior to the war. He met her for the first time that evening, and on their third date, he asked her to marry him. They corresponded during the war and then after returning to the United States, Hurley formally asked Admiral Wilson for his daughter's hand. "I just couldn't keep from marrying her," he informed his sister. It was not quite so simple, however, for her father was not certain of Hurley's credentials, and, moreover, Ruth Wilson had other suitors; Hurley himself reported that an ex-congressman offered to settle fifteen million dollars on her if she would marry his son. She chose Hurley. "I claim Ruth has good judgment. Knows the goods when she sees them," he wrote.[17] They were married on December 5, 1919, in what was for Hurley one of the most fortuitous developments in a career singularly marked by good luck.

Following his marriage he once again established his home in Tulsa, where he devoted his energies to making money, dabbling in politics, though not as candidate for office, and contributing to local civic affairs. In the 1920's Tulsa was well on its way to becoming a major city and the nation's "oil capital." Fed by the oil industry with its refineries and the attendant machine shops, tank manufacturers, rig and derrick companies, and tool makers, the city really boomed. It grew from a small town of 1,300 in 1901 to about 70,000 in 1920; in the twenties its population more than doubled. The newly paved streets in its growing business district bustled, as new banks, hotels, and office buildings dotted the way. The city now had two daily newspapers, an emerging cultural life, including after 1927 a civic symphony, and a private university; it also developed a beginning residential sprawl and some social problems. Hurley's home, which he himself built and called Elmwood, was one of the most beautiful in the city and was ideally located in an area surrounded by elm, ash, hackberry, and walnut trees.

In Tulsa, Hurley continued his practice of law, making an

17 To Mackey, n.d.

ample annual salary, much of which he used to procure additional real estate. When not busy with his practice he was managing his properties. He also became a coreceiver of the Gilliland Oil Company which was buffeted by problems connected with price fluctuations in the industry and jittery creditors. Through cajolery, shrewd judgment, and persistence he made a moneymaker out of the firm, and in 1927 when it merged with another company it showed a profit of better than a million dollars. By 1929, from this enterprise and from stock as well as his real properties he had assets of well over a million dollars. He developed large equities in the Ambassador Hotel in Tulsa, the Commodore in Wichita, Kansas, the Boulder-Park in Tulsa, and in 1931, had a $450,000 equity in the Shoreham building in Washington, D.C. As a result of his business activity in the twenties he became, to say the least, financially comfortable.

Although he and Mrs. Hurley were socially among the most prominent Tulsans throughout the decade, his most notable "civic achievement" occurred in 1921 when he helped quell the city's race riot. In late May and early June of that year disturbances occurred after a racial incident; then the Negro community, bitter and frustrated after years of overt discrimination, isolated and armed itself and was in turn challenged by angry whites; scores of people were killed in the resulting melee and over a hundred wounded. Hurley, never the faint heart, offered his services to the community to help bring order. He had himself deputized by the sheriff, then organized a group of vigilantes comprised of former roughriders and other adventurers ready for action: a very large force. The group helped seal off the city with orders from their leader to shoot to kill, and then, in a move to "secure" the area, marched on the Negro quarter where Hurley demanded that the blacks encountered surrender their weapons or be promptly slaughtered. The overwhelming force at his command allowed Hurley thus to disarm a segment of the Negroes and to contribute to the imposition of order; eventually calm returned and the city went on about its business. Interestingly, though not too surprisingly, in that era, Hurley manifested no concern—or at least left no record of any concern—for the injustice which may have prompted the violence.

Politically, Hurley was active during the twenties in the Republican organization but did not run for office. He was suggested as a possible candidate for governor in 1918 and for a federal judgeship a couple of years later. In 1926 he was again boomed as his party's candidate for governor, but he refused. Two things determined his decision not to seek office within Oklahoma: it was a Democratic state which had never elected a Republican governor and, through the twenties, only two Republican senators. State Republicans seemed for the most part less interested in creating a strong organization and winning state elections than in maintaining their own prominent positions within the national party, unchallenged by strong rivals (this applied later to Hurley as well). Secondly, Hurley was concerned primarily with, as the saying went, "getting himself well fixed," before he entered public service. He did, however, go to the national convention in 1924, where he cast his ballot for Calvin Coolidge; he was also on the delegation appointed by the national convention to notify Coolidge of his nomination and was president of the Coolidge and Dawes club in Tulsa. In 1928, he was a real force in the Hoover campaign for the presidency.

In the mid-twenties Hurley recognized Herbert Hoover as a figure with a future in American politics. He saw the Secretary of Commerce as a bright, energetic, and efficient administrator, indeed a "wonder boy," as Coolidge sarcastically referred to his subordinate. What he knew of Hoover's political philosophy he also agreed with, though this was secondary with Hurley. Consequently, when Hoover began his drive for the nomination after Coolidge made his "I do not choose to run" statement, Hurley thrust himself into the task of running his preconvention campaign in Oklahoma, not without some thought to his own political future. He stumped the state, working day and night in an attempt to secure the state delegation for Hoover. Ultimately he failed, as the state convention gave its support to Senator Charles Curtis of Kansas as its first choice, and to Frank Lowden of Illinois as its second. Curtis was popular in Oklahoma primarily because of his Indian ancestry, because he had been a leader in the congressional drive to make Oklahoma a state, and because he had business interests in the state; many Oklahoma Republicans also liked him for his staid conservatism and his steadfast party regularity. In any case, as a result of the convention's action, Hurley was not a member of the Oklahoma delegation to the national convention in Kansas City.[18] Undaunted, he went anyway.

At the convention, Hurley wormed his way into the inner circle of Hoover supporters, using as leverage the fact that he was one of the early boosters of the Secretary of Commerce; Hoover did not need Oklahoma to secure the nomination but obviously was anxious to carry the state in the November election. The convention and subsequent campaign proved a dramatic turning point in Hurley's career. It would perhaps be erroneous to suggest that no one would have heard of him nationally had it not been for his appointment by Hoover, for he was sufficiently brash and able enough that he might well have gone on to prominence in any case. At the same time, however, his work for Hoover was what brought about his appointment to the cabinet, national publicity, and access to centers of power in Washington.

Interestingly, Hurley may have played a decisive role at the convention in getting Senator Curtis to accept the number-two spot on the ticket after Hoover locked up the nomination for the presidency. Prior to the convention Curtis stated that he believed his party would be apologizing for years for Herbert Hoover and that Hoover's nomination would "immediately place the party on the defensive." [19] Curtis also stated that he would never accept

[18] Don Lohbeck, *Patrick J. Hurley* (Chicago, 1956), pp. 80–81, and Parker LaMoore, *"Pat" Hurley: The Story of an American* (New York, 1932), pp. 93–97.

[19] *New York Times,* June 13, 1928; Harris G. Warren, *Herbert Hoover and The Great Depression* (New York, 1959), p. 38.

the vice-presidency under Hoover, and the *New York Times* reported that he grew "white with anger" at the suggestion. Hoover scholars discuss the antagonism which existed between the two men, and Hoover himself, in his memoirs, implies that Curtis disliked him intensely.[20] All suggest that whatever ill feeling existed suddenly evaporated when Curtis was proffered the vice-presidential slot and that the Senator went on to be a loyal and staunch Hoover supporter. No Hoover scholars, however, discuss adequately the circumstances associated with the nomination or the reason for Curtis' agreement to take the secondary position on the ticket.

On this latter point a letter written February 6, 1959, to former President Hoover by Hurley appears revealing. Upon the occasion of the presentation of a bust of Curtis to be installed in the Indian Hall of Fame in Oklahoma, Hurley was requested to make a speech. He wrote to Hoover asking about and commenting on the manner of Curtis' selection on the 1928 ticket. Hurley stated that after it became clear that Hoover would get the presidential nomination, James Good, former congressman from Iowa and manager of the Hoover campaign, approached him and asked him "to sound Charlie out on the subject" of the vice-presidential nomination. Hurley said he then went to Curtis but found the senator very "antagonistic" toward Hoover and not interested in the second position. At this point, Hurley reported, "I suggested to him that if he did not accept, I thought possibly Bill Borah would be the nominee, and he immediately changed his attitude." Hurley stated that he believed the possibility of the Borah nomination convinced the Kansan but went on to ask Hoover if he could provide additional details.[21]

Hoover replied on February 11 that he "knew fully of his [Curtis'] personal antagonism toward me up to the last minute of

[20] Herbert Hoover, *The Memoirs of Herbert Hoover: The Cabinet and the Presidency* (New York, 1959), p. 192.

[21] To Herbert Hoover, Feb. 6, 1959, AK-1/5, Hoover Papers, Hoover Presidential Library, West Branch, Iowa.

his nomination. The Convention managers submitted the proposed nomination of Curtis to me to conciliate his Senatorial friends, and I of course agreed." Hoover also stated, however, that he had not known of the manner in which Curtis was approached, but that after the nomination Curtis "never flagged in his loyalty to the administration." [22]

What seems most important here is that Hurley's comments about the possibility of Borah as Hoover's running mate may have convinced Curtis to change his mind and accept the nomination himself.[23] Why would this prospect alarm the senator? The answer is not apparent in the papers of any of the people involved, but several things can be suggested.

In the years after 1923 President Coolidge had sought Borah's counsel more and Curtis' less, even though the latter was majority leader in the Senate, and the former was a political maverick who alienated party regulars with reckless abandon. One clear manifestation of this curious relationship between the extremely conservative president and the old Idaho progressive appeared in 1924 when Coolidge offered Borah the number-two spot on the Republican ticket. It seems reasonable to conclude that Curtis would resent Borah's access to the president. Moreover, in 1924 when Coolidge suggested Borah as his running mate, he overrode the party wheel horses who had earlier decided upon Curtis. It appears certain that Curtis was privy to this information and was affected by it.[24]

In 1927 and early 1928, while Curtis was running, Borah was himself considered one of the contenders for the presidential nomination. He clearly did not expect to be nominated but, even so,

[22] To Hurley, Feb. 11, 1959, *ibid.*

[23] On this point one comment is appropriate. Borah was not a candidate for the vice-presidency in 1928, and there seems to be no record that he was very seriously considered for the position. Moreover, it appears to have been Borah who first suggested Curtis' name for the vice-presidency, and the Idaho senator made the speech nominating Curtis. However, what Curtis thought when Hurley spoke with him is what is important; in 1924 when the Kansan was considered for vice-president the party did briefly turn to Borah.

[24] Marian McKenna, *Borah* (Ann Arbor, 1961), p. 209.

encouraged the boom. When it became apparent that he had no chance, he jumped on the Hoover bandwagon, one of the first notable figures to do so. He then campaigned actively for Hoover against Curtis and the other contenders.[25]

Two other factors may have influenced Curtis' thinking: an open letter written him by Borah in January 1928 and Borah's irregularity as a party man. In January 1928, Borah wrote Curtis and the other contenders for the nomination a public letter asking specifically for their views on prohibition. The letter was a surprise to the Kansan, and in his reply he was sufficiently vague so as to be chided on it by congressional Democrats. The criticism may have hurt his candidacy. In any event, he was clearly irritated by the Idahoan's move.[26]

Noted for actions such as this, Borah had little to endear him to staunch party men like Curtis. In contrast to the chairman of the Foreign Relations Committee, Curtis had never been ruffled by the liberal west wind. Populism and Progressivism had blown across Kansas without affecting him much; he was so regular, said Oswald Garrison Villard, that "only the crack of the party whip, or the sound of the dinner bell ever moves him." [27]

Clearly, something changed the Kansan's mind about the vice-presidency. It may have been party pressure or personal choice unrelated to external factors; but it may well have been, as Hurley suggests, the prospect of Borah's candidacy.

At any rate, the Republicans emerged from Kansas City with Hoover and Curtis and a unified party, and went on to defeat Governor Al Smith of New York, the Democratic contender. Hurley was even more vigorous in Hoover's behalf than he had been prior to the convention, and, when the election was over, Oklahoma was in the Republican column; the political reward was not long in coming.

Shortly after the election Hoover began to be bombarded by

[25] Claudius O. Johnson, *Borah of Idaho* (New York, 1936), pp. 417–418; McKenna, pp. 251–252.

[26] *New York Times*, Jan. 24, 1928, and Jan. 26, 1928.

[27] In "Presidential Possibilities," *Nation*, 126 (Apr. 11, 1928), 402.

advice that he consider Hurley for a major position—not all of the advice entirely independent of Hurley's knowledge. The *Lawton News Review* came out with an editorial which it sent to the president-elect, saying that Hurley was a first-rate man responsible for carrying the state for Hoover.[28] The *Daily Oklahoman* of Oklahoma City editorialized to the same effect. Hampton A. Steele of the Prairie Oil and Gas Company, a friend of Hurley's, wrote that he had been a leader of the Curtis forces in Oklahoma, and thus he and Hurley had been rivals. Hurley had been tactful in his almost single-handed work for Hoover prior to the convention and had made many friends for him everywhere. "I believe that to him more than to any other man credit should be given for the swing of sentiment in this state from opposition to support of our national ticket."[29] The U.S. Minister to Guatemala, Arthur H. Geissler, former chairman of the Republican State Committee in Oklahoma, informed Hoover that Hurley was the man, if he was considering a cabinet appointment from Oklahoma. "His appointment would help greatly to keep Oklahoma in the Republican column."[30] Scores of letters containing similar advice came to Hoover's attention.

Actually, however, the president-elect and his advisors were already considering the Oklahoman. And evidence in the Hoover papers tends to indicate that as early as the previous summer Hurley was approached as a possible assistant Secretary of War, for his name for this position appears on a sheet, in Hoover's Secretary Lawrence Richey file, entitled appointments and offers made—preconvention.[31] In any case, in early 1929 he was formally offered the post, which he promptly accepted. He then moved his family, which at that time consisted of a son and two daughters, to Washington where they occupied the house formerly rented by Vice President Charles G. Dawes at 1620 Belmont

[28] Charles Campbell to Hoover, Nov. 16, 1928, Hoover Papers.
[29] Hampton A. Steele to Hoover, Jan. 27, 1929, *ibid.*
[30] To Hoover, Jan. 16, 1929, *ibid.*
[31] Lawrence Richey File, 1-G/936, *ibid.*

Street. As a member of the "Little Cabinet," he, and Mrs. Hurley, entertained frequently and made a striking appearance; they quickly rose to social prominence in the city. *Time* magazine reported that they practiced entrances and exits in front of a mirror before going to parties.

Hurley barely had time to get settled into his new post and his family located in the capital, when dame fortune again smiled on him. When the Secretary of War James Good died in November 1929, Hurley promptly had his friends in the Republican party recommend him for the job. President Hoover, impressed by Hurley who very capably handled the duties of the War Department during Good's illness and immediately after his death, in December appointed the Oklahoman as Good's replacement. The position catapulted Hurley into national fame. He appears to have administered the office ably enough; he earned the respect if not always the affection of employees in the Department and of official Washington. Through his public speaking, which he did very well with his powerful voice, extemporaneous style, and magnificent presence on the platform, he became a leading spokesman of the administration. His wealth, his rugged good looks, military posture, his beautiful wife and attractive young family made him the envy of many in and out of public life. And the Hurleys continued to entertain, on a much more lavish scale than when he was an assistant secretary.

As Secretary, Hurley confronted a variety of items, some of lesser import, like the deliberations of the War Policies Commission, decisions relative to military bases, appointments, and so on, and some of considerable significance and much controversy like the Bonus March and Philippine independence. After the beginning of the Great Depression he also became Hoover's political spokesman within the cabinet, spending a good deal of time on the circuit, especially in the election years of 1930 and 1932.

One of his first actions in his new position was to serve the interests of his native Oklahoma. He refused to sign an order transferring the United States Army artillery school from Fort Sill near

Lawton, Oklahoma, to Camp Bragg, North Carolina, and eventually was successful in getting the order reversed. Another of his early moves was to urge Congress to approve a joint resolution creating a War Policies Commission, of which he was to be a member, which would study ways to "promote peace and to equalize the burdens and to minimize the profits of war," [32] the obvious motive for the move being that too many people had profited unduly in World War I and that the war effort was not equally shared. The Commission, which Hurley chaired, and which was comprised also of four Senators and four Congressmen and the Secretaries of Navy, Labor, Agriculture, and Commerce, and the Attorney General, held hearings and met periodically for two years before finally submitting a report in March of 1932. It advocated Congress' delegating the president a broad range of extraordinary powers in the event of a future emergency (not unlike those that devolved upon him in running the economy during World War I). Among these were to be the power to set prices, to expand executive departments, and to continue to allow the president to commandeer property. Another interesting feature, which Hurley backed, was a recommendation that the revenue law permit taxation at a rate of ninety-five percent on any income earned during wartime above the previous three-year average. The remainder of the report included suggestions in favor of peace-time planning for future emergencies and for building and purchasing procedures to be followed by the government.[33] How much responsibility for all facets of the report may be ascribed to the Secretary of War it is difficult to say; however, Hurley was most instrumental in getting the Commission organized, and the group's conclusions accurately reflected his own genuine concern that future wars be met with greater domestic planning than in the past so as to avoid economic confusion and unfair advantage to some citizens.

[32] U.S. Congress, *Congressional Record,* June 27, 1930.
[33] Report of the Commission created By Public Resolution No. 98, 71st Cong., approved June 27, 1930, Mar. 5, 1932, Hurley Papers.

Easily the most controversial of the matters with which the Secretary of War had to deal was the Bonus Expeditionary Force. The Great Depression of 1929 had interrupted America's prosperity and brought the nation to its knees, while threatening a final mortal blow. President Hoover's campaign rhetoric about eliminating poverty through continued business expansion looked like nonsense in view of the circumstances. Unemployment was staggering; people were literally starving; and by the early thirties, considerable national unrest manifested itself in farm strikes, picketing of the White House, and hunger marches on Washington. Like millions of other Americans, thousands of World War I veterans saw the depression eat up their savings, deprive them of their jobs, and leave them virtually helpless to feed and clothe their families. Despair drove them to Washington to petition the government for immediate payment of a World War I bonus due in thirteen years.

The question of the veterans' bonus was one long debated. Every president through the twenties opposed any assault on the federal treasury to pay soldiers a bonus. But there were strong pressures. In 1919 Congress consented to giving severance pay of $60 to men leaving the army. As veterans increased their lobbying activities, Congress in 1924 passed, over the President's veto, a comprehensive bonus bill which provided every veteran with an endowment policy, the sum to be determined by days of service. The United States treasury was to pay the premiums on these policies until they matured in 1945. With the advent of the depression and the attendant suffering, veterans began proposing various schemes providing either for immediate payment of the bonuses or the right to borrow larger amounts of money against them. Originally, a veteran could borrow up to twenty-two and one-half percent of the value of his bonus at six percent interest, forfeiting his bonus in 1945 if he could not repay the principal and interest. In 1931, veterans demanded the right to borrow up to fifty percent, and Congress passed a bill in February 1931 permitting it. President Hoover vetoed the measure as extremely expensive (it ultimately cost $1,386,828,621), but Congress overrode him, and veterans thus got some relief—many who did not need it along with many who did.

While the depression continued and unemployment remained high, however, agitation for immediate payment increased. Several bills were introduced in Congress in early 1932; finally Representative Wright Patman of Texas introduced legislation which reached the floor of the House. Meanwhile veterans gathered petitions and assembled at the Capitol in support of the bill. Immediate payment would have cost about $2.4 billion dollars, and this made it unthinkable in Hoover's view. But the veterans, many of them really destitute, came to look upon payment as a prescriptive right, as just compensation for their World War I efforts through which they had sacrificed much. Moreover, they were not moved by the protestations about cost from a President who could create a Reconstruction Finance Corporation that loaned vast sums of money to banks, insurance companies, and railroads.

In the spring of 1932 the veterans began to organize. In Portland, Oregon, and in other cities they began talking about a trip to Washington en masse to apply pressure for favorable congressional consideration of Patman's bill. In late May they began arriving in the capital; on May 29 there were about 1,300 men in Washington; in early June about 8,000; by mid-July about 20,000. Superintendent of Police General Pelham D. Glassford gave them an hospitable greeting as they arrived and helped set up facilities for them on Anacostia Field and at some twenty other places in the District of Columbia. Many of the billets were located on or near Pennsylvania Avenue not far from the Capitol. The veterans then set up a lobbying committee to get passage of the Patman legislation, a committee which was successful in getting House debate and ultimate passage of the measure. The Senate was another story. After brief debate, this august body soundly rejected the measure, while the representatives of the Bonus Expeditionary Force, some 8,000 strong, sat hopefully around the Capitol.

There was concern that an unfavorable Senate action might bring trouble, so General Glassford raised the drawbridges to Anacostia to prevent others from joining the crowd. Ironically, when the Senate decision was announced, the veterans sang "America" and dispersed. But this was not the end, though Congress thought it had settled the matter.

President Hoover and his advisers, acutely aware of the embarrassment of the B.E.F. and fearful of violence, now decided on June 18 that the group must be put out of Washington. The President asked Congress to appropriate $100,000 (to be deducted from the sums to be paid in 1945) to pay the veterans' way home. The time limit for them to get out was set as July 25. Many then left, but thousands stayed; by July 26 perhaps as many as 10,000 to 15,000 were still in Washington. Eviction, the administration concluded at the end of July, would have to be forcible. In policy developed by the President, Chief of Staff General Douglas MacArthur, the District Commissioners, Secretary of the Treasury Ogden Mills, and Hurley—though it is very difficult to consign individual ideas—it was decided that the Treasury Department would order an evacuation of the buildings occupied by the B.E.F. on Pennsylvania Avenue, giving as the reason that demolition of them was to begin on July 25. The camps at Anacostia could be dealt with later.[34]

When on July 28 the veterans had not evacuated the buildings in question, the District police surrounded them and forced the men out. Brief scuffles occurred in the process of the eviction but nothing very major. In the afternoon of that day a melee developed, the origin of which is impossible to establish, and the police fired upon and killed two of the veterans; several others were wounded and a number of men arrested. The crowd of veterans and onlookers and some "Communists" grew larger, prompting

[34] Account based on Warren, pp. 224–236; Arthur M. Schlesinger, Jr., *The Crisis of the Old Order, 1919–1933* (Boston, 1957), pp. 257–265; Frank Freidel, *Franklin D. Roosevelt; The Triumph* (Boston, 1956), pp. 326–328.

the president of the Board of Commissioners of the District, L. H. Reichelderfer, to request federal troops: "It is the opinion of the Major and Superintendent of Police, in which the Commissioners concur, that it will be impossible for the Police Department to maintain law and order except by the free use of firearms which will make the situation a dangerous one; it is believed, however, that the presence of Federal troops in some number will obviate the seriousness of the situation and result in far less violence and bloodshed." [35] Federal troops then moved in with such organization and dispatch that one cannot escape the conclusion that the administration and the Commissioners, as part of their policy, hoped to precipitate a scuffle between police and veterans to justify the request for the use of the army.

Whatever the agreed formal policy, at 2:55 P.M. on July 28, Hurley issued an order to General MacArthur calling out the army:

> The President has just now informed me that the civil government of the District of Columbia has reported to him that it is unable to maintain law and order in the District. You will have United States troops proceed immediately to the scene of disorder. Cooperate fully with the District of Columbia police force which is now in charge. Surround the affected area and clear it without delay.
>
> Turn over all prisoners to the civil authorities.
>
> In your orders insist that any women and children who may be in the affected area be accorded every consideration and kindness. Use all humanity consistent with the due execution of this order.[36]

Hurley, who wanted Hoover to declare martial law to enable the military to take more decisive action, exceeded the President's

[35] To Hoover, July 28, 1932.
[36] To MacArthur, July 28, 1932 (press release).

instructions. In authorizing the Secretary of War to use the army, the President ordered him only to see to it "that the disturbing factions are returned to *their camps* outside the business district"; in other words, he wanted the business district cleared but did not wish the veterans "driven from their camps." [37] Hurley understood the President's instructions, for on July 28 he drafted an order to MacArthur stating them rather precisely—with one exception; his draft message called for General MacArthur not to return the veterans to their own camps out of the business district but to drive them across the Anacostia bridge into the largest of the camps, Camp Marks.[38] Hurley did not communicate this draft order to MacArthur, neither the part relaying the President's instructions nor his own directive in excess of these instructions. It is significant, however, that while he chose not to inform MacArthur of the specific limitations of the President's order, he did tell him orally to push on to the Anacostia bridge.[39]

The President then informed the press that he had asked the army to restore order "to put an end to this rioting and defiance of civil authority." In a revealing comment, he further stated that the veterans had been given "every opportunity of free assembly, free speech and free petition to Congress," and that Congress had made provision for the return home of the force. Many took advantage of the offer. "An examination of a large number of names discloses the fact that a considerable part of those remaining are

[37] Hoover, *The Memoirs of Herbert Hoover: The Great Depression, 1929–1941* (New York, 1952), p. 227. Hoover's explanation of the affair in his memoirs, in which he mentions that his directive was not strictly followed, may be taken as an attempt to cleanse his record and as an essentially accurate accounting of what happened. But it does not change the fact that he wanted the B.E.F. out of Washington and that, while he did not envision such a rapid move, he assumed complete responsibility for the eviction.

[38] To MacArthur, no date, Box 48, Folder 6. For an excellent account of this point, see Donald J. Lisio, "A Blunder Becomes Catastrophe; Hoover, the Legion, and the Bonus Army," *Wisconsin Magazine of History*, 51 (Autumn, 1967), 37–50.

[39] Report from the Chief of Staff to the Secretary of War, Aug. 15, 1932, Hurley Papers.

not veterans; many are Communists and persons with criminal records."[40] Hoover indicated that the administration had had enough of the B.E.F.

Shortly thereafter, 600 U.S. troops arrived, armed with machine guns and six tanks and led by General MacArthur. The soldiers drove the veterans from their camps within the city and, using cavalry charges and tear gas, chased them off across the Anacostia bridge. MacArthur paused briefly at the bridge, while the President, already aware that his original order to Hurley had been exceeded, discussed the next move with the Secretary of War. He decided that MacArthur's forces should not cross the bridge and instructed Hurley to so inform the chief of staff; whereupon, the Secretary of War dispatched his personal assistant and Deputy Chief of Staff, George Van Horn Moseley, to relay the order. Moseley completed the mission, making sure that MacArthur understood the Secretary's directive; shortly thereafter, Moseley sent Colonel Clement B. Wright, Secretary to the General Staff, to repeat the message. MacArthur, with the same contempt for civilian authority which later ended his career, simply disregarded the order, crossed the bridge and continued the rout. He dispersed the remaining veterans, who offered no resistance, and proceeded to destroy their "town" which had already been torched by the retreating veterans.[41] Fortunately, the only fatality resulting from the military action was an infant at Anacostia who succumbed from the inhalation of tear gas.

Concerned about the casual disregard for his instructions and the possible political repercussions of the rout, President Hoover immediately requested that Hurley and MacArthur either publicly admit their responsibility in the affair or apprise a loyal Republican congressman who would defend the administration.

[40] Press release by President Hoover, July 28, 1932, *ibid.*

[41] George Van Horn Moseley, "One Soldier's Journey," Vol. II, pp. 144–145, Moseley Papers, Library of Congress. Cited also in James F. and Jean H. Vivian, "The Bonus March of 1932: The Role of General George Van Horn Moseley," *Wisconsin Magazine of History,* 51 (Autumn, 1967), 34.

They refused to do so, arguing that the totality of the action was just, that nothing need be said, and that, in any case, it would sound like they were "bragging," since the public generally supported the action.[42]

Although he had plenty of reason to demand compliance or, for that matter, to exact the resignation of MacArthur and Hurley, Hoover did not insist. He was more disturbed about the chief of staff's indiscretion than Hurley's, for the Secretary of War had altered the President's instructions only slightly. The two men, Hoover and Hurley, spent the evening of the 28th together, during which time Hurley was able to present a defense of the need to push the B.E.F. across the Anacostia bridge into Camp Marks.[43] And, though MacArthur openly disobeyed an order directly and explicitly communicated to him, the President also refrained from reprimanding him. Like President Monroe when faced with General Jackson's precipitous action in Florida in 1818, Hoover, one must conclude, ultimately supported his subordinates because, while he may have disagreed with their methods, he was not displeased with the result.

Citing the lack of bloodshed and the "radical" or "Communist" composition of the B.E.F., Hurley and others within the administration then proceeded enthusiastically to defend the move. Hoover saw the use of troops as necessary to avoid mob rule; the challenge to U.S. institutions had to be met "swiftly and firmly." [44] MacArthur said: "that mob down there was a bad looking mob. It was animated by the essence of revolution. It is my opinion that had the President not acted today, had he permitted this thing to go on twenty-four hours more, he would have been faced with a grave situation which would have caused a real battle. Had he let it go another week I believe that the institutions of our Government would have been very severely threatened." Later, he

[42] Memorandum by Lawrence Richey, July 30, 1932, Bonus Files, L-E/300, Hoover Papers.

[43] Moseley, "One Soldier's Journey," Moseley Papers, p. 144.

[44] Statement by President Hoover, July 29, 1932, Hurley Papers.

said: "There were few veteran soldiers in that group we cleared out today; few indeed." Moreover, "I have never seen greater relief on the part of the distressed populace than I saw today . . . the President played it pretty fine in waiting to the last minute; but he didn't have much margin." [45] F. Trubee Davison, Assistant Secretary of War, said the B.E.F. was mainly comprised of "tramps," "hoodlums," and "Communist agitators."

Hurley, on his part, in statements on July 29 and August 3, offered a more definitive defense. Prior to the use of force, he said, inspection of the various camps "proved" that only about two-thirds of the men present were veterans, and many of them had already received some sort of compensation. Those remaining were creating sanitation problems and were a general menace to the city. Then the group "became more and more under the influence of the number of so-called red, radical agitators after many of the genuine veterans had left." Furthermore, a riot led by the remaining veterans was ensuing on July 28 which could not be handled by the District police (though it is interesting that Glassford did not himself request federal troops) and only the army could save the situation. "After the arrival of the United States troops . . . not one shot was fired and no person was seriously injured." Law and order, Hurley further stated, was restored with "unparalleled humanity and kindness." In any event, "there was no reason for the continuance of these marchers in Washington except to carry out the orders of propagandists and radicals to harass, obstruct, intimidate and coerce the officials of the Government." [46]

Indeed, the influence of radicals and Communists on the B.E.F. was a theme on which administration officials hammered throughout. They exaggerated wildly. The Communists, much to their own chagrin, had played no part in the organization of the Bonus March, which was, essentially, a spontaneous movement. However, at the insistence of Moscow they quickly got involved, rec-

[45] Press interview, July 28, 1932, *ibid.*
[46] Statements, July 29 and Aug. 3, 1932, *ibid.*

ognizing the great chance thus offered to promote the cause of disorder and revolution. They organized the Ex-Servicemen's League, under the leadership of Emmanuel Levine of New York, which was to order a march on Washington in early June; the Communists would infiltrate the B.E.F., capture it, and foment a violent confrontation with the army. John T. Pace of Detroit, a Communist (since 1931), then led some 400 so-called reds to Washington where he became the leader of the Communist force; new recruits were brought in from other cities as well. The Communists plans were big. And in late July, more Communists came to Washington; most of them were present at the riots on the 28th and were responsible for much of the trouble. On the 29th they met to map strategy for resisting the army. But the fact is that at no time did the Communists have more than 500 to 600 men in Washington, and their effectiveness in inciting the veterans, most of whom were pitiful, despairing men with "no stomach for fighting," was almost nil. Neither the Attorney General's office nor any of the other government agencies investigating the matter could find any more than nominal Communist influence. And Police Superintendent Glassford testified to the paucity of evidence indicating Communist domination of the veterans.[47]

Of the administration's position and Hurley's part in evicting the veterans, several additional points might be made. The administration was jittery, perhaps with some justification, regarding the *potential* of a large group of veterans encamped in or near the nation's capital, especially in view of its reports about the number of Communists involved. Certainly the force added embarrassment for an administration already harassed by burgeoning depression problems, an administration that was seeking re-election in the fall. But crowds do not constitute riots; the veterans were essentially a peaceful group; the policy formulated for dealing with the B.E.F. had at its core the need for a pretext. The Attorney General of the District of Columbia wrote MacArthur

[47] Testimony to Grand Jury, Aug. 1, 1932, Hoover Papers; see also Warren, pp. 229–235.

asking him whether any high officials of the District Police Department asked him to move his troops to the scene of the disturbances. He wanted to know "the attitude of police authorities respecting the need for troops." [48] MacArthur replied: "To the best of my recollection at about 4:15 P.M. Superintendent of Police Glassford contacted me on the Ellipse. He came from the Pennsylvania Avenue rioting area and I asked him as to the immediate situation there. He stated the condition of the policeman whose skull he feared had been fractured. General Glassford had apparently seen the man on the operating table at the hospital. He inquired as to my plan for moving the troops. I explained it to him and requested him to return to the Pennsylvania Avenue area and notify the rioters that an Army detachment would be there within a few minutes; that I hoped they would evacuate the grounds peaceably and not make it necessary to use any unnecessary force." [49] MacArthur does not say that Glassford requested the use of troops; in fact he curiously avoids a specific answer to the question. The force used to drive them out of the District, for all its vaunted humanity, was hardly necessary; the rhetoric associated with the action—largely the work of MacArthur and Hurley—was misleading and not defensible. In Hurley's case there seems to have been little recognition of the plight of the veterans, of their right to petition their government in behalf of a cause they deemed just. Moreover, neither he nor any other figure within the administration suggested a possible comparison between the lobbying tactics of the B.E.F.—which were described as *intimidation*—and those long employed by American corporations.

The episode was hardly over before it became a campaign issue. Much of the nation's press favored the Hoover administration's action; approximately 70 papers with a 4.5-million circulation came to the President's defense. The *New York Herald Tribune* stated that "whether these men are really communists or not

[48] To MacArthur, Aug. 5, 1932.
[49] To the Attorney General, Aug. 6, 1932.

is immaterial; they are agitators, and their object is to foment trouble and make headlines." The *Cleveland Plain Dealer* wrote: "The capital cannot surrender to the B.E.F. or to any other group insisting on rights that do not exist." The *Washington Star* reported that there was "not one serious injury during General MacArthur's movements." The *Philadelphia Evening Bulletin* said "the government . . . must maintain itself against the mob and anarchy." The *Richmond News Leader* saw the "trespassers" as finally "ejected from ground they should never have been permitted to occupy." The *Boston Herald* believed that "the riffraff mob would not understand argument any milder." The *Washington Post* also upheld the President's action in similar terms.[50]

At the same time, some twenty-five newspapers across the country with a circulation of over 2.5 million were critical of the President's action and his attitude toward the B.E.F.; among them were the entire Hearst chain and such other papers as the *Philadelphia Record,* the *Baltimore Sun,* the *Washington News,* the *Akron Beacon Journal,* the *Cleveland Press,* the *New York World Telegram,* the *St. Louis Post Dispatch,* and the *Milwaukee News.*[51] The *Baltimore Sun* in a biting editorial said: "Panic, especially in high places, is usually contagious. It may be that after the demonstration of yesterday cooler heads will prevail, but it is all too likely that the disease will spread its virulence. In that event, as in yesterday's instance reason will depart; passion will masquerade as intelligence and vehemence as conviction."[52] Paul Y. Anderson, of the *Nation,* scathingly observed that Hoover and Hurley had opened Hoover's campaign for re-election on the issue "he saved the country from the radicals."[53]

The Democrats lost no time in berating the President for his

---

[50] See editorial pages of the papers mentioned between July 29 and Aug. 5, 1932.

[51] Confidential summary of editorial comment for the President, Aug. 3, 1932, Hurley Papers.

[52] July 29, 1932.

[53] *Nation,* Aug. 6, 1932.

use of troops. In fairness to Hoover and the Republican position, much of the reporting on the episode was gross exaggeration and malicious falsehoods. As might be expected, the Communists invented all kinds of atrocity stories to feed their propaganda mill. But the Democratic party, in its zeal to capture the White House in November, also propagated numerous untruths, especially in regard to the methods employed by the army in evicting the veterans. More critical, of course, were the veterans' organizations around the country, some of which were opposed to the force tactics used by the administration and some simply upset that it denied them the bonus.[54]

In any case, numerous of these groups, the most important being the American Legion, passed resolutions at the state and local level censuring President Hoover and Hurley and Mac-Arthur for their part in the affair. The American Legion National Convention meeting in Portland, Oregon, also threatened to endorse a statement to the same effect. Because he feared the effect this would have on the President's campaign for re-election and because of his concern about the criticism of himself, Hurley traveled to Portland to address the group. The move required courage (a trait he could never be accused of lacking), for at previous Legion meetings administration spokesmen had been hooted off the speakers' platform and threatened with bodily harm. Friends and family and the President counseled against the trip. Arriving at the Convention hotel, where the feeling was indeed so intense that there was great concern that the feisty delegates might not let him speak, Hurley promptly mounted the rostrum and informed the assembly: "at the meeting of the Oklahoma delegation this morning, I instructed them to cash my vote for the payment of the bonus."[55] When the jeers, catcalls, and some cheering subsided, he then went on with a typical Memorial Day or Fourth of July speech, filled with froth and sentimentality

[54] See, for instance, the Hurley Papers, Boxes 47 and 48, which contain much correspondence from and in regard to veterans' groups.

[55] Josephus Daniels to Franklin D. Roosevelt, Oct. 8, 1934, Roosevelt Papers, Roosevelt Presidential Library, Hyde Park, New York.

and a sprinkling of patriotic bluster, never once mentioning the Bonus March. The speech was generally well received.

Later, he "gave them both barrels." In a prepared "impromptu" statement at a banquet honoring the guests at the Convention, he answered a brief speech by war correspondent Floyd Gibbons who had condemned the administration's action. "When any man tells you," Hurley began, "that when the lives of two human beings are snuffed out, when 60 people have been wounded, when the District of Columbia advised the President that they had lost control of civil government and could not protect life or maintain law and order, when any man tells you that that was orderly procedure, he is not stating the facts." He passionately recounted the "facts," closing with avowals of love for his Legion "comrades" and a comment that what the country needed was "patriotism above politics . . . I recognize but one government, and that is the government of the United States. I recognize in this broad land of ours but one army, and that army is the Army of the United States."[56]

How much assistance, to Hoover, Hurley's efforts in Portland proved to be, is impossible to assess. He probably changed some minds or at least convinced many they should harbor less ill-will toward the administration. The convention did defeat an attempt to censure the President. However, on another but related issue the delegates censured Hurley himself; one of Hurley's friends in the War Department, unknown to the Secretary, mailed out to the Legionnaires copies of his reply to Gibbons on War Department stationery, prompting the Convention to respond with a ringing condemnation.[57] The Legion may have been slightly less hostile toward the President, but thousands of veterans cast their votes for Roosevelt in 1932 because of Hoover's treatment of the bonus question.

Realizing that because of the depression, re-election of Hoover

[56] Statement to the American Legion National Convention, Sept. 12, 1932, Hurley Papers.

[57] J. P. O'Neil to Hurley, Sept. 15, 1932, and Hurley to Evan L. Davis, Sept. 20, 1932.

would be a tremendous struggle regardless of the bonus issue, Hurley took the stump early and often for his chief; he recited the Republican interpretation of the causes of the depression which "originated in Europe," the "accomplishments" of the President, and the measures taken to end the economic catastrophe. Every depression emergency, Hurley stated, had been met "promptly, courageously and intelligently" by the President; the President was "an inspiration to us all." Also attacking the opposition, Hurley asked: "is the New Deal to substitute for individual effort, individual enterprise, some form of bureaucratic collectivism. . . . Just what is this New Deal?" "No dictator," he charged in Philadelphia, "has had the power that would enable him to redeem the promises that have been made to the people by Governor Franklin Roosevelt." The Democrats, he charged, were guilty of "vicious character assassination" and "smear tactics"; they were "indecent" in their vilification of President Hoover, and so on, and so on.

There may have been an ulterior motive for Hurley's vigor in behalf of his chief. Though he put out the familiar protestations that he did not want it, there was a strong move to make him the vice-presidential nominee in 1932; and while the position was perhaps not overtly sought by Hurley, he would have been delighted had Hoover chosen him as his running mate. Notwithstanding any personal ambition he may have harbored, and hoped to serve through the President, "Hoover," he wrote a friend, "is the greatest personality with whom I have ever come in contact." And, he believed, "when you work for a man, for God's sake work for him." [58]

[58] Hurley to Victor Locke, Jr., Apr. 7, 1931. In July 1949, former President Hoover wrote to Hurley in regard to an article published in *McCall's* magazine by Eleanor Roosevelt about the Bonus March. The article was extremely critical of Hoover and his handling of the affair, and Hoover requested Hurley to "scotch this perpetual myth the New Dealers are trying to build up about the Bonus March." Hurley responded with a long letter to *McCall's* defending the policies of his former chief (Hoover to Hurley, July 8, 1949; *McCall's* [Nov., 1949]).

In addition to his work as a political campaigner and with the
B.E.F., Hurley spent much of his time dealing with the question
of Philippine independence. Because the islands were administered by the War Department, he became a major formulator
of policy on their future status—a matter which rivaled the Bonus
March in generating domestic controversy, and, in view of the
international situation at that time, one important to the national
interests of the United States.

# III

## Philippine Independence

Since 1945, the countries of the West have been confronted with the task of formulating policies adequate to deal with strident nationalism in the underdeveloped areas of the world. Most have reluctantly withdrawn control over their colonies because of these nationalistic pressures. The United States, in the case of its Philippine possession, faced the same problem fifteen years earlier and responded then with legislation providing for ultimate independence of its ward. But, as in the case of the nations of western Europe, the move to effect withdrawal of American sovereignty by no means received unanimous support. Indeed, in the critical period between 1929 and 1932, during which time Congress acted on the matter, the Hoover administration stood solidly against independence. As Secretary of War and close adviser of the President, Hurley became a chief spokesman of the opposition.

The question of Philippine independence arose in the late twenties for a variety of reasons. Agricultural pressures in the United States, labor interests wanting to exclude the Filipino, idealistic concern on the part of certain members of Congress, a surging nationalism in the islands, previous promises by the United States and the Cuban sugar lobby: all these contributed to the movement.

When the United States entered the world arena in 1898 and warred with Spain, it did so ostensibly to free Cuba from Spanish control. And to prove that its motives were pure, as a part of the declaration of war, it made a self-denying pledge in the famous Teller Amendment that the United States had no intention of annexing that island. A by-product of the war with Spain was her Philippine colony. But in the case of the Philippines the United States had made no self-denying pledge. And so, because of increased interest in the United States in the markets of the Far East and in part because the United States saw a need now to exert more pressure in that region vis-à-vis the European powers, in 1899 she annexed the islands.

Annexation brought great disappointment to those Filipinos who were politically conscious. A nationalist movement there, led by Emilio Aguinaldo, had taken an early stand against Spanish rule, and indeed it was this element which helped the United States to achieve Spain's rapid defeat. Once the war was over many of these same Philippine leaders assumed that since Cuba had been granted its independence so too would the Philippines. When independence was not forthcoming, they rebelled against the United States, their effort not being crushed until 1903.

While the United States thus engaged in an imperialistic venture, it was not an imperialistic power without conscience. Consequently, during the first two decades of the twentieth century, beginning with the leadership of the first Governor General, William H. Taft, it began conducting a systematic census, establishing a system of public education, creating a modern currency, separating church and state, effecting sweeping changes in transportation and health facilities, and politically preparing the islands for independence through the creation of a National Assembly. During the Wilson administration, a greater effort was made in the direction of Philippine self-government. In 1913, Francis Burton Harrison, Wilson's liberal Governor General, began granting Filipinos more voice in the legislative process by alloting them more positions in the cabinet and the civil service. This meant that many of the reforms, particularly in health and economics of the previous Republican era, came under the control of the Filipino leaders, sometimes to the detriment of those programs.

When the Republicans returned to office in the United States in 1921, Harrison was replaced by General Leonard Wood, whose policies were less liberal politically and who was intent on maintaining stability and restoring the social and economic gains made down to 1913. Often contemptuous of Philippine nationalism and frequently undiplomatic in dealing with sensitive issues, he incurred the wrath of Filipino leaders who saw him as an obstacle to independence. Yet even Wood's program, which lasted until 1927, did not lead people to doubt that the islands would some day soon separate from the United States.

The American record in its colonial venture is obviously mixed. On the positive side, the United States enacted land and corporation laws making it impossible to establish huge plantations and cartels within the islands. Compared to the other imperialist powers, the United States established almost no bureaucracy in its colony; it spent far more money on health and education than did the British, French, and Dutch in their Southeast Asian ventures; it used no insular taxes to maintain a military force in the Philippines, as did the European powers in their colonies, instead placing the burden entirely on the American taxpayer; it imported no coolie labor as in Borneo and Malaya, encouraged no Muslim separatism as in India, and maintained no opium concession; it tolerated and even encouraged nationalist agitation to its rule, while the French in Indochina and the British in India were imprisoning thousands of Vietnamese and Indians.

At the same time, the United States committed numerous errors. It refused to consider equal status for the Filipino and manifested the same kind of racial attitudes toward the natives as toward American Negroes. Americans in the Philippines took Filipino mistresses but no wives; they established separate schools, churches, and social clubs; they refused anything more than minimal social intercourse with the islanders. Through its tariff policies the United States dominated Philippine economic life and fostered a strict dependence in the islands; the great bulk of the islands' imports and exports were with the United States, and, accordingly, the Philippines produced large amounts of agricultural products for export while most of its manufactured goods were imported. Because the United States did not discriminate against Japanese and Chinese minorities living in the islands, Filipinos were placed in competition, often disadvantageously, with these oriental businessmen. Thus, to the Filipinos, there were negative economic aspects of American rule. Militarily, the United States prevented the creation of a military establishment, which was good in that it channeled capital into other more desirable areas, yet it left the islands virtually defenseless in the face of an enemy—even during the American presence.

Perhaps the most significant determining factor in American policy toward the Philippines was that the United States, even from the beginning, did not need the islands economically. Therefore independence was never doubted on principle, only in practical terms related to time. What ultimately gave impetus to the struggle for independence was the early preparation for self-government and the encouragement given to Filipino nationalists, as well as that by the end of the twenties more and more Americans not only believed that the United States did not need the islands economically, but saw them as a distinct liability. Vigorous agitation for immediate independence by Filipino leaders began in 1919 and continued intermittently through the twenties. With the beginning of the Great Depression, American pressure groups demanded, as some put it, independence from the Philippines.[1] It was this combination of forces which made the question a compelling one for the Hoover administration and for Hurley.

Because the great economic depression threatened disaster for many American farmers, agricultural lobbies applied strong pressures in favor of independence, thus hoping to shut out seemingly competitive imports from the Philippines. This group, frequently labeled by historians as the most important in the independence drive, sought enactment of tariffs on such items

[1] See Theodore Friend, *Between Two Empires: The Ordeal of the Philippines, 1929–1946* (New Haven, 1965), pp. 1–9.

as coconut oil. American dairymen screamed that coconut oil hurt American dairy interests, the National Dairy Union and the National Cooperative Milk Producers Association taking the lead.[2] Actually, the farmers' protests served primarily the interest of another element of the economy. In the case of coconut oil, copra, from which coconut oil is made, entered the United States free of duty from all tropical countries, the Malay states, and elsewhere, as well as from the Philippines. This being the case, Philippine coconut oil perhaps competed with the oil produced in the United States from copra, but such competition was a matter of concern for those controlling the American mills, not the American farmer. Moreover, the amount of coconut oil available to American industry could not have been affected by this competition unless a tariff were placed on copra as well, which was unlikely. To illustrate further the farmer's erroneous thinking, when a tariff became operative on a reciprocal basis, the farmer would have been hurt, because the Philippines was one of his best customers for flour and dairy products. In any event, the farmer lobbied for Philippine independence so the United States could place a two-cent-per-pound duty on coconut oil.[3]

The American farmer also lobbied for a duty on Philippine sugar. Most of the sugar-beet-producing states went on record through the National Farm Bureau, the National Grange, and the National Beet Grower's Association as favoring Philippine independence for this reason. In this case, the farmer served primarily the Cuban sugar interests. Philippine sugar competed with Cuban sugar, and abundant Cuban sugar with its preferential tariff rate determined the domestic price. American producers could not have captured the market unless a high tariff were placed on all sugar. As it was, if Philippine sugar were sold for a lower price, those who had invested heavily in Cuban sugar

[2] See Grayson Kirk, *Philippine Independence: Motives, Problems, and Prospects* (New York, 1936), pp. 73–80, and Friend, p. 82; see also U.S. Senate, *Hearings before Senate Committee on Territories and Insular Affairs on S.3377*, 72nd Cong., 1st Sess., Feb. 11 and 13, 1932, pp. 34–35, hereafter cited as *Senate Hearings*.

[3] *Milwaukee News*, June 6, 1931; *Senate Hearings*, pp. 34–35.

would be hurt the most. They therefore had an interest in independence. Ironically, the National City Bank of New York, the Chase National Bank, the Royal Bank of Canada, and some Boston banks lobbied energetically along with the farmer for freedom of the islands.[4]

Allied with the agricultural community and certain banks in promoting the cause of independence was American labor. Filipino laborers had emigrated to the United States in ever-increasing numbers through the twenties, settling mainly in California. Not immediately viewed as a threat, by 1930 the economic depression had created mass unemployment and placed the Filipinos in direct competition with Americans for jobs. Because the Filipino clearly manifested a lower living standard, he was able and willing to work for significantly less than his American counterpart. Like the farmer, the laborer wanted a "tariff" enacted to exclude his foreign competition. Accordingly, the A.F.L., joined by numerous ultranativist groups, agitated against the "nonassimilable" Filipino.[5]

Not to be neglected in the account of the agitation is the idealistic concern of American congressmen, more notably Senator Harry Hawes of Missouri. Often overlooked by historians, such motivation is frequently very important. Although "Beets" Hawes was characterized at the time as being a mere lackey of sugar-beet interests, he appears to have shown a sincere concern for the Philippine cause. Records left by the Philippine delegation whose members had been in direct contact with the Senator, indicate that he evidenced a desire simply to contribute to the "happiness of a large section of mankind" before he retired. Moreover, no record exists tying him to the sugar interests. Hawes worked hard for independence and authored a bill to provide it, but he did not advocate premature tariff or immigration laws.[6]

While the various pressures were building in the United States

---

[4] Friend, pp. 82, 83.
[5] *Ibid.*, pp. 83, 84.
[6] *Ibid.*, p. 71.

to sever connections with its Far Eastern possession, Filipino leaders began contacting American officials to negotiate the question. Alternately, Manuel Quezon, President of the Philippine Senate, on the one side, and Manuel Roxas, Speaker of the House, and Sergio Osmeña, Acting President of the Senate, on the other, sought out American congressmen and officials of the War Department for consultation. Each side was suspicious of the other, and neither, because independence had become so tangled in Philippine politics, could permit the other to secure the prestige attendant to success. To complicate the question further, all realized that economic separation could be extremely detrimental to the islands, yet none could afford not to accept independence "on any terms" because of political repercussions at home. Thus in November of 1931, Quezon, though he had reservations about independence, wired Secretary Hurley that the United States would have to include a statement establishing a date for independence in a plan that would envision restriction of immigration and imports. The efforts of these Philippine leaders led ultimately to the introduction of independence bills in each house of Congress.[7]

In June 1930, the Senate Committee on Territories and Insular Possessions reported the Hawes-Cutting Bill—a measure named for its sponsors, Harry Hawes and Bronson Cutting of New Mexico. The bill called for the creation and ratification of a constitution and, after a five-year period, independence. Lacking sufficient support, Hawes and Cutting did not get a vote on the measure before Congress adjourned in March 1931. In March 1932, the House Committee dealing with the subject reported the Hare Bill for consideration. Calling for immediate independence and "economic adjustment," this bill won speedy approval.[8]

In the meantime, between March 1931 and the passage of the Hare Bill both opponents and proponents of independence worked

[7] *Ibid.*, pp. 59–92.

[8] Garel Grunder and William Livezey, *The Philippines and the United States* (Norman, 1951), pp. 191–197.

to consolidate their positions. Harry Hawes made a trip to the Philippines where he was wined and dined enthusiastically. Patrick Hurley also made such a trip. Predisposed against independence, Hurley went on a "journey of inquiry," ostensibly flexible in his outlook; actually, he sought corroborating evidence for his position.

The Republican party had not been the party advocating early severance of Philippine-American ties. And during the administrations of Warren G. Harding and Calvin Coolidge much of the liberal political effort of the Wilson administration had been stopped or reversed, and General Leonard Wood became a hated symbol of American rule. Moreover, no suggestion was made by the Hoover administration that independence would be forthcoming until the Filipino had been "adequately prepared." In fact, in one of the first expressions of the Hoover administration's position, Hurley, in a letter to Hiram Bingham, chairman of the Senate Committee on Territories, said independence "would be disastrous" at that time and indicated that the President wished to maintain the "status quo." [9] Hurley frequently echoed these sentiments, but he had many reasons for opposing independence.

It is not inaccurate to say that the Secretary of War shared many of the views of the turn-of-the-century imperialists. Usually careful about manifesting blatant racist attitudes, Hurley did from time to time cast aspersions on the Philippine "brown brother" and indicated that the United States was in this case carrying the "white man's burden." More particularly, he considered it the task of the American to impart civilization to the Filipino. The United States had already spent millions of dollars there and had produced significant results in education, health, and political unity, none of which the Filipino could have done on his own. "I wish no one to understand me to claim," he wrote, "that these splendid achievements could have been made without the intelligence, courage and industry on the part of the Fili-

[9] To Hiram Bingham, May 17, 1930, Hurley Papers.

pinos themselves. However, the achievement was brought about under American leadership and guidance which have been intelligently exercised and without which, in my opinion, this progress would not have been made." [10] Paternalistic and nationalistic, Hurley said frequently that the United States won the islands by force of arms and had therefore a valid claim which it should not surrender. In his opinion, the United States also had an obligation which had to be fulfilled; it would be dishonorable to free the islands prematurely.

A memorandum prepared for the President indicates clearly the Secretary's thinking along these lines. First, Hurley stated that the United States had never really promised complete independence to the islands at the time of the approval of the Treaty of Paris. Since that time it had been wisely decided that freedom would be granted only when the United States considered the Filipino ready. Obviously, through the period of the Wilson administration and the twenties, they had not manifested such readiness; and they still seemed as backward in many regards as in 1899. Filipinos could not maintain public order; they could not support the cost of independence; the United States would fail its obligation to the Philippine people unless it made "a declaration of purpose to continue American sovereignty in the Philippine Islands until the task to which we have committed ourselves there shall have been, in our best judgment, completed." [11]

Moreover, Hurley did not believe that the independence movement there was popularly inspired. His view of America colored in part by the rapid strides he had made in life, the Secretary considered his country the land of opportunity unequaled in the world's history; and that its government was the best and most

[10] Memorandum by the Secretary of War, Feb. 18, 1930, and Hurley to Charles East, Sept. 7, 1931, *ibid.*; *Civismo*, Sept. 7, 1931; and U.S. House of Representatives, *Hearings before Committee on Insular Affairs on H.R.7233*, 72nd Cong., 1st Sess., Feb. 10, 1932, p. 389, hereafter cited as *House Hearings*.

[11] Memorandum to the President, Feb. 18, 1930, Hurley Papers.

just ever created, he did not question. The United States was conducting in the Philippines "a colonial experiment," the creation of a "self-governing, self-sufficient nation." It therefore did not occur to him that any sizable portion of the island population could seriously consider removing itself precipitously from the cloak of such a nation once exposed to its magnanimous rule. He stated frequently in 1930 and 1931 that in fact the Filipino did not understand independence if he agitated for it. And in early autumn of 1931 on his tour of the islands he queried the population on the matter, concluding that less than one-fourth of the people there really wanted freedom from the United States and that the majority was being muffled by a powerful minority. Those who opposed the severance of ties, the Secretary said, came to him "in the night" with such statements as "my business will be destroyed, I will be ostracized if I tell the truth about this." [12]

If his personal prejudices were sufficient to convince him of the imprudence of the movement, the Secretary's hard-headed concern for economic questions made him doubly certain. He, of course, realized that the agricultural community and the Cuban sugar interests wanted independence in order to enact high tariffs on Philippine products. And he believed that if such levies occurred the Filipino would be placed in a decidedly disadvantageous economic position. Filipinos needed American markets, and, if they did not have them, their trade would collapse, banks would fail, property values would diminish, capital would leave the country, currency reserves would soon be dissipated, and the government would soon be bankrupt. Attendant problems would be unemployment, political disorder, public chaos, revolution, and perhaps absorption by a stronger power. [13]

Hurley was much concerned about the latter. And his concern

[12] Note by the Secretary on a Memorandum for the Secretary of War, dated July 27, 1931, *ibid.; New York Times*, Sept. 18, 1931; *Time*, Sept. 14, 1931; *House Hearings*, p. 390; and *Senate Hearings*, pp. 29–30.

[13] Hurley to the President, Dec. 22, 1932, and Hurley to Cameron Forbes, July 6, 1932, Hurley Papers; *Senate Hearings*, pp. 7–28.

reflects understanding of the power situation in the Far East perhaps beyond the level achieved by President Hoover. In February 1930, the Secretary warned that an expansionist-minded power like Japan would swallow up the islands in no time if the United States departed. He also recognized that withdrawal would cause the British to reconsider their position on the naval disarmament question since she considered American presence in the Far East a stabilizing factor—a fact that only later impressed Hoover after a discussion with Secretary of State Henry Stimson and Cameron Forbes. It therefore was not just a question of retention or independence. In Hurley's mind, "if the United States had a policy in the Far East, the Philippine islands were essential to that policy." Secretary of State Stimson believed that "no matter under what verbal profession the act of withdrawal were clothed, to the realist observers of that part of the world it would inevitably assume the aspect of abandonment of the wards we had undertaken to protect."[14]

Hurley's fear was also based on some knowledge of increased Japanese influence, influence which had grown by the month until in late 1930 and 1931 Japanese controlled much of the Philippine lumbering, hemp, and fishing industries. Indicative of the developing Japanese position was the action of the Japanese Consul at Davao who posted a map on his wall listing Mindanao as a "domestic" island.[15] When later asked by his friend Will Rogers if he thought Japan would move in "the day we got out," Hurley said no; he believed they would wait until the "following morning."

Japanese aggression in eastern Asia was the paramount topic after September 1931. Because she needed the raw materials to be procured there, and because she sought new markets, avenues of investment, and an area to which to send surplus population, Japan had long manifested a "special" interest in Manchuria. In 1931, her domestic life marked by a struggle between the mili-

[14] Memorandum by the Secretary of War, Feb. 18, 1930; Cameron Forbes to Hurley, July 1, 1932, Hurley Papers; and *Senate Hearings*, p. 28.
[15] Friend, p. 76.

tary and the civilian, and needing economic respite from the depression, Japan acted—or rather her military acted against China. Over the next year and one-half, she consolidated control over Manchuria, threatened China proper and menaced all other foreign investments in the region. She showed signs, moreover, that her designs would extend beyond China.

Hurley was in the Far East when Japan began her effort. Arriving at Manila on September 1, 1931, on board the U.S.S. *President Cleveland,* Hurley, his wife, and daughter Ruth were greeted by a throng of 10,000 well-wishers, including Governor General Dwight Davis who had declared a national holiday in honor of the Secretary. As Hurley walked ashore, whistles of the other vessels in port sounded their shrill notes, reminding him, he said, of the work alarm at number six mine in the Choctaw Nation. The Filipinos, already aroused by their leaders and by Senator Hawes who preceded Hurley to the islands, were enthusiastically proindependence, and their welcome was undoubtedly based on the hope of convincing Hurley of the righteousness of their cause. A fact quickly apparent was their desire to demonstrate unity on the independence question.

Seeking confirmation of his position, the Secretary then traveled about the country interviewing as many Filipinos as possible. He always asked a series of stock questions of those with whom he spoke: Do Filipinos want a tariff wall erected against them? Do Filipinos realize that independence would mean such discrimination? What will Filipinos have after independence that they do not now have? Can the Philippine people really compare their situation with that of Americans in 1776? Have not Filipinos attained progress and happiness under the United States? Will not taxes be higher if independence is granted? Can Filipinos defend themselves? What about the millions of dollars the United States has spent in the Philippines? Do not most poorer and apolitical people in the islands want the United States to stay? [16]

[16] Statement by the Secretary of War, Sept. 26, 1931, Hurley Papers; see also *The Philippine Herald,* Sept. 15, 1931, Hurley Clipping Book, p. 65, Box 6, *ibid.*

The last question of course indicated that the Secretary did not consider the movement to be one with broad support. The preceding questions revealed clearly Hurley's ideas. When he left the islands, the Philippine legislature, angered at his "closed-mindedness," passed a resolution requesting "immediate" independence. Hurley returned more convinced than ever to oppose it.

On his way back to the United States, Hurley, indicating great concern about Japanese intentions and with his anti-independence view firmed up, asked the State Department, the Commerce Department, and the Army and Navy to state whether they considered the Philippines a liability.[17] The State Department, with Secretary Stimson taking the lead, maintained that they were indeed very important to the American position in the Far East, that in fact the whole policy of the United States in taking a stand against Japan was predicated on the retention of the islands. To leave them would be tantamount to scuttling and running from the Far East and would make the policy of protest absolutely meaningless. Preparatory to writing his famous letter of February 1932 to Senator William E. Borah reaffirming non-recognition of Japanese conquest in China, Stimson wrote to Senator Hiram Bingham suggesting that an anti-independence stand on the Philippines needed to be linked to policy toward Japan.[18]

Actually American policy in China in the twentieth century had always been linked intimately with her position in the Philippines. She took the islands in the first place partially to insure a better position vis-à-vis China. Later, when Japan periodically threatened the Open Door policy in China by achieving increased special privilege, the United States and Japan in discussions often

[17] To the Secretaries of State and Commerce and to Army and Navy Departments, Oct. 2, 1931, *ibid.*; see also Friend, p. 77; and Memoranda for the Secretary of War, 1-G/984, Hoover Papers, Hoover Library, West Branch, Iowa.

[18] U.S. Congress, *Congressional Record*, Apr. 4, 1932; see also Secretary of State to President Hoover, Feb. 13, 1932, 1-F/838, Hoover Papers.

spoke of American position and military strength in the islands in one breath and Japanese interests in Manchuria in the next.[19] American willingness to stay in the Philippines and to fortify them went a long way diplomatically toward achieving temporary accommodation with Japan.

There were others besides Hurley and Stimson who worried that premature abandonment of the islands would have an adverse effect on the general Far Eastern situation. Newspaper publisher Roy Howard, critically assessing Japan's intentions, feared that Japan would fill the vacuum created by American withdrawal, and Nelson T. Johnson, American Minister to China, made positive statements that the United States should retain possession. Johnson did not believe that a mere pronouncement to this effect would force Japan to end her aggression. But, if coupled with denunciation of the treaties concluded in Washington in 1921 and 1922 and a rearmament program, it would give her pause and perhaps persuade her to negotiate a political settlement in China which would not preclude preservation of some American interests.[20]

That some of the American people held similar views is suggested in mail which Hurley received after completion of his journey. Many writers congratulated the Secretary for the stand he was taking on the independence question and then went on to cite Japanese aggression as an important reason for retaining the Philippines. These correspondents were concerned about a Japanese invasion of the islands, but some also believed that American presence was necessary to check Japan, to maintain a semblance of a balance in the Far East, and to avoid weakening the position of the other colonial powers. If the United States were to leave

[19] See, for instance, the Root-Takahira Agreement, the Taft-Katsura Agreement, and the Four Power Treaty.

[20] See Nelson T. Johnson to the Secretary of State, June 12, 1933, U.S. Department of State, *Foreign Relations of the United States, 1933*, III, 360–362, hereafter referred to as *F.R.*; see also Johnson to Stanley Hornbeck, June 1, 1933, and Aug. 6, 1933, and Johnson to Roy Howard, Aug. 29, 1933, Nelson T. Johnson Papers, Library of Congress.

the Philippines, the action would be a signal to other nationalist movements in Indochina, Burma, and Indonesia to pressure their colonial masters to leave. Such a development would redound even more to the benefit of Japan. One wrote: "Might I suggest that the peace of the Pacific today depends upon the United States remaining in the Philippines." Another indicated that he mentioned "the Japanese affair in this letter in as much as *it is* our Philippine problem." "The minute we walk out," another opined, "Japan walks in; everyone ought to know that much." "We should," averred one writer, "send 75,000 men to Manila, with large supplies, and the other nations should do likewise." The *Vancouver Sun* in a piece sent to Hurley editorialized: "Is the United States any less a guardian of the world's peace than Britain has been for the past 300 years? . . . Does the United States think it any less worthwhile to try to save Asia in 1932?" [21] Hurley's mail did not necessarily reflect the view of most Americans. But one thing is certain; the Secretary retained the letters which supported his position.

In cabinet meetings held shortly after his return to the United States, Hurley reiterated his view that American strength was needed in the Far East if Japan were to be blocked. He believed that "notes and diplomatic representations were not going to do much good unless backed by force." [22] Later he informed his colleagues that the United States would have either to accept Japan's ascendancy or be prepared physically to do something about it. [23] Hurley's thoughts were not based on historical knowledge of United States interests in China nor on a particularly sophisticated appraisal of current affairs there, but rather on a

[21] See W. W. Bronson to Hurley, Feb. 23, 1932; S. T. Cameron to Hurley, Feb. 15, 1932; Joseph Gray to Hurley, Feb. 17, 1932; Herbert Malone to Hurley, Feb. 25, 1932; *Vancouver Sun*, Jan. 20, 1932, and others, Box 40, Hurley Papers.

[22] Henry L. Stimson and McGeorge Bundy, *On Active Service in Peace and War* (New York, 1948), p. 243.

[23] Joseph Grew, *Ten Years in Japan* (New York, 1944), p. 49.

simple assumption which he then held that aggressive nations, like individuals, could only be checked by countervailing power manifesting itself in some overt way.

Thus committed, Hurley, in discussions with Philippine leaders both before and after his trip, and with proindependence congressmen, worked hard to preserve the American colony. When the Filipinos suggested immediate independence, the Secretary turned them down; when they pushed for a gradual plan with a definite date, he also balked.

But Hurley was willing to discuss dominion status for the American colony, hoping thereby, in giving half a loaf, to silence the nationalists and to undercut the position of those in the United States supporting independence. The Secretary's proposal entailed postponing indefinitely the independence question and provided for an elective governor general; American control over defense, health, and finance; reciprocal trade and immigration restrictions if mutually agreed upon; and creation by the Filipinos of a dominion or state form of government. The idea of dominion did not originate with Hurley but rather with Henry Stimson when he was governor general. Taken up by several Filipino leaders, it was embraced most enthusiastically by Manuel Quezon. However, pleased as they were privately at Hurley's suggestion, because of political repercussions, these Filipinos could not accept anything not guaranteeing independence. Consequently, they rejected the plan.[24]

In another move, in late July 1931, Hurley wrote to Governor General Dwight Davis urging him to advise the Philippine legislature to begin consideration of laws to prevent emigration of Philippine laborers to the United States and to limit the amount of sugar exported to this country. Such legislation, the Secretary believed, would make unnecessary discriminatory economic action by the American congress. Knowing of the economic force

[24] Hurley to Manuel Quezon, Dec. 3, 1931, Hurley Papers; and Friend, pp. 65–67.

behind the independence drive, Hurley hoped it would also make independence unnecessary.[25] Through the remainder of 1931 and 1932 Hurley continued his efforts to prevent congressional action.

Congress proceeded undeterred. The House approved the Hare Bill in April of 1932, and the Senate was considering the Hawes-Cutting Bill when it adjourned in June. Hurley testified before committees in each house, stating his position strongly, and his comments in the Senate touched off an angry exchange between him and Senator Hawes: "The purpose of the Hawes-Cutting-Hare Bill," said Hurley, "is cowardly". "Just a minute, just a minute," shouted Hawes. "I'm making this speech," Hurley replied, "you wait until I finish." Hawes then asked the Secretary if he was stating that he (Hawes) and Senator Cutting were cowardly, whereupon Hurley said: "the bill has not in it one of the elements  of courage. It is an attempt to tear down all that has been built up over a period of years." When Hawes then asked if this meant that the Secretary did not withdraw the word cowardly, Hurley said, "No, I don't." Hurley then went on to re-iterate his belief that the Filipinos were not ready for indepen-dence. He also indicated that a time could not be fixed for the ultimate withdrawal of American sovereignty. In his view, revo-lution would occur if independence were given in the immediate future. Since that was the case, he therefore would have pre-ferred immediate and unconditional independence so that the revolution did not take place under the American flag. Hurley hated the thought of independence, but he would have favored that to a drawing out of United States responsibility under im-proper conditions. As an alternative, Hurley believed that the United States should continue "preparing" the Philippines for independence. It could perhaps encourage the limitation of sugar imports from the islands and thus spur crop diversification; it could develop better relations between rural tenants and land-

[25] To Dwight Davis, July 31, 1931, Hurley Papers.

owners, justly determining who owned certain lands. And it could help develop a more informed citizenry.[26]

In December, the Senate again took up the matter, ultimately passing the Hawes-Cutting Bill which provided for a commonwealth period of fifteen years, with ten years of free trade to be followed by enactment of increasing tariff duties. After a compromise between House and Senate leaders, it was finally agreed that there should be a commonwealth period of ten years, after which independence would be granted and tariffs enacted. A bill to this effect passed congress on December 22, 1932.[27]

Hurley immediately drafted a memorandum reiterating his objections and urging the President to veto the measure. He stated first that he believed that the bill committed the United States to a position of "dangerous responsibility" without its having the power to back the commitment. Moreover, the bill would bring economic collapse in the islands; disrupt the system of government operating there and substitute an experimental type; bring chaos near the end of the ten-year period; bring disrepute to the United States, for it did not provide fulfillment by the United States of bonds previously sold by the Philippine government and ostensibly backed by congress; and disavow the "obligation" to non-Christian peoples living there. "A specially objectionable feature," said the Secretary, was "the proposed delegation to the Filipino people, the final acceptance or rejection of a procedure involving not merely the question of Philippine independence, but *the future international position and basic trade and other policies of the United States in the Orient.*"[28]

Accepting the Hurley criticisms of the bill as well as those of Secretary of State Stimson, Secretary of the Treasury Ogden Mills, and Secretary of Commerce Roy Chapin, President Hoover vetoed the measure and returned it to congress on January 13,

[26] See *Senate Hearings,* pp. 7–28.
[27] Grunder and Livezey, pp. 195–209.
[28] To President Hoover, Dec. 22, 1932, Hurley Papers.

1933. His comments reflect accurately those made to him by the Secretary of War, consisting of remonstrances about American "responsibility," "obligation" to non-Christian peoples, "aggression" in the Far East, and possible "chaos" in the islands.[29] Congress was as unimpressed as it had been earlier during the Hurley testimony and, on January 17, passed the bill over the executive veto. Ironically, because it got caught in the whirl of Philippine politics and because some Filipinos were dissatisfied with its tariff feature, the Philippine legislature rejected the Hare-Hawes-Cutting Bill; independence legislation mutually acceptable came only with the advent of the New Deal in the form of the Tydings-McDuffie Act.

Thus the Hoover administration, with Hurley playing the major role, resisted, however unavailingly, the Philippine independence drive. Significantly, all the Secretary's objections had some substance. In the light of Japan's later action there were compelling reasons to retain the islands, and to fortify them heavily. Similarly, it did not take one versed in economics to recognize the adversity to be confronted by the Filipinos after they left the American fold. Moreover, the Secretary recognized that selfish and powerful economic interests within the United States helped initiate the movement, that Filipino leaders themselves were actuated by political ambition rather than a sincere desire for independence,[30] and that therefore the whole affair seemed a "bit sordid."

But Hurley's position, if subjected to closer scrutiny, reveals some important weaknesses. Implicit in his remarks about stability as a prerequisite for independence was the assumption that the islands needed to become relatively independent economically. Such a position was not possible to attain nor was it then

[29] U.S. Congress, *Congressional Record*, Jan. 16, 1930, 72:2.

[30] According to Hurley, Manuel Quezon informed him on several occasions that he (Quezon) had mixed feelings on independence but that politically he had to remain its staunchest friend. See Hurley to Herbert Hoover, Jan. 26, 1961, ARI/5, Hoover Papers.

enjoyed by more than a handful of nations. When questioned on what he meant by economic advancement, the Secretary remained vague. On the question of defense, he was equally hazy. He stated that Filipinos should be able to defend themselves prior to gaining their freedom, yet it surely was clear to him that they could never hope to resist the advances of a determined large power. What constituted a proper defense posture he did not say. More important than each of the Secretary's individual objections, however, is his reasoning was based in large part on a fundamental lack of understanding of the Philippine desire for independence, or the spirit of nationalism developing there. Most of the Filipino leaders remembered the struggle against Spain and the later battle with the Americans. Some like Quezon had themselves been revolutionaries, only at the last surrendering to the Americans; others like José Laurel, had seen the Americans torture their fathers in a concentration camp; Carlos Romulo, when he was three years old, saw the Americans hang a good friend and neighbor in the village where he lived. These Filipinos and countless others resented the manifestations of racism overtly displayed by the Americans and rebelled against the omnipresent paternalism. They were also impatient at the slow rate of progress toward self-government. Hurley was insensitive to the above and sympathized with none of it, nor did he recognize the nationalist winds then growing stronger across much of Asia. As Theodore Friend points out in his excellent study of the Philippines, it is significant that, in Hurley's report to the President, which he submitted upon completion of his trip to the Philippines, he placed little emphasis on the term nationalist.[31] Unfortunately, and ironically, given his later vehemence in opposing the colonial policies of the British and French, one must conclude that had Hurley had the last word, the Philippines would still be an American colony.

[31] Friend, p. 45; see also *draft of the report of the Secretary of War to the President relative to his trip to the Philippine Islands,* 1931, National Archives, Record Group 350.

# IV

## Saving Sinclair's Chestnuts: Hurley and the Mexican Oil Expropriation

After the American voters repudiated the Hoover administration in the election of 1932, Hurley relinquished his cabinet post and returned to his law practice. He continued to work vigorously for the Republican party and spoke frequently in defense of his former chief, but these were Democratic years. Essentially he occupied himself managing his property, putting his financial affairs back in order, and serving the interests of the Sinclair Oil Company.

Because most of his investments were in real estate, the depression had hit him very hard, and he came out of the cabinet gasping for breath financially. His service in the government did not permit him to give proper attention to his affairs or to continue his law practice, which had always earned him a generous income. And to live in the manner to which he, Mrs. Hurley, and their four children had grown accustomed was expensive indeed. To get "back on his feet," therefore, he began accepting retainers, while at the same time he worked on various projects for independent oil firms. Harry Sinclair paid him a regular fee of $2,000 per month, not including remuneration for special jobs, while other assignments brought in similar sums. In this way he gradually "discharged his liabilities" and restored his modest fortune. Not until 1938, however, as a result of the Mexican expropriation of American oil company assets did Hurley again receive national recognition. Serving then as Sinclair's "diplomat," he successfully negotiated a settlement with the government of

Lázaro Cárdenas in a manner which proved to be the basis of settlement for all the major oil companies and the way out of a difficult and deepening crisis in Mexican-American relations.

Although immediately precipitated by a labor conflict between the Mexican government and the various companies, the oil expropriation had its roots deep in the Mexican revolution. Under Porfirio Diaz, who ruled that country with an iron hand from 1877 to 1911, American and other foreign nationals were encouraged to invest in various enterprises in Mexico, including oil. However, with the overthrow of Diaz and especially with the promulgation of a constitution by Carranza in 1917, Mexico began a reform movement designed to improve the lot of all Mexicans; to do so she sought to reacquire control over natural resources so essential to national well-being.

One of her efforts was directed at land reforms or, more specifically, to restoring lands to the hands of Mexicans. During the Diaz regime many of the common lands or *ejidos* became part of larger holdings, often in the control of foreigners, many of them American. Between 1920 and 1940 successive Mexican governments carried out varying degrees of redistribution to restore these properties to those considered rightful owners. In most cases where land belonged to foreign investors the property was simply expropriated with payment promised at an early date. Lengthy and difficult negotiations ensued through the 1930's between the Mexican government and American interests over payment of compensation for these lands.

But the land question never caused the animosity generated by oil. In the Mexican constitution of 1917 it was stated that all subsoil minerals in Mexico were to be the property of Mexico, not of the person or corporation that happened to own the surface area. Controversy immediately erupted, because foreign investors in oil during previous administrations had acquired subsoil rights and deplored the prospect of losing them. Serious Mexican-American discussions on this point occurred throughout the early 1920's with the Mexican government finally agreeing that the "positive acts" principle would determine ownership; that is, if an oil corporation made an effort to tap the oil to which it had presumably acquired a right, its ownership would not be questioned. This arrangement proved satisfactory temporarily, though it was soon repudiated by President Calles; then, through the efforts of American Ambassador Dwight Morrow, more negotiations occurred, as a result of which the "positive acts" principle was once more affirmed in an understanding known as the Morrow-Calles Agreement of 1928.

When Lázaro Cárdenas, a northerner much more radical than his predecessors, came to power in 1934 he redoubled the effort at achieving "Mexico for the Mexicans" and thus increased the expropriation of foreign lands and organized powerful and radical labor unions. His directive, aimed at the oil industry, came in 1938 as a result of a labor dispute in which the government-backed union made demands that the oil companies rejected as exorbitant. In 1935, the Mexican president organized the National Petroleum Workers Syndicate, which in 1936 demanded, among other things, an eight-hour day, double pay for overtime, inclusion of office staffs in the union, paid vacations, and a significant wage increase. When the companies, acting together, refused to comply, the syndicate in 1937 called a strike—a strike into which the Cárdenas government intervened shortly with forced arbitration through the facility of the Federal Board of Arbitration and Conciliation. The board, in August, in a sweeping ruling, came out in favor of the union, in particular advocating a 27 percent wage increase and union status for "confidential" or office personnel. Again the companies refused to comply but instead appealed to the Mexican courts, arguing that the award would be prohibitive economically and, with the inclusion of office or confidential employees, would undermine their management of the industry. When the Mexican Supreme Court ruled in favor of the workers, the companies began to negotiate, attempting to get the best terms possible. Ultimately negotiations broke down over the companies' insistance on an ironclad agreement with the Mexican government—a demand which Cárdenas considered a slur on national honor—and the companies' refusal to obey the Court ruling while negotiations ensued. Cárdenas then nationalized the oil property on March 18, 1938.[1]

Angered but probably not surprised at Cárdenas' action, the oil companies reacted in two ways: they appealed to the U.S. State Department to encourage Mexico to restore the property; and they appealed to the Mexican courts, challenging the legality of the expropriation. They alleged that the decree of March 17 and the expropriation law of 1936 on which it was based were both in conflict with the Mexican constitution. However, in a series of decisions rendered in 1938 and 1939, the Mexican courts, with a few minor exceptions, ruled in favor of the government, thus closing this avenue of appeal.

The companies' main hope lay with the State Department. Immediately upon hearing the news of the expropriation, the State Department began to move, as Under-Secretary of State Sumner Welles discussed the matter with the Mexican Ambassador to the United States Castillo Nájera. Welles informed Nájera that the action was deplorable, was an act of ingratitude on the part of the Mexican government, and one he hoped she would reconsider.[2] United States Ambassador to Mexico Josephus Daniels made a similar protest to officials there.[3] Shortly thereafter the State Department was to begin a policy which was to represent the extent of its action in the affair. On March 25, Secretary of State Cordell Hull proposed that the United States alter its silver-purchasing agreement with Mexico, which agreement committed the United States to the purchase of quantities of Mexican silver, thereby bolstering the Mexican economy. In other words,

[1] Account based on Howard F. Cline, *The United States and Mexico* (Cambridge, 1953); E. David Cronon, *Josephus Daniels in Mexico* (Madison, 1960); and Bryce Wood, *The Making of the Good Neighbor Policy* (New York, 1961).

[2] Memorandum of conversation, Sumner Welles and Castello Nájera, Mar. 21, 1938, *F.R., 1938*, V, 729–733.

[3] *Ibid.*, 728–729.

Hull hoped to bludgeon the Cárdenas government into reconsidering its action. Officially the United States did so change its silver-buying policy; but actually over the three years of the crisis it bought just as much silver as formerly.[4]

Continuing his efforts, on March 26 Hull sent a strong note of protest to Mexico condemning the expropriation. Daniels, on the scene in Mexico and cognizant of political feeling there, immediately indicated that the note should not be publicized as it would lead to a hardening of attitudes, and Hull agreed. Then, acting on his own, Daniels agreed to a suggestion of Cárdenas that the note be delivered, not as a formal protest, but rather as a series of informal questions to Mexico. When Hull learned of this action he was furious with the American representative, but Daniels' move probably prevented the breaking of diplomatic relations and worsening of the crisis. Daniels suggested frequently in dispatches to Washington that the United States should act with caution in its dealing with Mexico and should not question Mexican sovereignty or her right to expropriate foreign property. In his view, all the United States or the companies could hope for was adequate compensation.[5] Fortunately his advice was accepted in Washington.

Harsh protest and ostensible change of its silver-purchase policy were as far as the State Department went in its defense of American oil "rights." Two factors were primarily responsible in precluding stronger action. In 1933 the Roosevelt administration vowed to eschew intervention as a policy in its Latin American relations and committed itself to being the Good Neighbor. In view of this, President Roosevelt was not interested in the use of force against Mexico, and, indeed, force was never contemplated. Second, in 1938, 1939, and 1940 there was considerable fear of the deepening crisis in Europe and Asia and concern about the actions of the Axis powers. To adopt a hard line toward Mexico could drive her into accommodation with Japan and Ger-

[4] *New York Times,* Mar. 28, 29, 31, 1938; Wood, pp. 225–226.
[5] Daniels to Hull, Mar. 27, 1938, *F.R., 1938,* V, 736.

many, for Mexico needed oil markets, and the latter needed oil for their war machinery. Because a more vigorous policy therefore seemed out of the question, the State Department limited itself to attempts to facilitate negotiations between the oil companies and the Cárdenas government with a view to adequate compensation.

The burden was on the oil companies to reach a satisfactory settlement. The problem was, however, that satisfactory settlement meant payment for the property expropriated, which Mexico expressed a willingness to provide, but accepting payment meant agreeing that expropriation was valid. Such an agreement the companies did not want to give, nor were they anxious even to place a value on their property, for this would indicate that they were weakening in their stand. Hurley, serving as the representative of the Sinclair company conferring with President Cárdenas late in 1938, adequately expressed the company position when he stated that "when we talk valuations, we are admitting the validity of the expropriation and that the companies will not do." Moreover, Hurley stated, on the question of compensation, there was little worth in discussion, for "Mexico can't make it." [6] In view of their appraisal of the situation, the companies determined that it would be well to delay settlement, hoping that bankruptcy would bring a revolution in Mexico. Their representatives in Mexico sent frequent messages predicting the imminence of the overthrow of Cárdenas, and the Hurley correspondence contains a number of such documents.[7] But revolution did not occur, nor was the United States willing to encourage one, notwithstanding the oil company position.

Even though not prepared to place a valuation on their property and settle with Mexico, the oil companies working with the State Department did carry on discussions with Cárdenas through the remainder of 1938. In May, the Mexican government com-

[6] Memorandum by T. R. Armstrong entitled "Mr. Richberg's Verbal Report on his Negotiations in Mexico," Mar. 31, 1939, Hurley Papers.

[7] See Box 61, Folder 1, and Boxes 70, 71, 72, *ibid.*

municated to the State Department a proposal under which Mexico would organize a trust to run the oil industry. A commission of experts would evaluate the oil property, decide on a fair price to be paid the companies; then the government trust would sell oil to the companies at a discount price which they in turn could export and sell at a higher price. Under these arrangements the companies would ultimately be paid in full. The companies refused the offer.[8]

Mexico in turn began producing oil and proceeded reluctantly to sell as much as could be marketed to Germany, Italy, and other interested countries. She found difficulty in marketing, however, because the oil companies that controlled most of the world's supply of tankers refused to permit shipment of what they termed "stolen oil." The companies also launched a propaganda drive against the Mexican government in the periodical press in the United States and remained united in an attempt to boycott Mexican oil and oil products. They still hoped to see revolution and the overthrow of Cárdenas; economic pressure, they believed, would hasten it.[9]

In the autumn of 1938, the companies began to negotiate more seriously with the Cárdenas government, for they saw clearly by then that President Roosevelt was not disposed to act in their behalf and that it was perhaps unwise to base their policy on the thin hope of revolution. Moreover, in November, Mexico settled the acrimonious dispute over agricultural lands which had earlier been expropriated, thus proving that she could produce payment. Accordingly, Hurley, Sinclair's lawyer, acting as one of the two envoys employed by the united oil companies, journeyed to Mexico City to converse with the Mexican president. Hurley probed "the difficulty of President Cárdenas' economic mind" and found the president anxious to talk about valuations, if not in a formal sense, at least in terms of "unofficial estimates." Hurley, however,

[8] "Analysis of the situation leading up to and following the conferences of Mr. Richberg in Mexico," Box 3, Mexican Oil Expropriation, *ibid.*

[9] Cronon, pp. 208–211.

expressed the companies' reluctance to delve into that question. What he was authorized to discuss, as was Donald Richberg later, was an arrangement whereby the companies would sign a long-term contract for the management of the oil property—a contract which provided for "reasonable" labor guarantees, few restrictions on company operations, and compensation for losses suffered since the seizure. With the expiration of the contract the oil property would go to the Mexican government, the settlement not including anything that would imply the legality of expropriation.[10]

Hurley returned to the United States and reported to his employers, then prepared to go again to Mexico City along with Donald R. Richberg to renew discussions. Richberg, an old progressive and New Deal Democrat was hired by Standard Oil in the same capacity as Hurley with Sinclair. The two were kept apprised of all events postdating the seizure and participated in various company conferences. In March 1939, however, just prior to their departure for Mexico City to reopen direct negotiations, Standard Oil requested that Richberg be permitted to proceed alone to Mexico, suggesting that more progress could be made with a single representative working in behalf of the concerted companies. Hurley and Sinclair agreed, and, in March, Richberg alone began talks with Cárdenas.

Richberg began the discussions by reiterating the proposals earlier proffered by Hurley, but Cárdenas refused to countenance any plan not providing for compensation. The Mexican president countered with a proposal calling for a combined enterprise to be managed by the government and effectively under governmental control—a plan in which valuation would be placed on the property, the oil companies would assist in producing and marketing oil, and a reasonable profit would be reserved for use in liquidating the companies' claims. In short, the plan called for recognition of expropriation as a first step, but through joint man-

[10] "Richberg's Verbal Report," and "Analysis," Hurley Papers.

agement the companies were to be allowed the right to insure that the oil industry would continue to profit and therefore that they would be fully compensated.[11] Because the plan differed from that which he had put forth and because of his fairly rigid instructions which would not permit agreement to a proposal of this kind, Richberg temporarily suspended the talks and returned to the United States.

With his return, intracompany talks began with Richberg about his recent exchange with the Mexican government. Recognizing that discussions had reached an apparent impasse, William Farish, president of Standard Oil of New Jersey, asked Richberg what the next step should be. Richberg implied strongly that the only recourse at the moment was to appeal to the State Department, which he said he did indirectly while in Mexico City. Hurley, present at the meeting concurred in this, stating further that the important thing was the attitude taken by the administration on the "confiscation" of American property. He added that, if the companies and the administration admitted the validity of the Mexican seizure, "our position throughout Latin America will be ruined"; what was most important, he thought, before anyone returned to Mexico was to "devote attention to Washington. . . . Unless we have very definite support from Washington, conversations will be futile. President Cárdenas' term of office has twenty months left and if he can get by without settlement, it will be looked on as a successful administration; the chances for a revolution diminish as the end of his term approaches."[12] As a result of the Hurley-Richberg remarks, it was decided to send a memorandum to the State Department setting forth the company views. The memorandum stated that Mexico's act was confiscation and that: "It is the companies' earnest belief that the Department of State should stand on international law and formally demand a return of the properties to the management of their owners."[13]

[11] "Analysis," *ibid.*
[12] "Richberg's Verbal Report," *ibid.*
[13] "Analysis," *ibid.*

Subsequent to this appeal, Richberg in April returned to Mexico City for further discussions. In a slightly different proposal, but one which still denied the placing of a value on oil property, he suggested that the companies and Mexico agree to the creation of a four-company oil industry with each of the companies having Mexican majorities on their boards of directors. The companies would then produce oil with satisfactory labor guarantees from the Mexican government for a long-term period, and at the end of the period the property would revert to Mexico. Richberg returned then to the United States thinking he had established the basis of a satisfactory agreement, but the Mexican government did not concur, and again negotiations reached an impasse. When, by autumn 1939, a compromise solution put forth by the State Department failed to win support, it became apparent that the matter was no further along than it had been in March 1938.[14]

In the meantime a message, conveyed to Hurley on March 28, 1939, indicated that the Cárdenas government wished to make "a separate peace" with the Sinclair company. The report stated that Ed Skeet, a Sinclair representative in Mexico, was invited on March 26 to the home of a prominent Mexican senator, who happened to be a very close friend of President Cárdenas. After lunch the senator took Skeet on a tour of his estate which adjoined that of the Mexican president, and the two men talked of various mundane matters. During the course of the tour, however, they "ran into" Cárdenas who just happened to be sitting on a "rustic" bench near a bridge connecting the two properties. Cárdenas joined the two for conversation, which for awhile skirted the oil topic but then settled down to a frank discussion of a settlement. The Mexican president stated that Mexico was going to stick to her guns, but that she was now in a good position to settle, especially since she had recently completed with Germany a deal providing for German cash purchases of Mexican oil. Indeed, Cárdenas stated abruptly: "Why don't the Sin-

14 Cronon, pp. 241–242.

clair Companies make a settlement with us independently of the other people," and do so at the earliest opportunity. He went on to say that it occurred to him that Sinclair was suffering needlessly by making common cause with the other companies, because Mexico had always looked with favor on the actions of that company; the matter could be corrected if discussions were begun quietly between him and Sinclair representatives.[15]

Hurley later said that Sinclair broke the united front because he learned that Richberg had informed the Mexicans that the Consolidated Oil interests were meager and that, if the Cárdenas government settled with Standard and the other large companies, Sinclair would have to settle. Thus, according to Hurley, Standard Oil was guilty of a breach of faith, and it became clear that, if Sinclair were "to save its chestnuts," it would have to act alone. Hurley had in fact long been suspicious of Standard Oil. In late May of 1938, not long after the expropriation, the Secretary of State held a lengthy conversation with representatives of the oil companies, but he met only with three delegates from Standard. Hurley promptly telephoned the State Department to complain that he had just learned of a meeting between Hull and the oil companies but that "among those present he had not seen any representative of the Sinclair interests."[16] Then, in March 1939, Standard Oil had insisted on the wisdom of sending Richberg to Mexico City alone. Whether or not Richberg actually violated Sinclair's trust at this time cannot be substantiated; however, it seems probable that it was an excuse rather than a reason in view of the Mexican initiative of March 28.

In any event, as a result of this communication, when negotiations finally broke down completely between Richberg and the Mexican government, the Sinclair company began secret discus-

---

15 Unsigned memorandum, Mar. 28, 1939, Box 3, Confidential Reports, Mexican Oil Expropriation, Hurley Papers.

16 Memorandum of telephone conversation, May 31, 1938, Department of State, File 812.6363/4090; and Statement by Hurley before Texas Railroad Commission, Aug. 1, 1940, Hurley Papers.

sions with Mexico, with Hurley serving as the chief negotiator. In October and November of 1939, he and Ambassador Nájera dickered over the price constituting proper compensation for the Sinclair property; Hurley asking Nájera for forty million barrels of crude oil or roughly thirty-two million dollars as payment; the Mexican ambassador offered far less than that. Hurley then admitted that he had started with that figure for "bargaining purposes." [17] Significantly, both sides remained willing to continue talks and ultimately to compromise, and in December a new round of discussions were held with Secretary Suarez, Nájera, and Jesús Herzog on the one side, and Hurley and John L. Lewis, president of the United Mine Workers, on the other. Lewis' presence was, to say the least, a kind of mystery. He informed the Mexican ambassador that he was attending the meetings for three reasons: he wished, for patriotic reasons, to further good relations between the United States and Mexico; he hoped to keep the United States from adopting a too harsh posture toward Mexico; and he wanted to insure that the United States did not push for arbitration of the dispute as he considered it premature. Hurley, however, informed the Mexican ambassador that Lewis had a close "business interest" in Mexican oil and that Lewis' assertions were untrue.[18] Again, the two positions seemed irreconcilable, but again both retained an open mind and expressed a desire to continue. Through January and February of 1940 proposals and counterproposals were made. Sinclair scaled down its request to fourteen million dollars, more than cutting its earlier demand in half. By the middle of March both sides were hopeful, as signs pointed toward an early settlement; [19] Hurley had apparently won the friendship of his Mexican counterparts. Cárdenas,

[17] Jesús Silva Herzog, *Petróleo mexicano historia de un problema* (Mexico City, 1941), p. 173; *F.R., 1939*, V, 710–711.

[18] Memorandum of conversation between Sumner Welles and the Mexican Ambassador, Feb. 5, 1940, Department of State, File 812.6363/6487.

[19] Memorandum of conversation between Hurley and Hull, Mar. 1, 1940, Department of State, File 812.6363/6451,/6594; see also Herzog, 173–176.

liked him for what he thought was his Indian background, and Ambassador Nájera was won over by his affability.

In an apparently "cordial atmosphere," talks resumed on April 1 with Hurley still serving as the chief negotiator. This round of discussion produced an agreement satisfactory to both sides, a pact consisting of two parts. Mexico agreed to pay Sinclair the sum of eight and one-half million dollars to be paid in installments of one million dollars over the succeeding three years. Then, in addition, she would sell to Sinclair at a discount price, twenty to thirty cents below the market price, twenty million barrels of oil during the succeeding four years. What this meant was that the Cárdenas government agreed in effect to the fourteen million figure suggested by Hurley during the March conferences. In settling for this sum Hurley tacitly recognized the fact that, while Sinclair would not receive compensation "in full," the expropriation would not be revoked, and therefore Sinclair was getting what it could.[20] Josephus Daniels, American Ambassador to Mexico, said that Hurley had succeeded because he had not made demands or advocated forceful intervention, and because "he was a realist and knew that the interest of his company depended upon the policy of give and take. President Cárdenas and his cabinet members liked him and his desire to reach an understanding. Cárdenas, who is an Indian, was pleased to learn that Hurley likewise had Indian blood. Hurley also played up the fact that he, like Cárdenas, was a soldier. They both talked directly, brusquely, shouted at each other, disagreed, agreed, exchanged an *abrazo*, and parted as fast friends. The result was that Hurley received a fair price for the Sinclair Company and did not join in the campaign of vilification of all things Mexican."[21]

The Sinclair settlement did not end the oil controversy, for

[20] *New York Times*, May 8, 1940; Hurley's testimony before House Subcommittee Hearing on Amendment to National Stolen Properties Act, Aug. 6, 1940, Hurley Papers. Hereafter cited as *Hurley testimony*.

[21] Josephus Daniels, *Shirt-Sleeve Diplomat* (Chapel Hill, 1947), p. 265.

the other major companies, angry at the move, sought to discredit the agreement. They put their propaganda machines to work grinding out news to the effect that Sinclair's importation of Mexican oil was exceedingly damaging to the price of crude oil in the United States, and moreover that the settlement was a breach in faith. In testimony before the Texas Railroad Commission, precipitated by specific charges of Sinclair damage to oil markets in Texas, Hurley eloquently defended the agreement and explained the reasons for making it. He said that it was the view of his company at the outset that expropriation was invalid and that they disagreed with the State Department which said that Mexico did have this right if payment for the property were made. Moreover, even if one had accepted the correctness of the Department's position, Mexico seemed unable ever to pay for the property, and therefore she could only make restitution by restoring the oil property. However, as events progressed, the Cárdenas government insisted that it could pay and was anxious to be given the opportunity; never did that government try to deceive Hurley during the course of discussions on the matter. In view of the position adopted by the State Department, which precluded a return of the property unless through magnanimity on the part of the Mexicans, the only realistic thing to do was to settle. The Sinclair company broke the united front, said Hurley, because Richberg disregarded its interests in negotiations with Cárdenas.[22]

Concerning the agreement itself, Hurley maintained that it was legal in Mexico, in the United States, and in international law, and did not represent a threat to oil markets in the United States. The importation of Mexican oil by Sinclair amounted to only one barrel out of every twenty-two which entered the U.S. market from all sources; how the one barrel of Sinclair oil destroyed the market, and the other twenty-one, imported mainly by Standard Oil, did not, Hurley said was hard to figure. Sinclair's competitors

[22] Statement by Hurley before Texas Railroad Commission, Aug. 1, 1940, Hurley Papers.

imported oil and did so under the beneficial low tariff enacted under trade agreement quotas, but Sinclair's Mexican imports received no such consideration. And these competitors were importing oil from Colombia and Venezuela at four times the ratio of Sinclair imports from Mexico. In a final thrust at his accusers Hurley stated: "I might say, in closing, there is one Christian doctrine that all Americans, including Catholics, Protestants, Jews and non-believers seem to accept completely. That is the doctrine of vicarious atonement. We all like to have some noble spirit who will suffer for the expiation of our sins. Sometimes we do not place this disposition on our part on the high plane of vicarious atonement. We simply admit that we are looking for a goat. In this breaking of the market by foreign importations, the Sinclair companies must respectfully decline to become the goat." [23]

Sinclair was also accused of accepting "stolen property" as payment, and, accordingly, Hurley one week later testified before a House Committee on the question. The purpose of the testimony was discussion of an amendment to the Stolen Properties Act of 1934. In the summer of 1940 an amendment to the act was approved by the Senate upon the urging of Texas Senators Tom Connally and Morris Sheppard, an amendment that would have prevented the importation to the United States of any product or property expropriated by a foreign government. The measure was sponsored in the House by John McCormack of Massachusetts, a Catholic, because of his intense feeling about the Cárdenas regime and its anticlerical position. Clearly, however, the real support behind the amendment was provided by the Standard Oil Company. Hurley stated: "We are informed and believe that the proposed legislation does not originate in the Texas delegation, nor with Congressman McCormack of Massachusetts. We are convinced that it originated in the propaganda bureau of our competitor, the Standard Oil Company of New Jersey." [24] Regardless of its origin, the measure was an attempt

[23] *Ibid.*
[24] *Hurley testimony.*

to undermine the Sinclair settlement which Hurley had negotiated; but in testimony Hurley insisted that the amendment could not apply in this case because all of the oil that his company was accepting as payment came from wells formerly owned by the Consolidated Oil Company. Searching for a way to refute his testimony, his questioners asked if Sinclair oil was not transported in part in pipelines and therefore comingled with oil of other companies which could be regarded as "stolen," and was impossible to identify. Hurley said facetiously he would make no attempt to say "that oil comingled in one pipeline is properly separated after it has been in the pipeline" but reiterated that stipulated amounts of oil were coming from former Sinclair property.[25]

Interestingly, in October, Hurley had a sharp exchange with Colonel Frank Knox, Secretary of the Navy, over this matter of "stolen oil." The Navy Department refused to accept a low bid by the Sinclair company to supply 550,000 barrels of oil on the grounds, as Knox put it to Hurley, that it was "stolen." The Sinclair representative replied strongly that it was not stolen and then called the State Department for support, since that department had approved of the Sinclair-Mexican settlement. Assistant Secretary Adolf A. Berle then drafted a memorandum for Secretary Hull stating that, in his view, "Hurley is entitled to some support." The State Department, said Berle, encouraged the companies to settle with Mexico, and Sinclair did so. "It is obviously absurd to call oil under this settlement 'stolen' . . . The real complaint against the Sinclair Company," Berle continued, "undoubtedly comes from Standard Oil of New Jersey, and its quarrel is that Sinclair, using Mexican oil is underselling them. Bluntly, it is not 'playing ball' on a price maintenance arrangement."[26]

Though vigorously attacked by Standard Oil, the Sinclair agreement, defended strenuously by Hurley, stood. Heartened by their

25 *Ibid.*
26 Memorandum by Assistant Secretary A. A. Berle, Oct. 11, 1940, Department of State, File 812.6363/7160.

successful break in the united front, Mexican officials then hoped for settlement with the other companies on a similar basis. Accordingly, in June, they once again expressed a desire to compensate, agreeing to permit the joint United States-Mexican appointment of a commissioner to determine the kind of compensation. The offer was rejected both by the State Department and by Standard Oil because of the impending national elections in Mexico and the required change in administrations. When General Manuel Camacho, the liberal candidate, won the election, and, when it became increasingly clear to the United States that it needed to do all possible to settle western hemisphere differences in view of the dangerous European and Asian situations, a new effort was made. Consequently, as Mexico and the United States moved toward rapprochement on economic and defense matters, it became increasingly difficult for the oil companies to remain intractable. Moreover, a report of the Interior Department revealed that the company claims against Mexico were exorbitant and that they did not have the case they claimed to have; indeed the Interior Department estimate, it was later revealed, agreed with the companies' own report of the value of the property to Mexican officials for tax purposes. As a result, and after difficult negotiations, an agreement was signed on November 19, 1941, providing for a general settlement of United States-Mexican claims including oil, which stipulated that Mexico would make a down payment of $9,000,000, and each government would supply an expert to determine the total payment due. The companies ultimately received about $29,000,000 for their property.[27]

Significantly, Hurley, in working with Mexican officials, manifested a realistic appraisal of the oil expropriation not shared by his compatriots from the other oil companies. He indicated a healthy respect for the sovereignty of Mexico, recognizing its right to move as it had, and his action appeared to reject the notion that U.S. intervention in Latin American affairs was

[27] Cronon, pp. 254–71.

proper or even acceptable. Indeed, this is the view one gets from his authorized biographer, and from a superficial perusal of the documents. Whether or not Hurley was truly motivated by such concern; whether his thinking was that the United States and the oil companies needed a more beneficent Mexican policy, however, is another matter. The record demonstrates that he early condemned the Mexican action and, along with Armstrong, Farish, and Sinclair, worked diligently to commit the State Department to play a more active role in securing a return of the oil property. Only when he saw that there was no hope of the latter, when it became clear that the only route open was to accept compensation, did he approve the idea of settlement. Then, because Sinclair saw the need to pull its chestnuts out of the fire, Hurley began negotiation secretly with Mexico and reached an agreement—an agreement which may be deemed proper and appropriate but one based essentially on expediency.

# V

## Itinerant Envoy: Hurley in the Southwest Pacific, Russia, and the Middle East

As a former Secretary of War and well-known Republican wheel horse, whose name again made headlines in connection with the Mexican oil expropriation, Hurley was considered a possible candidate for the Republican presidential nomination in 1940. He and Mrs. Hurley were prominent in Washington society during the Hoover years, and he was well known there to all in Republican circles. Moreover, his long service to Republican candidates around the nation, made through frequent speaking engagements in their behalf, gave him as many outstanding political I.O.U.'s as anyone in the party. His friends urged him actively to seek the nomination; he declined, but evidence indicates that he would have welcomed a draft. No boom developed, however, as backers could not capture the delegation from his home state.[1] Hurley actually was not disappointed for he realized, once Roosevelt declared for a third term, that he could not beat the President; indeed, in all probability no Republican could.

For all his displeasure at the President's decision to break political tradition, and all his rhetoric to the contrary, Hurley was on good terms with Roosevelt. When Roosevelt was first elected, Hurley stated that he was "convinced that the success of the Roosevelt administration is essential to the welfare of the

[1] Hurley's secretary to Merryl Shaver, June 11, 1940; Hurley to Fred L. Foster, July 16, 1940; to George McKinnis, Jr., July 16, 1940; to Ben Lawless, May 23, 1939; to Alexander Johnston, May 25, 1939; to Alexander Johnston, June 20, 1939; and to Neal Sullivan, Sept. 23, 1939, Hurley Papers.

country." Later he supported the N.R.A. and other New Deal measures aimed at stabilizing the economy, while he urged his fellow Republicans to give Roosevelt a chance. He called on the President in person and telephoned him several times during the thirties about appointments, and he and Roosevelt had several contacts during the Mexican oil expropriation controversy.

Though in 1939 he had expressed fears of the consequences of a more active U.S. role in world affairs, as more storm clouds appeared on the international horizon, he also drew closer to the President's position on foreign policy. Japan continued its offensive in China, capturing its major eastern cities and a good portion of the interior, and forcing the Chinese government to flee to Chungking; Germany invaded Poland and, in 1940, the Low Countries and France. With the fall of the Netherlands and France to Nazi power, Japan prepared to move southward into Southeast Asia. In 1940 and 1941, American relations with Japan deteriorated, as the United States responded with economic sanctions, while American aid to Great Britain brought the country nearer to a confrontation with Germany. Hurley advocated a program of national defense and repeal of the neutrality acts which he saw as "cowardly." He later applauded Lend Lease, the destroyer-bases deal, and other of Roosevelt's prewar measures. A Republican internationalist like Wendell Willkie, Hurley could move gracefully from partisan politics to service under Roosevelt.[2]

In the months preceding the bombing of Pearl Harbor, Hurley, a colonel in the reserves since World War I, began requesting assignment to active duty, and in November took military training with U.S. troops in South Carolina. He continued his pleas after December 7, requesting a command assignment, but General George Marshall would have none of it; he had little need for an overaged and undertrained former Secretary of War as a field commander. Though rejecting Hurley's appeal to overturn

[2] Hurley Speech, Nov. 11, 1939; Hurley to Bailey Bell, Feb. 5, 1940; to William Hard, Oct. 30, 1941; to Frederick Bartlett, July 8, 1940, *ibid.*

Marshall's decision, President Roosevelt, who had genuine affection for the Oklahoman, vowed to find a suitable assignment. In January he asked Hurley to undertake the first of many wartime military-diplomatic missions, this one to the Southwest Pacific.[3]

Hurley's assignment combined sufficient amounts of danger, adventure, and intrigue to satisfy the dramatic spirit of the brash Westerner; he was to coordinate an effort already begun by a Colonel John A. Robenson to run guns and ammunition to General MacArthur in the Philippines. The Japanese, after their treacherous attack on Pearl Harbor, fanned out across the Southeast and Southwest Pacific, purging territory after territory of Western influence and control in quest of their New Order in Asia. In January, as they beseiged the Philippine Islands and trapped the American force on Bataan Peninsula, General Mac-Arthur requested large quantities of guns, ammunition, and medical supplies to enable him to repel the invader—materials which would be taken in through the Japanese blockade. Although the allies early in 1942 had decided to center their strength in Hawaii and Australia and abandon the Philippines, MacArthur's valiant resistance became symbolic to Americans, and U.S. policy makers consequently decided some assistance should be rendered to the beleaguered Philippine force. Because he had previously worked with MacArthur and was recognized as "a man of energy," Marshall chose Hurley for the assignment as head of the mission led thus far by Robenson.

Promoted to brigadier general and named U.S. Minister to New Zealand to shroud the mission in secrecy, Hurley as "Personal Representative of the Chief of Staff" was to go first to Australia, where he would continue the requisitioning of supplies and boats, contract support with allies in the East Indies, and then begin the move toward the Islands. His military experience obviously did not justify the rank, but the United States, as

[3] Hurley to the President, Dec. 24, 1941; Marshall to Hurley, Jan. 17, 1942, ibid.

President Roosevelt put it, had "a great many make-believe generals."

He arrived in Australia in early February and began his job immediately. The task was not as simple as outlined on paper, however, as he experienced early difficulty in procuring the six ships needed for the mission and had an even greater problem securing the necessary trained manpower. He did eventually get together six ships and their crews in Australia and arranged with the British and Dutch for twelve more in the East Indies. However, at the last minute the American-British-Australian-Dutch Command at Surabaja, without explanation, refused permission for the use of the twelve vessels, and in mid-February Hurley had to fly to Java to pry them loose. Successful in this, though it was agreed that the ships would sail directly from Java rather than go first to Australia, Hurley flew back to Australia, braving the hazards of a Japanese attack in airways largely in their control. Back in Port Darwin, Australia, where on February 19, he suffered a minor head wound in a Japanese air raid, Hurley removed the remaining administrative obstacles and implemented the mission. Loaded with guns, ammunition, medical supplies, and some food, the six ships which the U.S. envoy had assembled at Port Darwin, minus one sunk in the Japanese air raid, were dispatched for the Philippines. The effort proved a failure. Most of the ships, including those sailing directly from Java, were either sunk or captured, and in the end only three reached the islands. The Japanese noose around the Philippines was simply too tight; and when Hurley realized this fact, he advocated abandoning the effort. The point soon became moot, for MacArthur was driven off the islands and to Australia.[4]

Although named Minister to New Zealand, Hurley as of March 1 had yet to present his credentials or even to set foot on New Zealand soil; he wanted to stay where the action was—in Australia—even after the failure of the gunrunning mission. He set

[4] See Secret Mission X by John A. Robenson, Box 79, *ibid.*

about the task of ingratiating himself with Australian and American officials, ultimately getting to know them well enough so as to be included in some military discussions. He also attempted, with the aid of U.S. General George Brett and Australian military officials, to secure appointment as U.S. Minister to Australia to replace Nelson T. Johnson. Hurley later thanked General Brett: "I remember distinctly how you went your limit for me when I tried to be changed from Minister to New Zealand to Minister to Australia. I have never forgotten that." Johnson, it was alleged, did not have command of military problems, and Hurley did. However, Roosevelt, who later evoked a storm of protest over the Australian mission when he attempted to remove Johnson in favor of New York politician Edward Flynn, at this point stuck by his Minister.[5] When this attempt failed, Hurley tried to get MacArthur to keep him around; he enthusiastically greeted the general upon his arrival in Australia, joined him in his ceremonious entry into Melbourne, and hinted on several occasions that MacArthur use him as an administrative aide. When all his maneuvering failed, Hurley reported to New Zealand on April 1.

In his short and insignificant stay in the New Zealand post (there is nothing printed in *Foreign Relations* relative to this period), the U.S. envoy performed two primary functions—that is, when he was not busy trying to get back to Australia. A fairly good public speaker and an impressive figure, Hurley did a good deal of speaking around the country, exhorting New Zealanders to more sacrifice and greater war effort. Whenever possible he invoked the need for cooperation between his country and the people of New Zealand, citing the danger posed by Japan to all democracies: the two nations working together would destroy the Japanese menace. Hurley also intervened somewhat in domestic politics to suggest greater support of the Labor government

[5] Hurley to George Brett, Jan. 20, 1945; Marshall to Hurley, Feb. 22, 1942; General Brett to Marshall, Feb. 17, 1942, *ibid.;* and Russell D. Buhite, *Nelson T. Johnson and American Policy Toward China 1925–1941* (East Lansing: 1968), pp. 17–18n.

of Prime Minister Peter Fraser from dissident factions among labor not wholly committed to the war. And he persuaded the Labor government to take in members of the opposition, thus creating a truly national government. All the U.S. Minister's speeches seemed to be well received, and as a public relations man he did an outstanding job; newspapers throughout the country praised his efforts, even lauding his brief foray in New Zealand politics. "The New Zealanders," Hurley later remarked, "were great people. You couldn't tell the difference between them and the hillbillies of the Ozarks or the cowboys of West Texas or the Nesters of Oklahoma, except for a slight difference in accent, and in their methods of making coffee." [6]

The other matter of some importance to which Hurley devoted his time was the operation of the Lend-Lease program; bottlenecks sometimes developed because the distance between the United States and New Zealand was so great, and problems related to the operation of reverse Lend Lease occasionally appeared. Though these were questions of some magnitude, requiring skilled handling, they were "boring" administrative duties, and the U.S. Minister longed to put this sedate position aside for one filled with action. Consequently, in July, pursuant to an invitation proferred by the United States to the Australian and New Zealand Prime Ministers to go to Washington to discuss military and supply matters, Hurley asked to be allowed to accompany New Zealand's Minister, Peter Fraser. The State Department concurred, and in August he left New Zealand, never to return. [7]

Arriving in Washington on August 26, after a stopover in Australia, Hurley immediately began conversations with the War Department, the State Department, and the President. An avid

[6] Hurley to Victor Locke, Jr., Aug. 8, 1942, Hurley Papers. For comment on Hurley's speeches, see for instance the *New Zealand Herald,* June 4, 1942, the *Auckland Star,* June 4, 1942, and the *Waikato Times,* June 5, 1942.

[7] Hurley to Secretary of State, Aug. 7, 1942, Department of State, File J./51; *New York Times,* Aug. 26, 1942.

supporter of the proposition of opening a major offensive in the Pacific, Hurley tried to convince General Marshall and President Roosevelt of the wisdom of the course and reinforced the arguments made along these same lines by both Fraser of New Zealand and his counterpart from Australia. The President obviously would not buy the argument, as war priorities calling first for the defeat of Germany were already established.

Cognizant of the fact that Hurley did not wish to return at once to New Zealand and apparently hoping to change his mind about the European theater, Roosevelt decided to give his envoy a new assignment. For no outstanding reason other than to convince Hurley of the need to defeat Hitler first and to have him convey this attitude when he finally resumed his job as Minister to New Zealand, he was to return to the Southwest Pacific via the Soviet Union and the Middle East; the mission was to be made under vague orders to serve only as a "fact finder." Interestingly, when Russian Minister to the United States, Maxim Litvinov, heard of the assignment he protested, suggesting that with a trip by Wendell Willkie just completed, and with the U.S. ambassador, U.S. naval and military attachés coming home, he failed to see why the trip was necessary; he wondered "what there was about his country that we still wanted to know." [8]

Overcoming the Russian ambassador's objections, Hurley began his trip to Moscow via Egypt and Iran. After brief stops in the latter countries, the U.S. envoy arrived in the Soviet Union on November 3. Marshal Josef Stalin was out of the city when Hurley first arrived, but he held several conferences with Foreign Minister Vyacheslav M. Molotov and then on November 14 a lengthy one with Stalin himself. Opening the remarks, Hurley told Stalin that he believed, though President Roosevelt did not, that the United States should attack and destroy Japan before she had an opportunity to exploit the resources she had recently

[8] Office Diary, Oct. 3 and 8, 1942; Marshall to Hurley, Oct. 5, 1942, Hurley Papers; and Memorandum by William Moreland to the Office of the Secretary of State, Oct. 8, 1942, *F.R., 1943,* III, 654.

brought under her command; ultimately such action would contribute greatly to Germany's defeat. Since Roosevelt disagreed
with this idea, Hurley was prepared to go along with the alternative. Stalin replied that of course he agreed completely with the
U.S. President, that Japan did not possess the requisite manpower
or knowledge to use effectively the resources she controlled,
that she was largely dependent on Germany for aircraft and other
technological materials, and that it would be at least eighteen
months before she could recoup her losses and develop the resources of Southeast Asia. But Stalin went on to recognize the importance of defeating Japan. As Hurley reported the conversation:
"At one point his discussion indicated that Russia intended in due
course to cooperate in the establishment of a mainland front
against Japan but further discussion of that subject so modified
his statement that it should not be taken as a commitment." [9] In
any event, this seems to have been the first indication by the
Soviet dictator that the Soviet Union would enter the Far Eastern
war.

Further discussion centered on the opening of a Russian offensive and U.S. supplies. Hurley stated: "I told him . . . he had not
yet given me a clear statement of Russia's strategy in Russia and
that I would like to know, for instance, what Russia now had
between her enemy and her oil, how much material Russia
would require before she could take the offensive, and where,
how, and when he contemplated the offensive." Here, Hurley
said, "I expected to be thrown out of the Kremlin." [10] Instead,
incredibly, since he had been to that time very secretive about
Russian military activity, Stalin invited Hurley to visit the "vital
fighting areas."

On November 26, Hurley along with his Russian hosts and his
aides, departed Moscow for a ten-day tour of the Stalingrad
front. There he witnessed the famed Soviet battlefield, scene of
some of the cruelest effects of the war. Russian officers explained

[9] Hurley to Roosevelt, Nov. 15, 1942, Hurley Papers.
[10] Ibid.

strategy to him, showed him their equipment and supplies, and guided him through fields strewn with horse carcasses and countless corpses of Rumanian soldiers, allies of the Nazis who participated in the battle; they also introduced the U.S. envoy to scores of Russian troops. Of little military importance, the trip did, however, have several significant results: it marked the first time any American had actually been to a Soviet battle zone and thus was a gesture the consequence of which probably was increased trust by the United States of its wartime ally; it allowed an appraisal of Russian material and equipment, which Hurley deemed poor by comparison to that used by the allies, elsewhere, and prompted the U.S. envoy to advise broadening Lend Lease; it also helped convince Hurley of the wisdom of the allied strategy in striking the Nazis first.

Before leaving the Soviet Union, Hurley viewed another Russian military zone. This time he traveled to the Caucasus, flying over the Baku oil fields and observing the military power Stalin had between "his enemy and his oil." Again, as at Stalingrad, Hurley was shown Soviet military equipment and was permitted to associate with junior-grade officers and regular Russian troops. Again, also, he witnessed the remains of Nazi armies that had only recently been driven from the field. The trip reinforced his belief that Stalin was an effective ally but needed increased U.S. support. As Hurley prepared to leave Russia in December he looked upon the two visits to important military zones and rapport with Stalin as marks of the success of his mission.[11] An individual to whom personal relationships were very important, he believed that, since he had seen the Soviet dictator to be a reasonable man, most of the problems of the wartime alliance could be settled amicably. In ensuing years, Hurley, like Roosevelt, was to place perhaps more stock than warranted in Stalin's commitments.

Following his trip to the Caucasus, Hurley, whose itinerary

[11] Hurley to the President, Dec. 8, 1942, and Dec. 29, 1942, *ibid.*

President Roosevelt changed to permit a trip back to Washington before going on to New Zealand, left the Soviet Union and after brief stopovers in Teheran, Baghdad, and Cairo, returned in January to the United States where he again conferred with State and War Department personnel and the President. He also spoke with Australian and New Zealand officials about the importance of the European front as opposed to the offensive they had hoped to inspire in the Pacific. And he fulfilled numerous speaking engagements, with the Army War College, the Quartermaster Corps, and other military groups as well as private organizations, each time reiterating the theme: that Stalin was a useful and trustworthy ally; that he would persevere and would not conclude a separate peace with Germany; that Germany was the major enemy and should be defeated first, and that therefore it was important to provide additional support for the Soviet Union. In his frequent conferences at the White House during this period he refined the latter, on one occasion to the dismay of Admiral William Leahy, who questioned Soviet intentions and believed Hurley may have been duped.[12]

Although still ostensibly Minister to New Zealand, it became apparent during this stay in Washington that Hurley would not return to the Southwest Pacific; President Roosevelt had still another assignment for his roving envoy. Deciding that he needed more knowledge about the Middle East, and, aware that Hurley did not want to return to New Zealand, the President in early March asked Hurley to go again to the Middle East, where he would once more serve as a "fact finder," reporting to the President on matters related to the "U.S. national interest" and general conditions in Egypt, Syria, Lebanon, Iran, Iraq, Palestine, and Saudi Arabia.[13]

Stopping first in Morocco, a French colony then under control of the Free French, Hurley held talks with certain nationals, with

[12] William Leahy, *I Was There* (New York, 1950), p. 147; Office Diary, Jan.-Feb., 1943, Hurley Papers.

[13] Roosevelt to Hurley, Mar. 13, 1943, Hurley Papers.

Sidi Mohammed Ben Youssef, Sultan of Morocco, and with Grand Vizier El Mokri about U.S. aims for the world as opposed to those of the imperialist countries and Russia; the United States, Hurley informed his hosts, stood for international "freedom of conscience" and provided a middle way, neither like the European colonists nor the Russians.[14] Departing Morocco, he then went to Cairo, where he briefly explored questions related to allied conflict in the region, particularly in regard to dissemination of news unfavorable to the U.S. by British forces, and of a more substantive nature, disputes related to major supply organizations. One of these organizations, the Middle East Supply Center, an allied agency dominated by the British, which facilitated supply of military and civilian goods to countries in the region, was alleged by American manufacturers to be prejudicial in favor of the British in orders for goods that it handled. Hurley found some of the charges true but also recognized that the organization had done some generally outstanding work, especially in the area of agricultural research.

Subsequent to exploring these questions, the U.S. envoy in early April went to Palestine where he involved himself in a major Middle Eastern problem—the Arab-Zionist question. Upon arrival he conferred with both Arab and Jewish leaders, learning quickly of the intense feeling on both sides. And the President's representative was not long in indicating with whom his sympathy lay. He had a lengthy conversation with David Ben-Gurion, Zionist leader in Jerusalem who eloquently defended the Jewish claim to Palestine and stated also that the United States was "committed" and "obligated" to the establishment of a Jewish state there. The United States was obligated, Ben-Gurion stated, because of the investment of American Jewish capital in Palestine which relied "on the protection of the U.S. government," because of U.S. support to the creation of a Palestine Mandate, and because of support given Zionists in a Congressional resolution of

---

[14] Hurley to Roosevelt, Mar. 26, 1943, *ibid.*

1922. Evidencing at least a partial knowledge of past American policy, Hurley told the Zionist leader that his arguments had appeal, but that they were "in fact incorrect." "It seemed wise," Hurley reported to Roosevelt, "to point out to Mr. Ben-Gurion that none of the evidence offered revealed any obligation of the U.S. Government or the American people to support the present Zionist demand for creation of a Jewish majority and establishment of a Jewish Political State in Palestine. The documents were produced, and it was shown clearly that the U.S. Government merely consented to the British Mandate for Palestine and, in Joint Resolution, favored only the establishment of a National Home for the Jews insofar as such a home would not trespass on the rights of Christian and other non-Jewish Communities in Palestine." [15]

In actual fact, the history of U.S. policy on the Zionist question reveals much of the same ambiguity as that of Great Britain. During World War I, in order to secure full cooperation in the war effort of her domestic Jewish population, as a kind of reward to Jewish chemist Dr. Chaim Weizman, a leading Zionist who during the war developed synthetic cordite, an explosive, and to appeal to Russian Jews who were mainly Zionists, Britain made the Balfour Declaration, named for Foreign Secretary Arthur J. Balfour, and a promise to support the idea of a national home for the Jews in Palestine. Also during that war, however, she made a conflicting commitment to the Arabs, promising independence to the Arab regions of the Ottoman Empire, including Palestine, in an effort to secure greater cooperation from them against the Turkish Empire, with whom Great Britain was at war. Though placed in charge of Palestine through the Turkish Treaty of 1920, Britain's policy remained vague in the twenties and thirties, while emigration of Jews to Palestine increased; her publication of a famous White Paper in 1939 setting a limit of 75,000 Jewish immigrants over the following five years did not

[15] Hurley to Roosevelt, May 5, 1943, *ibid.*

stem the tide, and the number of Jews there in 1943 rose to about 500,000.

In the case of U.S. policy, Woodrow Wilson, upon the urging of adviser Louis Brandeis, a leading American Zionist, had come out in favor of the Balfour Declaration. But he had also espoused self-determination of nations prior to and at Versailles thus, of course, revealing a dichotomy in the U.S. position. In 1922 in a joint resolution, Congress stated that it favored creation of a national home for Jews but only if this did not infringe upon the rights of Christians and other non-Jewish people in Palestine. In both the U.S. and Great Britain during the thirties and forties Jewish political pressure prevented a clear delineation of policy that might hinder the Zionist effort aimed at increased emigration.

During the forties several pro-Zionist committees were organized in the U.S. to apply pressure on Congress: in 1941 Senator Robert Wagner of New York reconstituted the American Palestine Committee, a unit which had functioned in the thirties but then became dormant; the Christian Council on Palestine was formed; and the American League for a Free Palestine came into being. Membership lists in these organizations read like congressional rosters; two hundred representatives and over sixty senators belonged to the American Palestine committee alone, and many more joined the other organizations. Purpose of the organizations was to commit the United States to the advocacy of unrestricted immigration into Palestine and the creation of a Jewish homeland. To this end, congressmen, sympathetic to the Zionist cause, to Jewish suffering in Europe, and concerned about their constituencies, introduced numerous bills and resolutions.

In his report to the President, Hurley also revealed his personal observations on the question. The Zionists, he believed, were committed to a sovereign Jewish state, comprising Palestine and Transjordania; to the transfer of Palestinian Arabs to Iraq; and to Jewish economic leadership in the entire Middle East. However, there was no unanimity of feeling among Jews on the Zionist question, and the possibility existed that once democracy was restored to Europe the movement would crumble. As for the Arabs, he did not see them as anti-Jewish, but there was among them deepseated "hostility to any immigration program intended to create a Jewish majority in Palestine and to the establishment of a Jewish sovereign state." The Arabs also viewed with evident distaste Jewish claims of being the "chosen people," likening this doctrine to that of the Nazis in Europe. Most Arabs, the U.S. representative suggested, would approve of the proposal of Nuri as-Said, Prime Minister of Iraq, providing for an Arab Federation comprising Palestine, Transjordania, Lebanon, Syria, Iraq, and the other Arab states, with limitations placed on Jewish immigration to Palestine, but granting Jews autonomy within regions where they were in the majority. Hurley indicated strongly that he liked the idea.[16]

Later in a conference with Ibn Saud, Hurley indicated more clearly his personal feeling on the controversy. Saud told the U.S. envoy that he despised the Zionists' position, that their claim to Palestine was a fake, that the Jews lost title to Palestine to the Romans the same way they had won it, by force, the only difference being that the Romans did not exterminate Jews the way the Jews had the original inhabitants. Hurley had never heard the latter point, but he agreed with Saud in principle. "I told him," Hurley stated, "that I personally am not in favor of the establishment of a Jewish political state in Palestine, that I think that a great majority of the Jewish people in the United States would be opposed to the establishment of such a state, but there are certain very rich, powerful, influential Jews who are using America's freedom of speech and freedom of conscience to conduct a great propaganda drive among the American people in an endeavor to compel America to obligate herself to establishing a Jewish political state in Palestine."[17]

As might be expected in view of his position on the controversy, Hurley quickly became embroiled in the acrimonious de-

[16] *Ibid.*
[17] Notes on Conference between Ibn Saud and Hurley, undated, *ibid.*

bate which raged in the United States. In the spring and summer of 1943, various noted Americans, among them Sumner Welles, Drew Pearson, Senator Robert Wagner, and Representative Emanuel Celler increased their agitation in favor of a Jewish national state; numerous Jewish-sponsored organizations did the same thing—thus applying pressure on the Roosevelt administration to support their position. At the same time Arab leaders like Nuri as-Said and King Ibn Saud began publishing their views in U.S. news media. On August 9, Drew Pearson published an article in which he charged that Hurley agreed with Ibn Saud's ideas on Zionism and that the U.S. envoy was supporting the impending visit of Saud to Washington to express his views against the Jews. Moreover, he alleged that, in conferences with State Department personnel and the President, Hurley had urged stifling the Jewish propaganda in the United States and any further discussion of the question. Though correct that Hurley agreed with Saud's ideas, the veracity of Pearson's other remarks was highly questionable at best; but this did not detract from their influence, and Hurley became the target of a violent Jewish reaction. Jewish individuals and organizations filled his mails so full of threats and warnings that he was finally moved to write Roosevelt that he "was being baited by the Jews." Emanuel Celler, Representative from New York, threatened to investigate Hurley and the entire Middle East contingent of the State Department; he also warned against shutting off discussion of the question. Hurley denied ever advising the State Department in the manner alleged by Pearson, and ultimately received the backing of the President, who advised him that the best way to deal with Pearson's "ill considered falsehoods" was to ignore them.[18] The storm quieted, but the deeper controversy remained.

In January 1944, James Wright, Democrat of Pennsylvania, and Ranulf Compton of Connecticut introduced in the House of Representatives a resolution to impel the State Department to

[18] Emanuel Celler to Roosevelt, Aug. 18, 1943; Roosevelt to Hurley, Aug. 20, 1943; and Roosevelt to Hurley, Aug. 30, 1943, *ibid.*

repudiate the British White Paper of 1939. A similar statement, the Wagner-Taft Resolution advocating unlimited Jewish immigration to Palestine, sponsored by Robert Wagner of New York and Robert Taft of Ohio, was introduced in the Senate. While also sympathetic to the plight of European Jews, the State and War Departments and the President were concerned lest the resolutions infuriate the Arabs and perhaps lead to fighting between Jews and Arabs in the Middle East, thus forcing the allies to keep additional troops in the area. Consequently, army officials were directed to testify before the Congressional committees dealing with the resolution that military necessity precluded their passage. And, further, Secretary of War Stimson wrote a letter to Tom Connolly, chairman of the Senate Foreign Relations Committee, voicing his opposition to them.[19] As a result, the resolutions were tabled.

Pearson, master of the use of innuendo and half-truth, stayed on Hurley's trail. In March 1944, after the U.S. envoy had made another whirlwind trip across the Middle East and reported his "findings" in Washington, the journalist published an inflammatory article stating that Hurley "connived" with Secretary of War Stimson and General Marshall to undermine the Wagner-Taft Resolution, and Hurley, Pearson alleged, hoped to stop completely Jewish movement to the region by urging the administration to adopt a restrictive policy. Again, Jewish organizations attacked the Oklahoman, stating that unless he vigorously denied the charges, his political future would be ruined. Hurley weakly branded them false, although they were partially true; he would indeed have liked to limit Jewish immigration to Palestine. As a result, leaders of the Jewish community were unconvinced.[20]

[19] Minister to Iraq to the Secretary of State, Feb. 14, 1944, *F.R., 1944,* V, 565; Memo by the Assistant Secretary of War to General Marshall, Feb. 22, 1944, *F.R., 1944,* V, 574; under Secretary of State to the Secretary of State, Feb. 19, 1944, *F.R., 1944,* V, 567–568; and Secretary of War to chairman of the Senate Foreign Relations Committee, Feb. 7, 1944, *F.R., 1944,* V, 563.

[20] Hurley Scrapbook, 1944; Office Diary, Feb. 28, 1944, Mar. 28, 1944, and Apr. 4, 1944; Abba Hillel Silver to Hurley, Apr. 7, 1944, Hurley Papers.

Hurley then reiterated his denials in a conversation with a leading Zionist, Rabbi Abba Hillel Silver, but the Jews still harbored doubts; in particular they were concerned that Hurley's oil interests were leading him to sacrifice the Jewish position in an effort to maintain good relations with the oil-rich Arabs. Though they undoubtedly assigned simpler motives to the U.S. envoy than were warranted by the facts, Hurley was indeed interested in oil.

The suspicions persisted. While he was in Washington in early 1944, the matter of the building of a U.S. government-owned pipeline from Saudi Arabia to the Mediterranean arose. The Oklahoman was definitely sympathetic to the idea, and speculation occurred as to whether he had negotiated an agreement with Ibn Saud to permit the line to be built—an agreement in which the U.S. would promise in return to attempt to limit the influx of Jews to Palestine. Hurley may have been involved with Saud in such negotiations, but no evidence other than circumstantial to confirm the fact is available, and was not available at the time. But again Hurley was criticized. Ultimately, he dropped his support for the plan, if not because of Jewish protests, perhaps because private oil companies (Hurley was still associated with Sinclair) cooled toward the idea. After 1943 the severe Nazi threat no longer existed, and they did not need U.S. government support. His ultimate rejection of the plan and its failure of realization did not suffice as far as the Zionists were concerned, however; Hurley's reputation with them was beyond repair. Consequently, one of the reasons Hurley was not returned to the Middle East in 1944—he was considered by Roosevelt as possible commander of that theater—was that it was an election year, and the President feared the animus his appointment would engender with U.S. Jews.

Related to this was the concern that Hurley's oil background would add fuel to the criticism already shrilly voiced by the Jewish community that the administration was reluctant to take a strong pro-Zionist stand because it was controlled by the oil companies. Secretary of the Interior Harold Ickes wrote to the President, who very much wanted to make Hurley chief in command in the area, that he could "see no good purpose that could be served by such an assignment. Personally, I have a high regard for him but the oil situation in that section of the world is so delicate that I would be disturbed by the injection into it of a new personality, particularly when he has had, and still has oil clients."[21]

Since the Middle East possessed a huge proportion of the world's supply of oil, concern for continued access to oil fields pervaded Hurley's attitudes and actions in the region in 1943 and early 1944. He visited all the major producers in the area, conferring with leading officials in each of the countries. Particularly was he interested in Saudi Arabia, for it was there that U.S. companies had their major concessions. Hurley conversed with Ibn Saud about the most efficient way to extract the oil in his country and yet secure fair treatment for all parties concerned. Saud said that American companies had done much good in his country in areas unrelated to oil production—in building hospitals, developing water resources, and the like—but he hoped to secure Arabian control of all foreign-based oil companies; U.S. companies could continue to pump oil, but he wanted to regulate them.

In an apparent attempt to reconcile the interests of all sides on the petroleum question, Hurley prepared an interesting recommendation for the President. He suggested that the U.S. government buy into U.S. companies, thus giving the government a vested interest in company operations. The government should then play a definite regulatory role in company affairs as they pertained to foreign operations. This would insure against the kind of malpractice which characterized much of the U.S. oil operation in the past in Latin America. At the same time it regulated corporations to prevent recurrence of imperialistic prac-

[21] Harold Ickes to Roosevelt, June 23, 1944, Roosevelt Papers, Roosevelt Presidential Library, Hyde Park, N.Y.; see also Office Diary, Apr. 10, 1944; and Hurley Scrapbook, 1944, Hurley Papers.

tices now passé in view of the Atlantic Charter, the U.S. government would work to prevent the summary nationalization of oil company property. This scheme should please the Arabs, since the U.S. government could play a role in their internal development, would probably be acceptable to the oil companies, and would insure continuation of the flow of oil.[22]

Hurley's comments were apparently based on some knowledge of policy being developed in Washington during the summer of 1943. As early as June the Joint Chiefs of Staff decided that the United States was faced with a serious shortage of oil reserves and that for national security purposes she should secure proven reserves in some other part of the world. Accordingly, they suggested that the Reconstruction Finance Corporation organize a government oil corporation which would secure a "controlling interest" in Saudi Arabian oil concessions.[23] At that time the California-Arabian Standard Oil Company, whose stock was owned 50 percent by the Standard Oil Company of California and 50 percent by the Texas Corporation, possessed the right to explore and develop the oil territory in Arabia.

Subsequently, the RFC on June 30 organized the Petroleum Reserves Corporation, which was to "finance, retain, develop, exploit, or lease" oil reserves outside the continental limits of the United States; the directors of this government corporation were the Secretaries of State, War, Navy, and as chairman, the Secretary of the Interior, Harold Ickes.[24] The corporation then began confidential negotiations with the California-Arabian Standard Company, with the full backing of funds from the RFC, to gain control of the Arabian concession. While the negotiations were in progress the U.S. Minister in Egypt wired the Secretary of State that he thought the actions of the California company

---

[22] Hurley to Roosevelt, June 9, 1943; and Notes by Hurley, Oct. 22, 1943, ibid.

[23] Memorandum from the Joint Chiefs of Staff to President Roosevelt, June 8, 1943, F.R., 1943, IV, 921.

[24] Letter to Roosevelt, June 26, 1943, ibid., 924–930.

were exemplary, that the company was held in high regard by King Ibn Saud, that a government-run operation in Arabia would make the United States like the European nations in the eyes of the world, and that the United States should give greater support to private corporations in their foreign enterprises.[25] Nevertheless, for a while the private company seemed receptive to the idea of government partnership.[26] But as the Axis threat lessened, it became more and more intransigent. The government tried first to purchase the entire stock of the company, then tried to secure majority control, and then tried to get one-third. Finally, at the end of 1943, an agreement seemed beyond reach, and the discussions were suspended.[27]

Hurley's recommendation represented no new commitment on his part to government-run enterprise, for he was still a firm supporter of the private oil corporations. In Egypt in October, he informed King Farouk that American oil companies paid the highest rates of any in the world to foreign governments, and, moreover, they built schools and hospitals.[28] Later he told Secretary of the Treasury Henry Morgenthau, who viewed the oil companies as "greedy" and "self-seeking," that his appraisal was inaccurate, the companies were doing a good job, and by and large served very generously the interests of Middle Eastern countries.[29] The companies also served the long-range national interest by acquiring new oil assets. It was, then, not to divest the private companies of their ownership that Hurley proposed partnership with government, or because he viewed the U.S. companies' practices in the Middle East with distaste. What he apparently wanted was a guarantee against nationalization, and protection against the enemy, while the war was on, and some regulation so

[25] Minister in Egypt to the Secretary of State, July 27, 1943, *ibid.*, 935–937.
[26] Memorandum by Wallace Murray to Secretary of State, Oct. 26, 1943, *ibid.*, 940–941.
[27] Memorandum by Wallace Murray, Dec. 14, 1943, *ibid.*, 948–950.
[28] Hurley's Notes, Oct. 24, 1943, Hurley Papers.
[29] Hurley's Notes, Oct. 26, 1943, *ibid.*

as to ensure that companies be certain of acquiring access to oil pools in the future from Arab leaders, who were very jealous of their national prerogatives.

Hurley continued for a time to urge government-industry co-operation. In November 1943, he made this point in discussions in Saudi Arabia with representatives of the Texas Oil Company and the California-Arabian Standard Oil Company. He was concerned about U.S. development of oil fields there—he had gotten assurances from Saud that the United States would be permitted to participate in oil extraction in his country—and he wanted government partnership. He was told by these representatives that negotiations were then proceeding in Washington along the same lines. Later he reiterated his view in discussions with Sacony-Vacuum representatives, arguing that cooperation would benefit the oil companies, the indigenous population, and the U.S. government. However, in early 1944, he became less enthusiastic about the idea and, as indicated above, opposed the government operation of a pipeline from Saudi Arabia to the Mediterranean; from this time forward he generally reflected the position of the oil companies, in particular in any dispute of theirs with Secretary of the Interior Harold Ickes and Secretary of the Treasury Morgenthau, both of whom he disliked intensely.[30]

Notwithstanding his concern about the "emerging" states of the Middle East, in all his opinions on oil Hurley did not deprecate the interests of U.S. oil firms, and thus his true motives may be subject to question. His interest was essentially a private one, however, and while he did make reports and enter discussions on the question, his role in shaping U.S. "oil policy" was peripheral. He had no love for Standard Oil. But throughout the period he

[30] Hurley's Notes, Nov. 17 and 20, 1943; and Office Diary, May 18, 1943, *ibid.* Hurley's animus for Ickes apparently originated in a personality conflict between the two men; it grew when Hurley began to hear reports that Ickes considered him an egotistical promoter whose estimation of his own importance did not accord with fact. His feeling toward Morgenthau is better explained in the context of the China question.

maintained contact with the Sinclair company; Sinclair continued
to pay Hurley's law firm a retainer, even though the Oklahoman
was not active in Sinclair's business. Moreover, Hurley in 1944
supported the oil companies in negotiations with the government
regarding oil reserves in California where the companies hoped
to retain their reserves in the face of pressure from the Navy
Department, which also wanted them.[31]

Interested in the Zionist question and in oil, Hurley also concerned himself with the position of the European nations vis-a-
vis the Middle East, that is, the burgeoning nationalism of the
region as it confronted the vestiges of imperialism. In the summer of 1943 Hurley was in Washington recovering from an illness that had forced him to return from the Middle East; he had
a prostate operation in June and was convalescing. He then
caught pneumonia, and from July to September, he rested at his
home in New Mexico. During this period the State Department
and the President contemplated his next assignment. He personally hoped to return to the Middle East, especially to Iran,
where he had visited after his trip to the Soviet Union; as a result,
in October the State Department indicated that it agreed. He
would go to Iran to help sort out and solve the problems created
by the occupation of the country—an occupation which was
made necessary in 1941 and 1942 because of the vital oil resources there and Iran's strategic position for carrying supplies
to the Soviet Union.

In 1941, the Soviet Union, which had a treaty of 1921 with
Iran specifying that in case a third power threatened Russia it
could send troops to Iran to reduce that threat, began applying
pressure on the Iranian government to expel the German influence from the country. In mid-August the British joined Russia
in the representations but received little satisfaction from Reza
Pahlavi, Shah of Iran, who was obviously impressed by the
hitherto unchecked German successes in the war. Consequently,

31 Office Diary, Apr. 27, 1944, and other entries 1943 and 1944, *ibid.*

on August 25, 1941, the British and Russians launched a coordinated attack on Iran, the Soviet Union driving in from the north and Great Britain from the south, and on September 9 imposed an agreement on Iran which placed Russia in control of the northern part of the country and Great Britain in control of much of the south and central region. Though not formally an occupying power, the United States, in 1942, in order to insure the continued flow of Lend-Lease materials to the Soviet Union, established a military mission in Iran; in 1943 it created the Persian Gulf Command, a noncombatant force of about 30,000 men which took over and operated Iran's railways and principal highways. During the period of American presence, the United States also furnished Iran with Lend-Lease goods.

As indicated in a report he submitted in May of 1943 after a brief tour of Iran, Hurley saw the actions of the occupying powers in that country as pointing the way to postwar policies in all the Middle Eastern countries; a beneficent position adopted by the powers toward Iran would have important implications for the entire area. Consequently, he advocated that guidelines be established to conform with the Atlantic Charter; in his view, Iran's postwar sovereignty should be guaranteed, Iran should join the United Nations in a declaration of war against the Axis, and the powers should cooperate to take her into the family of nations; the U.S. legation, moreover, should be raised to an embassy.[32]

Before Hurley could be formally assigned to Iran, President Roosevelt decided to send him on a trip to Afghanistan, India, and China for a variety of reasons: to check on supply matters, to locate sites for new air fields, to investigate disputes between British and U.S. military officials in the China-Burma-India theater, and to confer with Generalissimo Chiang Kai-shek about impending conferences with Marshal Stalin and Prime Minister

[32] See Adolf Berle to Stettinius, Oct. 6, 1943, *F.R., 1943*, IV, 392; Memorandum by Wallace Murray to Stettinius, Oct. 7, 1943, *F.R., 1943*, IV, 392–393. Also Hurley to Roosevelt, May 13, 1943, Hurley Papers.

Winston Churchill. In particular he was to seek Chiang's concurrence to attend a conference at Cairo in November.

To solve many of the outstanding difficulties in prosecuting the
war in Europe and to make important military decisions about
such things as a second front, President Roosevelt had arranged
to meet Stalin and Churchill at Teheran. But, as the United States
also had important questions to discuss regarding the war in the
Pacific, i.e., territorial aggrandizement of China at war's end,
terms for Japanese surrender, and questions of military procedure, it was necessary to confer also with Chiang Kai-shek. Since
the Soviet Union was not then in the Asian war, it would have
been awkward to include the Generalissimo in the meetings with
Stalin at Teheran; in fact, Stalin was afraid of an attack by Japan
while he was preoccupied with Germany. Consequently, two
conferences were to be held, one at Cairo between Chiang,
Roosevelt, and Churchill, and another, following it, at Teheran,
comprising Roosevelt, Churchill, and Stalin. Chiang in his talks
with Hurley agreed to attend the former conference.

In making this trip, Hurley, who left Washington on October
14, went again through the Middle East, stopping briefly to confer with U.S. officials. On this occasion, as before, he encountered
Anglo-American rivalry on Middle Eastern supply matters, the
position of the British enraging him constantly; he reported to
Roosevelt his belief that Great Britain was attempting to foster
imperialism in the area through distribution of Lend-Lease supplies, and, in his view, this should be stopped. Moreover, through
the United Kingdom Commercial Corporation, a completely British agency, they sold excess Lend-Lease goods. The U.S. should
take firm control of all supply matters, he believed, if it wished
to facilitate implementation of the Atlantic Charter.[33]

As Hurley took off for India and China to continue his mission,
the President decided he was needed in Cairo and therefore had

[33] To Roosevelt, Nov. 7, 1943, Hurley Papers.

the War and State Departments inform him to remain in the Middle East. Their communication came too late and only reached him in China some days later, whereupon after a three-day stop he returned to Cairo. Back in Cairo, he held two conferences with President Roosevelt. He informed the President of his friendly talks with Chiang Kai-shek, and of the information he received of the Communist-Kuomintang conflict in that country. He also spoke briefly, and without any new insight, of the dispute in the China-Burma-India theater between General Joseph Stilwell and General Claire Chennault, and of the British-American rivalry. In another session, he told Roosevelt of his suspicions regarding British intentions in the Middle East.

Present at the start of the Cairo conference, while the meetings were in progress Hurley was sent, on November 24, to Teheran to prepare the way for the arrival of President Roosevelt for the conference to be held there at the end of the month. Specifically, Hurley was to check into the matter of the use of facilities offered by the Russians in their legation as quarters for the U.S. President. Apparently Stalin, suspicious of a plot on his life, feared traveling the streets of Teheran, and thus wanted the meetings in his own headquarters; he may also have believed that his intelligence corps could operate more effectively, given this arrangement. In any event, Roosevelt first refused the offer, but, after Hurley arrived and inspected the quarters and after rumors circulated of an impending assassination attempt on the President at the U.S. Legation, a second Russian invitation was accepted.

Hurley had no part in formulating the policy emanating from the Cairo meetings; he did at those held in Teheran. At the Iranian conference, Roosevelt, Churchill, and Stalin in an amicable spirit, arrived at some important decisions. They agreed that there should be a cross-channel invasion, named "Overlord," instead of the thrust at the "soft underbelly" of southeastern Europe that Churchill proposed, and that this invasion would come in the spring of 1944. At the same time an invasion would be launched in southern France, and Russia would begin an offensive against Germany. Russia would enter the war against Japan soon after the defeat of Germany, as promised earlier in the Foreign Ministers Conference at Moscow, though exact conditions under which she would enter were left undetermined, only to be specified later at Yalta. The three also agreed to support Tito and his partisans in Yugoslavia. These were the major military agreements. Politically, the Big Three decided, quite inconsistently with the Atlantic Charter, that the boundaries of Poland should be revamped, with territory in the east being conceded to Russia in return for accession of some German territory in the west. In talks on the future of Germany there was no definitive agreement, but among the items discussed was Roosevelt's proposed division of that nation into five independent states. Finally, and most important as far as Hurley was concerned, the wartime leaders signed a three-power declaration on Iran.

The Declaration on Iran originated in the State Department's Division of Near Eastern Affairs in January 1943 and more specifically in a memorandum drafted by Foreign Service officer John Jernegan. The memorandum began by stating that the wartime weakness of the government of Iran and its poor internal structure, coupled with "past and present" attitudes on the part of Russia and Great Britain (Russia's desire for a warm-water port and Britain's interest for strategic reasons), could make Iran a significant "danger point" in any postwar settlement. Therefore, the document continued, the best course was to strengthen Iran, thus allowing her to stand independently, while at the same time the Great Powers would make self-denying pledges toward that country. Since the United States was probably the only power capable of giving assistance without arousing suspicion of its motives by either the powers or the Iranians, and had vital interest in the principles of the Atlantic Charter, the United States should take the lead in securing the affirmation of the Charter relative to Iran; the United States should "exert itself to see that Iran's integrity and independence are maintained and that she becomes prosperous and stable." There should be positive action on Iran not only to facilitate the war effort but for postwar development of the country.[34]

This memorandum was accepted by the Division of Near Eastern Affairs and by the State Department as comprising U.S. policy toward Iran and was conveyed to U.S. Minister Louis Dreyfus on March 13. Dreyfus saw it as an excellent statement of the United States position, and, in his dispatch to the Department on April 7, he agreed that Iran was "a proving ground for the Atlantic Charter." However, he believed that the United States should do some soul-searching to see if it lived up to these principles, particularly in view of its association with the Middle East Supply Center, an agency based on monopoly and compulsion.[35] Hurley, obviously apprised of State Department policy, reiterated many of these points in a message to Roosevelt on May 13, arguing for a positive U.S. approach based on the Atlantic Charter.[36]

On August 16, Secretary of State Hull also summarized the Jernegan memorandum for the President. He stated that Iran had been a battleground between Russia and Great Britain for a century, and said: "If events are allowed to run their course unchecked, it seems likely that either Russia or Great Britain, or both, will be led to take action which will seriously abridge, if not destroy, effective Iranian independence. That such action would be contrary to the principles of the Atlantic Charter is obvious." The note also stated that this would have world-wide repercussions; therefore, the United States should strengthen Iran and call upon its associates to reaffirm the Atlantic Charter.[37]

The reasons for American enthusiasm for the Atlantic Charter were perhaps expressed best by Jernegan in September 1943. The United States, he stated, had two interests in Iran, one practical and one idealistic. The United States was vitally interested in present and future oil development in Arabia. Her position

[34] Memorandum by John Jernegan, Jan. 23, 1943, *F.R., 1943*, IV, 331–336.
[35] Minister in Iran to Secretary of State, Apr. 14, 1943, *ibid.*, 355–359.
[36] To Roosevelt, May 13, 1943, Hurley Papers.
[37] Secretary of State to Roosevelt, Aug. 16, 1943, *F.R., 1943*, IV, 377–378.

could be jeopardized by a great power ensconced on the Iranian side of the Persian Gulf. The other interest, and he established no priority though he cited the practical one first, was in upholding the principles for which the United States was fighting. If Iran were to lose its independence, the result would be negation of the Atlantic Charter, and "such a negation would destroy the confidence of the world in the good faith of the United Nations and would begin the disintegration of the peace structure which we hoped to set up."[38]

Pursuant to formulating this policy, the United States attempted at the Moscow Foreign Ministers Conference to secure acceptance of it by Great Britain and the Soviet Union. The British proved willing to accept a compromise version, but all attempts to get a commitment from Russia failed.[39] Consequently, the matter was of some concern to U.S. officials at Teheran and became part of the agenda at the conference upon the insistence of Secretary of State Hull.

At the beginning of the Conference, Roosevelt asked Hurley to draft a declaration on Iran which might prove acceptable to all parties at the meeting. Subsequently, Dreyfus delivered to the U.S. envoy the State Department policy statements on the question, as well as Jernegan's studies from the Division of Near Eastern Affairs for the previous eleven months, and Hurley went to work. The fruit of his labor was a brief statement, which the three heads of state signed on December 1, acknowledging Iran's importance to the war effort and the difficulties for her arising from the war, and specifying agreement to cooperate to assist her economically during and at the end of the war. In addition, "the Governments of the United States, the U.S.S.R., and the United Kingdom are at one with the Government of Iran in their desire for the maintenance of the independence, sovereignty, and territorial integrity of Iran. They count upon the participation of

[38] Memorandum of conversation by John Jernegan, Sept. 21, 1943, *ibid.*, 386–388.
[39] George Allen to Secretary of State, Nov. 4, 1943, *ibid.*, 400–405.

Iran, together with all other peace-loving nations, in the establishment of international peace, security, and prosperity after the war, in accordance with the principles of the Atlantic Charter, to which all four Governments have subscribed." [40]

Though the declaration was little but a pious hope for the future, Hurley was gleeful at its signing. And because of his part in drafting it, he came to consider the policy thus enunciated as his and the President's alone. Actually, of course, it was policy developed by Jernegan and the Near East Division with Hurley's role a minimal one, except insofar as he became one of its publicists. Nonetheless, he had a close interest in the policy statement, and it reflected accurately his views regarding Iran.

More significant was Hurley's work after the Teheran Conference on the basic principles of the future relationship between Iran and the United States. At the close of the meetings, Roosevelt informed his envoy that he would like to see a plan defining U.S. relations with the Middle Eastern country which might be considered as constituting criteria for dealing with all "less favored and liberated nations." Hurley was concerned about this question, for he recognized that the United States, through economic concessions, could be as exploitative as other nations penetrating Iran. He told the Secretary of State that Iranian leaders were now anxious to have U.S. business enter all Iranian enterprise, in view of the good will engendered by the Declaration. But it was important to Iran, and should be also to the State

---

[40] Declaration regarding Iran, Dec. 1, 1943, *ibid.*, 413–414. According to Hurley and his official biographer Don Lohbeck, after the conference ended, and the Big Three met at an official dinner, Stalin entered the room where Churchill and Roosevelt were already seated and, as instructed by Hurley the year before, stated in English: "Hey, what the hell's going on in here" (Don Lohbeck, [*Patrick J. Hurley*, Chicago, 1956], p. 219). Actually, the story is apocryphal and was started by Hurley himself. The President's Secretary Stephen Early checked into it on behalf of Richard E. Lauterbach, Associate Editor of *Life*, and he talked with a number of people present, including Ambassador Charles Bohlen, and all said it was untrue (Richard E. Lauterbach to President Roosevelt, Jan. 12, 1945, Roosevelt Papers).

Department, to know the character and responsibility of these firms. He therefore advised that the Department "scrutinize" carefully all business groups wishing to enter Iran so as to avoid "shoestring promoters" and "exploiters." "Department in my opinion should, with assistance of other agencies of Government, be able to advise Iran definitely about character and qualifications of every applicant for a concession." [41]

On December 21, Hurley submitted an extended memorandum to the President comprising his plan for Iran. Semihistorical, semiphilosophical, the message contained six related parts. First, he restated the U.S. view that principles of self-government and free enterprise should be applied in Iran, and went on to suggest that the United States could help her achieve the basic "freedoms"; to accomplish this the United States would furnish expert advisers in various fields of government who would be paid by the Iranian government but who would work closely with the State Department. In this way the United States could help channel Iranian efforts toward building a modern nation. But to accomplish much would take patience and cooperation among the powers interested in Iran; and the principles espoused would conflict with traditional British and Russian imperialism. The United States would therefore have to commit these powers to its policy. The third and fourth sections dealt with the question of Lend Lease and the monopoly established by the British through the United Kingdom Commercial Corporation, which sold supplies in Iran. Hurley believed that the United States should take "complete control of the distribution of our Lend-Lease supplies in this area." Russia should not be permitted to secure U.S. rifles and other materials through Lend Lease and then agree, as they had just done, to sell Iran 50,000 rifles and quantities of tanks and airplanes—the Soviet Union was learning from the British. Finally, the United States should not, in formulating policies to help Iran in the postwar period, neglect its

[41] Hurley to Secretary of State, Dec. 20, 1943, *F.R., 1943,* IV, 417–419.

home front, particularly the economic problems involved in transition from war to peace.[42]

President Roosevelt liked the report and, on January 12, 1944, forwarded it to the Secretary of State with the note: "Enclosed is a very interesting letter from Pat Hurley. It is in general along the lines of my talk with him. . . . I was rather thrilled with the idea of using Iran as an example of what we could do by an unselfish American policy. We could not take on a more difficult nation than Iran. I would like, however, to have a try at it. The real difficulty is to get the right kind of American experts who would be loyal to their ideals. . . . If we could get this policy started it would become permanent if it succeeded as we hope during the first five or ten years. And incidentally, the whole experiment need cost the taxpayers of the United States very little money. Would you let me know what you think I should reply to Hurley? He is right that the whole Lend-Lease Administration should take complete control of the distribution of our own Lend-Lease supplies in the Middle East." [43]

Under-Secretary of State Edward Stettinius indicated his approval, particularly of the assistance arrangement proposed by Hurley, and wired the envoy that progress was being made in broadening the program. Also, the Department was beginning the scrutiny of U.S. business groups, as recommended, and hoped before too long to implement the "full report." [44] However, some second-echelon personnel in the State Department apparently did not view the Iranian plan so favorably. The Near East Division drew up a memorandum on the question of Lend-Lease control by the United States, stating that Hurley was correct, and closer control of supplies should be exercised. To this, Eugene Rostow attached a note before sending it on to Assistant Secretary Dean Acheson to the effect that, while the proposal seemed innocent, it could cause much confusion. In the spring of 1944 during a

[42] Hurley to Roosevelt, Dec. 21, 1943, *ibid.*, 420–426.
[43] Memorandum by the President to the Secretary of State, Jan. 12, 1944, *ibid.*, 420n.
[44] Stettinius to Hurley, Mar. 2, 1944, Hurley Papers.

visit to the State Department, Hurley ran across a memorandum also prepared by Eugene Rostow and initialed by Assistant Secretary Dean Acheson, in which the entire plan was called "hysterical messianic globaloney." Hurley became violently angry with Acheson and Rostow in the Assistant Secretary's office, and a bitter scene ensued. Hurley never forgave Acheson; later, in December 1945, before the Senate Foreign Relations Committee, he charged him with "undermining" U.S. policy.[45] Roosevelt backed his envoy, when informed of Rostow's memorandum, and continued to support his plan.

That some professionals in the State Department would not be as enthusiastic about Hurley's plan as was the President is perhaps not too surprising. As previously mentioned, they feared the "confusion" that might result in dealing with America's allies if drastic changes were made in the Lend-Lease distribution systems; in any case they did not believe the abuses as great as Hurley averred. For the United States to contemplate sending more "advisers" to build a "modern nation" in Iran would require a missionary zeal in diplomacy, which developed after the war, but which many, at this juncture, were not willing to envision. They were also highly skeptical about the prospects for "free enterprise" and "self-government" in Iran and undoubtedly wondered about the reasons for Hurley's sudden interest in the country. Moreover, many of them, and in this particular instance, Acheson and Rostow, viewed the formulation of U.S. foreign policy as a process in which first concern was granted the more immediate national interest. To use such terms as "freedom from fear," "freedom from want," freedom of speech and press, and to stand for freedom of conscience on an international plane was a fine expression of ideals, but one had always to reconcile these terms with the real world. To suggest that they might apply specifically to Iran, given traditional world-power interests in that country and the colossal problems there, one of which was

[45] Memorandum for the President by the Secretary of State, Feb. 18, 1944, and Memorandum for the President, Jan. 27, 1944, Department of State, File 891.00/3037; see also *Baltimore Sun*, Dec. 11, 1945.

over 90 percent illiteracy, was simply not very realistic. Even members of the Near East Division of the State Department like John Jernegan, who first authored the idea of invoking the Atlantic Charter, did so partly for perfectly practical reasons. Jernegan saw adherence to the Atlantic Charter at least in part as a way to preserve and protect the U.S. material and strategic position, for he feared the consequences to the U.S. oil interests in Arabia of the ascendancy of a major power in Iran.

The reasons for Hurley's enthusiastic advocacy of the Iranian plan are difficult to assess. He was suspicious of the British, and also to a certain extent though less so, of the Soviet Union, because of the abuse of Lend Lease, and because of the supercilious manner of the British, which as a southwesterner, he could not abide. Partially, his intent was a negative one; he wanted to deny Britain and Russia the postwar influence in the region which they so desperately hoped to preserve and expand. Though he did not articulate it, he may also have been concerned about the U.S. position in the Middle East because of his interests in oil. Sinclair, in 1944, worked vigorously for an oil concession from the Iranian government. While there is insufficient evidence to establish just how actively Hurley supported Sinclair, it may be significant to note that in 1943 and 1944 Hurley conferred with Sinclair forty-three times, often for a full day at a time.[46] Hurley, therefore, may have found a way to promote the oil company by appealing to idealistic concern for Iran. This is not to say that he had no concern for Iran or that he attempted to deceive President Roosevelt, for his desire to "help" Iran and his belief in the ideals of the Atlantic Charter seem genuine enough. A final supposition relative to the wording of the document is even less flattering to Hurley but may have some validity: he may have determined in conferences what the President's ideas were about future policy toward Iran and simply told him what he wanted to hear.

[46] See Office Diary, 1943 and 1944, Hurley Papers.

After authoring the Iranian plan, Hurley left Iran for a quick trip to Afghanistan where he hoped to spread good will and to check on the adequacy of airfields to handle planes en route between Cairo and Chungking. He went first to Karachi, whence he planned to fly on to Afghanistan. However, while there, bad weather set in, and he experienced difficulty with British officials in getting fuel—a fact that made him more the Anglophobe—so he motored to Kabul, arriving on January 8. Although he did little while there save converse briefly with government officials, the mission was a success; the Afghans had heard of his Iranian plan, seeing in it good will and economic assistance on the part of the U.S. for their own country, and, for what it was worth, better U.S.-Afghan relations resulted.

From Afghanistan, the U.S. envoy flew back to the Middle East where he made another whirlwind tour, again touching briefly upon all the important topics—oil, Zionism, Arab nationalism, supply problems. In mid-February, he returned to Washington. In Washington he conferred with Secretary of State Hull and the State Department's Near Eastern Division as well as the President about the various problems he had encountered in the Middle East; he was particularly anxious that Roosevelt implement the plan for Iran, and he so informed the President. He also spent large amounts of time explaining his position on Palestine and advising his clients on Middle Eastern oil. In the summer of 1944, Roosevelt, as previously mentioned, considered sending Hurley back to the Middle East in a command capacity, but the Oklahoman's outspoken opposition to Zionism and his oil connections had made him a controversial figure in the United States, and Secretary Ickes objected. Moreover, 1944 was an election year. Instead, the President asked his aide General E. M. Watson to discuss with General Marshall a suitable assignment for the Oklahoman; he then sent Hurley to China, where interallied squabbles threatened the effective prosecution of the war against Japan.

# VI

## The Recall of General Stilwell

In the summer of 1944 President Roosevelt called upon Hurley to undertake an important mission to China to mediate differences between General Joseph Stilwell and Chiang Kai-shek and to help stabilize the military situation there. Though Hurley knew little of China, the President apparently believed his personality suited to the task; he was to be the President's personal representative and was to report directly to him. On August 25, Hurley and Donald Nelson, former head of the War Production Board, departed for Chungking via Moscow, arriving in Russia on August 30 and in the Chinese capital on September 6. Hurley looked forward enthusiastically to his new job and, according to the colorful description left by Stilwell, deplaned "full of P and V."

The necessity for Hurley's mission can be understood only in view of developments in China dating back to 1937. On July 7, 1937, at the Marco Polo Bridge just outside Peking, Japanese troops on maneuver exchanged shots with Chinese forces in the area. Using the pretext that they had been attacked, the Japanese then waged a full-scale war on China, a war that continued for eight years. Japan in 1937 hoped to capture the five Chinese provinces just south of the Great Wall to add to the territory already seized north of the Wall in action beginning in 1931. After acquiring control of these provinces she would then force the government of Chiang Kai-shek to make additional economic and political concessions until Japan held all China in her grip as a colonial satrapy.

What Japan found easy in 1931 and 1932 was now considerably more difficult, for in 1937 China was unified in purpose as never before. The Chinese Communists, after completing their excruciating "long march" to Yenan in Shensi province to escape Kuomintang annihilation, changed their party line, and in 1936 and 1937 began to call for unity against the Japanese. Chiang Kaishek, after suffering the embarrassing "kidnapping" by Nationalist generals at Sian in December of 1936, emerged as a symbol to the people and with greater political strength than he ever previously possessed; though not deceived by the Communists, he accepted their promise of "cooperation" against Japan. The result was resistance to the Japanese military intrusion with far greater fury and determination than any demonstrated to that time. The Japanese drive in the north succeeded in that Japan captured the key railways and road junctions and, with savage attacks based on superb intelligence, put the ragtag war-lord armies to rout. But the Communist forces, which in 1937 became the Eighth Route Army of the Central Government, continued to fight; they took in those war-lord troops who wished to join their ranks; they added peasants and university students to their numbers; they broke their regiments into smaller units and battled the Japanese behind their own lines; they killed Japanese while increasing the size of their army and the countryside under their control.

Meanwhile, in August 1937, the Japanese attacked Shanghai in the lower Yangtze valley where they met furious fighting in the form of Chiang Kai-shek's best government troops. It took massive Japanese resources and better than two months to dislodge the Chinese troops from Shanghai. Finally, Japanese superiority in weaponry prevailed; they captured the city and moved on up the Yangtze where, in December, they took Nanking, the Kuomintang capital. The Chinese government then moved to Hankow farther up the river, at the same time continuing its resistance. Again, however, Chinese military strategy was only temporarily successful; in 1938, the Japanese captured Hankow, forcing the Chinese government still farther inland, this time to Chungking. At the end of 1938 Japan held the entire coast of

China, all of its industrial centers, the outlets of its three great-est rivers, nearly all of its railways and important highways, and a sizeable portion of its south central region. The Japanese con-tinued to hold this territory, and more, until the war ended in 1945.

Forced to flee the seat of its power and to abandon its re-sources, its eastern cities, and its transportation facilities, the government of China after 1938 confronted problems gargan-tuan in nature. Chungking, the new capital, was devoid of in-dustry, and what existed there during the war had to be carried in; it was not easily accessible to the West, a source of assistance; it possessed woefully inadequate facilities necessary for a func-tioning government. The city, as Theodore White and Annalee Jacoby described it, "was known even in China as a uniquely un-pleasant place."[1] Located in Szechuan province above the narrow rock gorges which separate central China from the interior region, Chungking was remote by Chinese standards; its people had little knowledge of or interest in the rest of China, and government was by semifeudal alliances held together by a super war lord. Its climate was something less than ideal. As Theodore White writes: "There were only two seasons in Chungking, both bad. From early fall to late spring the fogs and rains made a dripping canopy over the city; damp and cold reigned in every home. The slime in the street was inches thick, and people carried the slippery mud with them as they went from bedroom to council chamber and back . . . everyone shivered until summer came; then the heat settled down, and the sun glared. Dust coated the city al-most as thickly as mud during the wintertime. Moisture remained in the air, perspiration dripped, and prickly heat ravaged the skin. Every errand became an expedition, each expedition an ordeal. Swarms of bugs emerged; small green ones swam on drinking water, and spiders four inches across crawled on the walls. The famous Chungking mosquitos came, and Americans

[1] Theodore H. White and Annalee Jacoby, *Thunder Out of China* (New York, 1946), p. 5.

claimed the mosquitos worked in threes; two lifted the mosquito net, while the third zoomed in for the kill. Meat spoiled; there was never enough water for washing; dysentery spread and could not be evaded."[2] Sanitation was nonexistent; and garbage and human waste flowed into the same streams which provided drinking water.

Then the Japanese bombs came and smashed the primitive telephone system, deprived the city of light for days at a time, drove people into caves, and brought more squalor to an already squalid community. Government officials were jammed into dormitories; they worked in unheated offices; they got by on water rationed at a basinful per person per day; and they were hungry —most of the time.[3]

The tremendous influx of people, both government personnel and refugees from the Japanese advance, which transformed a city of 200,000 to one of well over a million, also brought tremendous inflation. Meanwhile, the Japanese blockade pushed prices upward at a dizzying rate in the entire area under Kuomintang control. Hoarding became a fact of life. Corruption in various forms touched every level of government in unoccupied China; often it was mandatory for survival, given the deteriorating economic situation. Moreover, the Szechuanese looked upon the refugees and the government as intruders, and Kuomintang control was based more on hatred of the Japanese resulting from the bombings than any allegiance elicited by the government.

As the war progressed, Chiang recognized the accumulating strength, in the north, of his old adversaries, the Communists, and their ultimate threat to his personal power. His deal with them was only a modus vivendi: the war with Japan had intruded and prevented the Generalissimo from achieving a final victory over the CCP. Nothing that had transpired so far had created any basis for permanent union. The Communists developed great strength, not only in Shensi, but along the coast, in the

2 *Ibid.*, pp. 9–10.
3 *Ibid.*, pp. 11–17.

lower Yangtze valley, and beyond the Yellow River; they expanded their operations behind Japanese lines as they won support and allegiance from the countryside. In 1937, they controlled about 35,000 square miles and about 40,000,000 people.[4] Increasingly they came in contact with government troops and clashed with them. After 1941, when Kuomintang troops trapped and wiped out the Communist new Fourth Army, even as negotiations were taking place between CCP and government officials, the breach was opened wide. China now suffered a war between the Kuomintang and the CCP as well as a war against Japan. Neither of these wars was Chiang prepared to win; neither, however, could he afford to lose.

Chiang's army was dreadfully incapable of meeting this test. Chiang often seemed more concerned about personal loyalty than for an officer's ability as a commander. There was no adequate central command, and the various armies ignored directives from Chungking; the government could not supply sufficient guns and ammunition from its arsenals; commanders were asked to raise their own supplies, which were then hoarded for future emergencies or sold. Local commanders, often incompetent militarily, became virtual governors in districts under their control, where they collected taxes and made laws, usually to the detriment of the peasant who bore the major brunt of the war effort. Many troops starved or suffered from malnutrition while profiteering from extortion; opium running and other corrupt practices were rife. Conscription was by seizure, with the rich buying their way out, and the poor carrying the burden; training was extremely brutal; there were almost no doctors, and disease of every sort sped through the ranks; there were few hospitals and almost no ambulances. The wonder is that the Chinese army did not completely collapse of its own weight, entirely independent of any external threat posed by the Japanese and the Communists.[5]

[4] U.S. Senate, Judiciary Committee, *Hearings on The Institute of Pacific Relations*, 82nd Cong., 2nd Sess., 1952, p. 2369.
[5] White and Jacoby, pp. 70–72.

The Japanese attack on Pearl Harbor brought these massive Chinese problems into sharp focus for American policy makers. The United States believed that China could be of assistance both during and after the war in several ways: air bases could be established there, from which to attack shipping and eventually to bomb Japan itself; if Chinese forces could be improved in efficiency and in combat effectiveness, their numbers could reap fierce casualties among the Japanese; short of this, if China could just be kept in the war, she would tie down a large Japanese army which could not be used elsewhere. In the postwar world, China, it was hoped, would be a major force in preserving the balance of power in Asia, and the United States would not herself be drawn into Asian politics.[6]

Accordingly, American wartime aspirations regarding China's contributions proved to be mother of an exaggerated estimate of her world stature; President Roosevelt lost no time in referring to China as a great power and insisted that she be considered as such in wartime deliberations. Ironically, however, while American diplomacy was predicated on the notion of China as a world power, military policy, which gave first priority to Europe, precluded sending her aid commensurate with her presumed status. In December 1941, the United States was sending Lend-Lease materials and weapons into China, was attempting to improve transportation there, and was supporting the volunteer air group under General Claire Chennault. But the real support for China, viewed against the total picture of the war, was thin indeed.[7]

The China-Burma-India command proved a manifestation of this dichotomy. At the Arcadia Conference in Washington in December 1941, President Roosevelt and Prime Minister Winston Churchill, cognizant of the need to work with China in the Asian war, proposed to Chiang Kai-shek that he become Supreme Commander of a United Nation's China Theater. Chiang concurred and then requested the appointment of an American officer to

[6] Tang Tsou, *America's Failure in China, 1941–1950* (Chicago, 1963), pp. 45–68.

[7] *Ibid.;* and Herbert Feis, *The China Tangle* (Princeton, 1953), pp. 4–5.

serve under him as Chief of Staff of the allied staff which the Generalissimo planned to organize to help command the China Theater. The United States nominated General Joseph Stilwell, a distinguished infantry officer in World War I and former military attaché who had spent many years in China, and he was promptly accepted by the Chinese. Under the arrangement thus devised Chiang Kai-shek was Supreme Commander of all United Nations troops in the China Theater, accountable only to God; General Ho Ying-chin was Chief of Staff of the Chinese Army under Chiang; and General Stilwell was the Generalissimo's joint or allied Chief of Staff. Actually an extremely complicated command arrangement was to devolve on Stilwell. He became Commander in Chief in the China-Burma-India Theater in which he commanded all Americans in the Theater; in India he became, in addition, deputy Commander of the Southeast Asia Command when it was created in 1943, serving directly under British Admiral Lord Louis Mountbatten.[8] His instructions were vague at best, and his relationship with Chiang Kai-shek, which ultimately proved to be his undoing, improperly defined. Strong willed, impatient, and suspicious of the motives of both the Chinese and the British, Stilwell, who arrived in Chungking in March 1942, quickly came into conflict with his new colleagues, and in particular with Chiang.

The defense of Burma in March and April 1942 occasioned the first flare-up between the two. The American general, who immediately assumed direct command of U.S. and Chinese troops in Burma, at first believed that he received inadequate support from Chiang; then when the Generalissimo did agree to send more troops, the Japanese continued their advance, and the military situation deteriorated further, Stilwell became convinced that Chinese troops were responsive only to secret orders from Chungking and were paying little heed to his directives. Finally, in late April, the allies, as Stilwell put it, got "run out of Burma" com-

[8] Charles F. Romanus and Riley Sunderland, *Stilwell's Command Problems* (Washington, D.C., 1956), p. 1; see also White and Jacoby, p. 149.

pletely. This he saw correctly as a tragic humiliation, a defeat which not only threatened India but isolated China as well, a defeat which, in Stilwell's view, could be ascribed primarily to Chiang's interference. Stilwell wanted to "go back and retake it." [9]

In the aftermath of this defeat, Stilwell proposed in May and June 1942 the creation of an elite force within the Chinese army comprised of numerous well-led, well-fed, well-trained divisions, supplied by U.S. Lend-Lease materials and weapons. Concurrently, he proposed that U.S., British, and Chinese troops begin an offensive to recapture Burma; and in July he put forward a detailed plan under which the allies would reopen the port of Rangoon and re-establish the supply line between Rangoon and Kunming. Once this had been done and the United States had created a powerful and well-supplied Chinese army, the United States could begin an air offensive against the Japanese home islands, and Sino-American forces could begin to drive the Japanese out of China. Had the Stilwell plan been implemented, the course of Chinese history might well have been different. As Tang Tsou suggests in his sophisticated analysis: "A strong Nationalist army might have come into existence and taken part in the offensive to drive the Japanese army from China. The economic and political deterioration in Nationalist China might have been arrested, and the Nationalist regime might have been in a better position to deal with the Communists. If there was ever a chance to make China a great power, such a chance depended on effective implementation of this plan in Burma." [10]

Because of the higher priority assigned to winning the war in Europe, however, neither the United States nor Great Britain could commit the necessary men or material to this operation in Burma. The British on their part were much more interested in the Middle East and in India, even as secondary fronts, and could not muster enthusiasm for an amphibious assault on Rangoon, without which they believed troops would bog down in

[9] Feis, p. 33.
[10] Tang Tsou, p. 63.

the Burmese jungles interminably. The United States would not assign combat troops on a large scale to Burma. In this situation, the Chinese themselves were reluctant to become committed to an all-out offensive for several reasons, not the least of which was Chiang's preoccupation with the preservation of his forces to keep himself in power. Consequently, the Burma campaign was long delayed and in scope much reduced.[11]

Meanwhile, Stilwell continued his efforts toward improving Chiang's army. He proposed reducing the number of divisions within the force, firing all inefficient or incompetent commanders, and training and equipping 30 to 60 crack divisions. Once these measures were taken, he was certain that China would become a more potent factor in the war against Japan and would find many of her domestic political problems diminished, especially that of provincial loyalty; it would also put her on the road to stability when the war was terminated. Stilwell made some progress, in that an infantry and artillery training program was set up in Yunnan in March 1943, and an American liaison staff was created for the Yunnan divisions. Generally, however, he met frustration upon frustration because of Chiang Kai-shek's reluctance to act; Chiang feared the animosity he might engender with his generals in any significant army reorganization. "The plain fact," Stilwell wrote, "is that he doesn't dare to take vigorous action—they are sure to be sulky and they may gang up. His best cards are in the air force, the artillery, and the ten armies whose training is under the Central Government. Why doesn't the little dummy realize that his only hope is the 30 division plan, and the creation of a separate, efficient, well-equipped and well-trained force?"[12] To follow Stilwell's program, Chiang realized, could upset the balance of political power in China by creating a new political force, while removing commanders wholesale would eliminate many who were loyal to Chiang. Therefore while the Generalissimo did not dislike the idea of a stronger Chinese army, he could

[11] *Ibid.*, pp. 63–65.
[12] Joseph Stilwell, *The Stilwell Papers* (New York, 1948), p. 157.

not accept military reform without careful deliberation unless willing to dangerously imperil his own position; he countered Stilwell's admonitions by requesting more U.S. aid. Stilwell in the face of Chiang's delays, concluded that the Generalissimo, whom he referred to as the "Peanut," was an "ignorant, arbitrary, stubborn man."

Chiang's obstinance, however, was not of itself responsible for the failure of Stilwell's program. As the American general advanced his ideas in favor of an early recapturing of Burma, Chiang put him off with the argument that more could be accomplished in China with an effective air force. Reinforcing him was the opinion of General Claire Chennault. Chennault believed that by concentrating on reform of the Chinese army the United States was losing valuable time and a good opportunity to blast Japanese forces and installations from the air; in other words, there were quicker, less costly, and more spectacular ways to defeat the Japanese in China. In October of 1942, Chennault put before President Roosevelt a plan under which he would utilize 105 fighters, 35 medium bombers, and 12 heavy bombers to "accomplish the downfall of Japan." He would simply bomb the Japanese in China, destroy their air force, and then launch attacks on the home islands.[13] Roosevelt bought Chennault's proposal, because it conformed with his prior commitment to fight the war first in Europe, and because it offered possible quick results, apparently not realizing that it tended to contradict his efforts to make China a great power.

When the so-called Trident Conference was held in Washington in May 1943, the Generalissimo urged the President to support Chennault, while the U.S. War Department backed Stilwell's approach. The two were obviously in conflict for supply tonnage. The War Department advised that, if Chennault's proposals were backed, the Japanese would be provoked into attacking the east China air bases from which the 14th Air Force operated[14]—

[13] Romanus and Sunderland, p. 5; Tang Tsou, pp. 75–78.
[14] Ibid.

which as events transpired was exactly what happened; and China's troops were ill-prepared to deal with this Japanese drive. Roosevelt refused to heed the War Department's arguments. The combined Chiefs of Staff also agreed at the Trident Conference not to undertake a reconquest of all Burma but only of the northern sector.

Stilwell was thus undercut on his Chinese army reform program and on the Burma campaign. His efforts were also undermined by the American decision made in the fall of 1943 to bomb Japan with B29's based in India, a plan staged through China and called the Matterhorn project. This bombing drained away supplies but did not reduce the Japanese steel industry as intended; it was, indeed, another example of an American decision in pursuit of a quick and spectacular victory. The island-hopping campaign confirmed at the Cairo conference in 1943 was another course of action which would make Stilwell's work superfluous; it was now obvious that the United States attached little importance to improving the combat efficiency of Chiang's army or to retaking Burma.[15] Stilwell, nevertheless, continued his efforts.

Responding to Stilwell's frequent pleas, the allies at Cairo, in November 1943, finally agreed to an offensive in Burma. The British were to land on the southern coast, the Chinese would attack across the Salween, and Stilwell would advance through northern Burma. At the Teheran Conference which followed, however, the allies made a commitment to a cross-channel invasion of the European continent, and this precluded a British landing in southern Burma because of a shortage of landing craft. Without the British landing, Chiang stated, he would not permit the use of Chinese troops across the Salween. In any event, Stilwell, in January 1944, began his north Burma offensive, while continuing to urge Chinese participation. Finally, as a result of pressure applied by President Roosevelt in April, Chiang agreed to launch the offensive; the United States threatened to cut off Lend-Lease

[15] Romanus and Sunderland, pp. 6–8.

supplies to China's forces designated for Burma unless he put them into action. Roosevelt in this case, and in rejecting Chiang's request in January for a huge loan, thus began the use of a quid-pro-quo policy in dealing with the Generalissimo—a policy reflective of his view of the new diminished military importance of China.[16] The President was no longer so concerned that Chiang would, as he so often threatened, conclude a separate peace with the Japanese.

During the winter, Stilwell's campaign in Burma made considerable progress, and in April the addition of Chiang's Yunnan troops helped. But the monsoon rains soon bogged the forces down, the Japanese fought furiously, and it became clear that a quick, decisive victory would be denied. Then the Japanese intensified their attacks in eastern China, thereby beginning the "East China Crisis" of 1944. The Japanese attacked a section of the Peiping-Hankow railway in April, drove toward Changsha in May, and in late June, began an offensive on Hengyang preparatory to advancing into Kweilin, a major air base in eastern China. Chungking itself seemed under imminent threat. Meanwhile, China's interior demoralization, caused by the evils of conscription, extortionistic and unequal taxation, and a disastrous famine in Honan, had weakened the government's position and its ability to resist. The situation reinforced Stilwell's belief that the Generalissimo should employ Communist troops.

Stilwell had long been of the opinion that Chiang should utilize the Communists, and this was one of the substantive issues between the two men. He had urged this course on the Generalissimo in April 1942 during the first crisis in Burma; in the face of Japanese pressures in the fall of 1943 in the Yangtze valley, he reiterated his view, suggesting that the Communist 18th Group Army could be of inestimable assistance if supplied and encouraged to launch an attack in north China. At this same time, Chiang was under increasing pressure by more conservative ele-

16 Tang Tsou, pp. 109–110.

ments in the Kuomintang not only not to use the Communists, but to attack them and settle that domestic problem once and for all; the Generalissimo in 1943 rejected Stilwell's advice. Now, though in the midst of the crisis of the spring of 1944, Chiang, realizing the dangers to his control, remained reluctant to use the Communists. On their part, the Communists, as they saw the crisis deepen with each Japanese advance, progressively raised their price for cooperation with the government. As Chiang proffered excuses, Stilwell grew more and more contemptuous. In the meantime, in early July the China crisis brought President Roosevelt around to demanding that the Generalissimo recall Stilwell from Burma, place him in command of all Chinese troops, and allow him to utilize Communist forces; this would involve a political accommodation between the two Chinese factions.[17]

It is thus clear that serious substantive issues arose between Chiang and his American Chief of Staff—proper strategy to be used in Burma, the revitalization of the Chinese army, the use of the Communists, to say nothing of conditions imposed by Washington which viewed the China area against the total picture of the war. What was of very great significance also, however, in the ultimate break, was the personality conflict that developed. Stilwell was abrasive, outspoken, impatient. As Tang Tsou writes: "Stilwell's policy and tactics might have had a better chance to succeed if they had been accompanied by tact, courtesy, and politeness. . . . As it was, the acid, abusive comments of Vinegar Joe on the Generalissimo and the Chinese government were soon known all over Chungking and aroused intense emotional reactions."[18] Chiang, slighted by the wartime allies, annoyed at Stilwell's constant admonitions, and cognizant of Stilwell's vituperative and disrespectful references to himself, grew equally distrustful and contemptuous of the American general. As a result of this mutual distrust and contempt, when Vice President Henry Wallace traveled to China in the spring of 1944 to promote more

[17] *Ibid.*, pp. 171–172.
[18] *Ibid.*, pp. 94–95.

serious CCP-government negotiations, Chiang took the occasion to inform him of his unsatisfactory relationship with the American general, and he suggested that Wallace inform Roosevelt that it would be well for the President to consider removing Stilwell and send a personal emissary to China to serve as a liaison official between himself and the Generalissimo.[19]

Wallace responded on June 28, urging the President to send the official Chiang requested. He painted a bleak picture of the politico-military situation in China, stating that the impending loss of eastern China would be extremely demoralizing to the Chinese, and that it would in part nullify the U.S. effort in the area. "With the right man to do the job," Wallace stated, "it should be possible to induce the Generalissimo to reform his regime and to establish at least the semblance of a united front. . . . What is needed is an American officer of the highest caliber in whom political and military authority will be at least temporarily united." [20] Joseph Ballantine of the State Department's Far Eastern Division then sent a short memorandum to the President, indicating that Ambassador Clarence Gauss in China shared Wallace's views of the situation and that the Department agreed with Wallace's request.[21] In early August, after the President decided to pressure Chiang to accept a broadening of Stilwell's duties, he selected Hurley for the sort of liaison assignment proposed by Wallace; Roosevelt's idea was for Hurley to work with both the Generalissimo and the American general.

Why Roosevelt chose Hurley is an important question. He had little Far Eastern experience, and he knew virtually nothing about China's history, language, politics, or about current problems there. (In 1931, for instance, he had written to Chiang:

---

[19] Chiang Kai-shek to Vice President Wallace, July 8, 1944, *F.R., 1944*, VI, 238–239.

[20] Vice-President Wallace to Roosevelt, June 28, 1944, *ibid.*, 236.

[21] Joseph Ballantine to the Secretary of State, June 29, 1944, *ibid.*, 237–238. Gauss indicated in July that he was willing to step down in the interest of effective coordination; see also Ambassador Gauss to the Secretary of State July 12, 1944, *ibid.*, 124–126.

"Mrs. Hurley joins me in expressing to you and *Madame Shek* our sincere appreciation for the flowers you sent to us." [emphasis mine.]) He had undertaken lengthy missions for the President in 1942 and 1943 but nothing of the magnitude of this important task; the President had sent him to Chungking in November 1943 to confer with Chiang and to arrange details of the Cairo Conference—this was his strongest Chinese connection up to this time. He was not a military man, regardless of his commission, except in the most liberal use of the term. But he had been Secretary of War, which gave him prestige, and he possessed a vibrant extraverted personality which Roosevelt perhaps believed would serve to ease the Stilwell-Chiang tension and induce the Generalissimo to promulgate reform. The idea of Hurley's appointment to China first originated in the War Department, with Secretary of War Stimson. After deciding not to send the Oklahoman back to the Middle East in a command capacity, the President asked General Marshall to find another assignment for him. Marshall and Stimson discussed the matter; then when the China mission was called for, Stimson suggested Hurley. Hurley and Stimson both held positions in the Hoover cabinet, Hurley as Secretary of War and Stimson as Secretary of State. They had worked closely on the matter of Philippine independence policy, were in agreement on that policy, and had remained in contact during the thirties when the Republican party was out of power. In any event, Stimson and Marshall were the first officials to approach Hurley about the mission.[22]

Shortly after the initial contact, Hurley telephoned Under-Secretary of State Edward Stettinius, suggesting that if he were to go to China he hoped to go as United States Ambassador. When the Under Secretary informed him that it was highly unlikely that an early change in representation in China would

[22] Under Secretary of State Stettinius to the Secretary of State, Aug. 3, 1944, *ibid.*, 247; Memorandum by General E. M. Watson, June 26, 1944, Roosevelt Papers, Roosevelt Presidential Library, Hyde Park, N.Y.; Hurley to Chiang Kai-shek, Oct. 3, 1931, Hurley Papers.

be made, he appealed to him to discuss it with Secretary Hull, implying that he would only go under the proper circumstances.[23] On August 9, Stettinius reported to Hull that Roosevelt had nearly made up his mind to send Hurley to work "between General Stilwell and the Generalissimo" but that Hurley would not be informed until the appointment was cleared with Chiang Kai-shek. The Under Secretary stated further: "General Marshall prefers that I not mention anything to Pat Hurley about being Ambassador until the appointment is made, so I shall have to postpone doing this until General Marshall gives us clearance."[24] Implicit in this statement is that the administration was seriously contemplating the relief of Gauss in August and that Hurley would be his replacement—an appointment which was ultimately made in November. Indeed, the Department twice asked Stanley K. Hornbeck, political adviser in the Department and longtime member of the Far Eastern Division to go to China as ambassador. Hornbeck refused, because he did not want it to appear as though he were undercutting Gauss.[25]

Hurley's final instructions from the President designated him the President's personal representative with the Generalissimo, assigned "to promote harmonious relations between General Chiang and General Stilwell and to facilitate the latter's exercise of command over the Chinese armies placed under his direction." His additional duties, connected with the dispersing of Lend-Lease supplies would be specified by the War Department; and he was at all times to maintain close contact with Ambassador Gauss.[26] As he interpreted his instructions, one other important function was to facilitate military unity in China. This aspect of Hurley's instruction was not explicitly spelled out, thus raising

[23] *F.R., 1944*, VI, 247.

[24] Under Secretary of State Stettinius to the Secretary of State, Aug. 9, 1944, *ibid.*, 247–248.

[25] Memorandum by Stanley Hornbeck, Aug. 19, 1944, Stanley K. Hornbeck Papers, Hoover Institution, Stanford University.

[26] Secretary of State to the Ambassador in China, Aug. 22, 1944, *F.R., 1944*, VI, 250–251.

questions as to whether he was authorized to seek a CCP-Kuomintang accommodation. Though there is no record of the conversation, it appears obvious that he talked with the President about the matter and that this was the reason for a side trip to the Soviet Union. At any rate, American policy makers recognized that he was correct in perceiving the need to bring the two Chinese forces together and soon reaffirmed their support of the policy, though not always of Hurley's tactics.

To accompany Hurley to Chungking, the President sent Donald Nelson, former head of the War Production Board, whose ostensible assignment was to study the deteriorating economic situation and to make a report to the President on the effects it would have on the war effort and on postwar development. Actually, Roosevelt dispatched Nelson to China because he wanted to get him out of the country and especially off the War Production Board, where he was in constant conflict with Charles E. Wilson. The President said he believed Wilson would stay with the Board if Nelson were moved out; it was necessary to take this action to avoid a further blowup in that agency.[27]

Apparently because he believed it important to the task of promoting unity, Hurley decided to stop in Moscow on his way to Chungking to learn of Stalin's intentions vis-a-vis the Chiang government and to inform him of the nature of his mission. Evidence indicates that this move was not explicitly sanctioned by the State Department or by the President and was made on his own. The State Department's Office of European Affairs indicated that the trip would create a bad impression on Chinese officials, and "it would not be in accord with General Hurley's position as personal representative of the President for him to consult with Russian officials for the purposes which he has indicated."[28] Hull stated that "the trip to Moscow was apparently an after-

[27] Roosevelt to Harry Hopkins, Aug. 7, 1944; and Hopkins to Roosevelt, Aug. 8, 1944, Roosevelt Papers.

[28] Deputy Director Office of European Affairs Matthews to the Secretary of State, Aug. 24, 1944, *F.R., 1944,* VI, 252.

thought," and he informed Ambassador Averell Harriman in the Soviet Union that the President told him that "while General Hurley and Mr. Nelson are his personal representatives to Chiang Kai-shek, neither is going to Moscow on instructions from him." [29] Nevertheless, when Hurley arrived in Moscow, Donald Nelson, who also accompanied him there, immediately informed Molotov that they stopped in Russia on the instructions of the President, and Hurley stated this several times thereafter. Harriman, who earlier received Hull's telegram stating that the trip was not officially approved, made no comment on Nelson's remarks in his report to Washington.[30] Had Hurley acted completely independently, it seems unlikely that Nelson would have concurred or opened discussions in this manner or that Harriman would have refrained from comment. It is obviously difficult to assess, but what seems likely is that Roosevelt, acting upon the advise of Hurley, who believed that the policy of the Soviet Union had to be determined prior to achieving a political solution in China, intimated privately that the two confer in Russia but informed Hull differently. In a letter of February 12 to the Secretary of State, which he drafted but did not send, Hurley emphasized that it was he who originated the idea of the stop in Moscow but that the President concurred.

Hurley and Nelson arrived in Moscow on August 30 and held discussions with Molotov the following day. The talks focused on the desire for the early defeat of Japan and the need for political and military cooperation within China toward this end. Molotov appeared most amenable to the ideas suggested by the two Americans, as he indicated that the Soviet Union had no wish to interfere in China's internal affairs to aid the Communists. In fact, Molotov stated that many of those who called themselves

[29] Secretary of State to Ambassador Harriman, Aug. 26, 1944; and Secretary of State to Ambassador Harriman, Aug. 30, 1944, *ibid.*, 253.

[30] Ambassador Harriman to the Secretary of State, Sept. 5, 1944, *ibid.*, 253–256. Hurley later stated that he convinced the President of the need to stop in Moscow; see Hurley to President Truman, Aug. 25, 1945 (unsent), Hurley Papers.

Communists "had no relation whatever to Communism," that the Soviet Union was not associated with these "Communist elements," and that his government would look with favor on the American effort to promote unity.[31] Hurley, who later was to predicate his actions on these assurances, traveled on to Chungking, much heartened by the Russian minister's remarks.

While unification and military efficiency were his ultimate concern, Hurley's immediate task was to alleviate the rapidly deteriorating Stilwell-Chiang relationship. Stilwell was chafing in Burma over lack of support from the Generalissimo and Chiang's failure to stabilize the military situation in central China. Chiang, who saw vindication for his position in the Japanese attack in the east, adamantly refused to listen to what he considered the unsound advice of the American general. However, it quickly became evident in early summer 1944 that Japanese advances in central China augured a very serious situation fraught with danger both for the Chinese government and the American position "unless drastic measures were taken." Consequently, on July 6, 1944, acting on advice of his Joint Chiefs of Staff, President Roosevelt sent the Generalissimo a sharply worded telegram stating that he was "fully aware" of his feelings toward Stilwell, but that "I am promoting General Stilwell to the rank of full general, and I recommend for your most urgent consideration that you recall him from Burma and place him directly under you in command of all Chinese and American forces, and that you charge him with the full responsibility and authority for the coordination and direction of the operations required to stem the tide of the enemy's advances."[32]

Clearly, Chiang did not want to make the appointment. To put Stilwell in the position would be to place one of his chief adversaries and critics who had personally offended him in a position of command over his armies. More than this, the move would undermine his prestige and perhaps his personal power, because

[31] Hurley to President Truman, Aug. 25, 1945 (unsent), Hurley Papers.
[32] Radiogram from Roosevelt to the Generalissimo, July 6, 1944, *ibid.*

Stilwell as commander would be concerned primarily about a general's military achievement, not his loyalty to the Generalissimo. Stilwell had in fact suggested Generals Pai Ch'ung-hsi and Li Tsung-jên of the Kwangsi faction of the Kuomintang as alternatives to Chiang for leadership in China.[33] Though this issue proved not the major factor in Stilwell's recall, the appointment would also place one of the early advocates of arming and utilizing the Communists at the head of the Generalissimo's forces; this was asking too much.

In his response on July 8, Chiang said he agreed in principle with the President's suggestion but that political conditions made it not that simple; directing Chinese troops would not be easy for Stilwell, and it would be best to have a preparatory period prior to his taking command.[34] Roosevelt replied that he understood the importance of political conditions to military decisions but that the grave danger justified "some calculated political risks," and he urged the Generalissimo "to take all steps to pave the way for General Stilwell's assumption of command at the earliest possible moment."[35] Chiang feared that if he gave command of his army to a foreigner, the people would think that he no longer held control, that the Communists would spread "malicious rumors" about his weak, ineffective rule, and that they would continue to seek to undermine the prestige of his government, and confidence would be destroyed. Moreover, appointment of Stilwell to the command was particularly onerous because of their poor relationship, and because to appoint Stilwell would be tacit agreement to the course Stilwell had recommended: the merger of Communist troops with those of the government. The Generalissimo admitted that the military situation was serious, but, "in almost every year since 1937 China has been confronted

---

[33] U.S. Senate, Committee on Foreign Relations and Committee on Armed Services, *Military Situation in the Far East*, 82nd Cong., 1st Sess., p. 2920, hereafter cited as *Military Situation in the Far East;* Tang Tsou, pp. 111–112.

[34] Chiang Kai-shek to Roosevelt, July 8, 1944, Hurley Papers.

[35] Roosevelt to Chiang Kai-shek, July 15, 1944, *ibid.*

with similar crises." [36] The situation was not so grave as to demand such a command position for Stilwell—at least not if it could be avoided.

In the face of growing pressure from Washington, Chiang continued to balk, insisting as conditions that Stilwell's authority would have to be defined, that he would not use the Communists if appointed, and that Lend-Lease come under Chinese control. Stilwell on his part insisted on meaningful control, which meant the right of punishment and reward, and the right to move and use all Chinese units as he saw fit. He also wanted the removal of General Ho Ying-chin as Chief of Staff. As the military situation continued to worsen, Roosevelt in part acceded to the Generalissimo's wishes. First, he appointed Hurley as the liaison officer as requested; then he indicated that Stilwell's new position, if agreed to, would be commander of the Armed Forces in China *subordinate* to the Generalissimo; and he "relieved" the American general of the "burden" of handling Lend-Lease supplies; another American official would be in charge. Roosevelt hoped that now he would get action before it was too late "to avert a military catastrophe tragic both to China and to our allied plans for the early overthrow of Japan." [37] Chiang still resisted and had not yet made the command arrangement when Hurley arrived in Chungking. Consequently, on September 7, Hurley, who knew little about the issues involved but nonetheless rushed blithely ahead, began daily discussions with the Generalissimo with a view to hammering out details; these negotiations were complex and lengthy, involving both Chiang and Foreign Minister T. V. Soong as well as Hurley and Stilwell, but ultimately proved to no avail.

In the meantime the military situation approached crisis proportions. In Burma, tough Japanese forces threatened not only to stop the allied offensive, but to put it to rout. In China, the Japanese continued to advance, threatening the U.S. air base at Kweilin and the early destruction of Chinese resistance. While

---

[36] Chiang Kai-shek to Dr. H. H. Kung, July 23, 1944, *ibid.*
[37] Roosevelt to Chiang Kai-shek, Aug. 22, 1944, *ibid.*

Hurley tried to persuade the Generalissimo to agree to terms under which the new command would be effected, Stilwell frantically appealed for Chiang to use the troops that he held in reserve blocking the Communists, and to commit more troops to the Burma campaign. He reported on the situation to Washington, and, in a note prepared for Dr. T. V. Soong but not delivered, he stated: "China is very close to collapse. Desperate conditions require desperate remedies, and unless the Generalissimo is prepared to administer them, my recommendation would be for the United States to withdraw entirely from China and India, and set up a base in Russia."[38]

Responding to the near-tragic developments in China, President Roosevelt on September 19, sent the Generalissimo a stern, reproving message designed to get some action. The message, which was, as Stilwell put it, "hot as a firecracker," stated that disaster appeared imminent unless Chiang sent reinforcements to north Burma to continue the offensive and reopen the Burma road and unless he took immediate action to put Stilwell in command of all forces in China to provide efficient military leadership and thus prevent the loss of critical areas of eastern China and the Kunming air terminal.[39] Because the note was transmitted by the War Department to the Military Mission in China, General Stilwell came into possession of it, and to him fell the task of delivering it to the Generalissimo. He was delighted, for therein he saw vindication of his position and a heavy blow to Chiang; he drove quickly to the Generalissimo's residence.

Before giving the message to the Generalissimo, however, Stilwell showed it to Hurley, who was already, on September 19, at Huang Shan, the Chinese president's home; he called Hurley out to the veranda to discuss the note privately. Hurley, who believed he was making some progress in negotiations with Chiang, urged him not to deliver it immediately but rather to go slow to permit

[38] Stilwell to Soong, undelivered memorandum, Sept. 16, 1944, *ibid.*; Feis, pp. 186–187.
[39] Roosevelt to Chiang Kai-shek, Sept. 16, 1944, *F.R., 1944*, VI, 157–158.

it to be interpreted to the Generalissimo first. He recognized that the note would be humiliating, for it constituted a kind of ultimatum seldom given to an ally; and he understood the bitterness between the two men. Stilwell went ahead undeterred, arguing that it was his duty to deliver it himself. Hurley until the last did all he could to limit the embarrassment for Chiang; when Stilwell presented the message, he requested that a Chinese translation be given him, and he presented it to the Generalissimo. Chiang read it without visible reaction, then terminated the meeting. Not long thereafter he requested Stilwell's recall.

The affair was regrettable in Hurley's view, because, as he informed Stilwell, he thought Chiang ready "to make every concession that we have asked. He had made them; he is ready to go; he is ready to bring troops down from the north to reinforce you on the Salween front; he is going to appoint you Commander-in-Chief."[40] Hurley's hopes far exceeded fact. Whether or not Chiang would ever have appointed Stilwell is debatable; and it is clear that Hurley and he had not yet hammered out the details on a new command arrangement like the one called for by Roosevelt.

Shortly after his arrival in China, Hurley had developed a ten-point agenda for discussions which dealt with a broad spectrum of issues ranging from military unity, to definition of Stilwell's powers, to control of Lend-Lease materials. His optimism was apparent in his first report to the President on September 7. However, dickering occurred on all these points; in particular Hurley remained adamant on American control over Lend Lease, and Chiang strongly opposed use of the Communists unless strictly controlled by him, while Stilwell insisted on adequate guarantees of his authority.[41] After the Roosevelt message, Hurley resumed discussions with the Generalissimo, still hoping to effect the desired command.

[40] *Military Situation in the Far East,* p. 2868.
[41] Ambassador Gauss to the Secretary of State, Sept. 28, 1944, *F.R., 1944,* VI, 256–259; Hurley to Roosevelt, Sept. 7, 1944, *F.R., 1944,* VI, 154.

It now was becoming clear to Hurley, however, that Chiang would not have Stilwell. Accordingly, he conveyed his thoughts to the President in a letter, one version of which he allowed Stilwell to edit, stating that the problem as he saw it was between two determined incompatible personalities.[42] On September 25, the Chinese president replied to Roosevelt's message, agreeing to place an American in command of the combined armies in China and to make changes in his officer corps but saying that Stilwell must go.[43] Then, in an aide-memoire to Hurley, the Generalissimo indicated that Stilwell was unacceptable to him, not only because of their mutual distrust, but because of Stilwell's lack of military judgment. This deficiency had been displayed, he said, throughout the ill-advised Burma campaign which drained off Chinese military reserves and supplies and made tenuous the defense of Chungking. However, he would work with the "right" American officer.[44]

Chiang's request for Stilwell's relief was the culmination of an extended period of animosity. Noting the animosity, Lauchlin Currie on a personal mission for the President, recommended in late 1942 that Stilwell be recalled; he cited the American general's attempt at pressuring the Generalissimo as constituting bad tactics. Chiang soon made a similar plea. In August and September 1943, T. V. Soong, the Generalissimo's brother-in-law, expressed to both Stanley Hornbeck and the President Chiang's desire that Stilwell be removed, and Roosevelt said he would comply if the Generalissimo himself requested the move. Chiang then did so, but General Somervell talked Chiang out of it, and Stilwell stayed on as misunderstandings were laid aside.[45] Now there was no turning back.

Roosevelt's response to the Generalissimo's request is interest-

[42] To Roosevelt, Sept. 23, 1944, Hurley Papers.
[43] Chiang Kai-shek to Hurley, Oct. 9, 1944, *ibid.*
[44] *Military Situation in the Far East,* pp. 2869–2871.
[45] Hornbeck to the Secretary of State, June 29, 1944, Hornbeck Papers; Feis, pp. 77–78.

ing. He first expressed surprise and regret at Chiang's reversal of his agreement, but then stated it was his opinion as of that date, that because of deteriorated conditions, the United States should not place an American officer in command of ground forces in China. Rather, because of the importance of maintaining the so-called hump-tonnage, it would now be better to have such an official in direct command, under the Generalissimo, of Chinese troops in Burma and Chinese ground forces in Yunnan Province; he urged that Stilwell be given this assignment. At the same time, Roosevelt stated that he was accepting Chiang's proposal that Stilwell be relieved as his Chief-of-Staff and of responsibility over Lend-Lease matters. This was clearly a partial capitulation by the President.[46]

The day after Roosevelt indicated this change in tactic, Hurley wrote to him, indicating Chiang's reaction and his current attitude toward Stilwell. Hurley stated that T. V. Soong informed him that H. H. Kung, in Washington, had cabled the Generalissimo on October 1 that Harry Hopkins had just told him the President intended to comply with the request to relieve Stilwell. This was important, Hurley believed, for it prompted Chiang to reveal to a secret government council his intentions and therefore put him in the position of not being able to compromise on Stilwell and still save face; it would, Hurley opined, determine the nature of his reply.[47]

Hurley proved correct. Chiang said he was willing and even anxious to appoint an American to the command position earlier discussed or to appoint such a person only in Burma and Yunnan, but the officer chosen would have to be one in whom he had confidence and with whom he could cooperate, and, as he had stated in his aide-memoire of September 25, he had no confidence in Stilwell; Stilwell was not acceptable even for the limited com-

---

[46] Roosevelt to Chiang Kai-shek, Oct. 5, 1944, *F.R., 1944*, VI, 165–166; Feis, p. 195.
[47] Hurley to Roosevelt, Oct. 6, 1944; and H. Hopkins to Hurley, Oct. 7, 1944, Hurley Papers. Hopkins later denied that he so informed Kung.

mand of troops in Burma and Yunnan. Along with this message, Hurley included the aide-memoire sent to him by the Generalissimo, in which Chiang recounted the differences between himself and Stilwell, questioned Stilwell's military judgment, and stated his constant readiness to comply with the President's wishes "as far as humanly possible." In a brief paragraph appended to the aide-memoire, Hurley himself "took a stand": "There is no other Chinese known to me who possesses as many of the elements of leadership as Chiang Kai-shek. Chiang Kai-shek and Stilwell are fundamentally incompatible. Today you are confronted by a choice between Chiang Kai-shek and Stilwell. There is no other issue between you and Chiang Kai-shek. Chiang Kai-shek has agreed to every request, every suggestion made by you except the Stilwell appointment." [48]

Now convinced that, if he were to accomplish anything in China, Stilwell would have to be relieved, Hurley on October 13 wired Roosevelt his views in greater detail. He said that in his opinion the Generalissimo reacted favorably to logical persuasion and leadership, but that he would not accept coercion or ultimatums—as Stilwell proposed to deal with him. Stilwell's intent was to subjugate Chiang, and this could not be done. Moreover, if Roosevelt sustained Stilwell in this controversy, he would lose Chiang Kai-shek and China with him, for Chiang had gone on record publicly for Stilwell's ouster. Hurley did not agree that the United States had no responsibility for China, and he was convinced that the United States could keep China in the war. The President should accept the Generalissimo's offer to appoint an American general to command all air and ground forces in China, and this general should be young, vigorous, a man of experience, but more important, acceptable to Chiang Kai-shek.[49]

While the President was clarifying the form of his reply to Chiang's rejection of Stilwell, he wired Hurley asking his advice on possible successors for the rejected American general. Hurley

[48] Hurley to Roosevelt, Oct. 10, 1944, *F.R., 1944*, VI, 166–170.
[49] Hurley to Roosevelt, Oct. 13, 1944, Hurley Papers.

contacted the Generalissimo and responded that the Chinese leader's preferences among those who would be available were Generals Alexander M. Patch, Albert C. Wedemeyer, and Walter Krueger.[50] As events transpired, the President chose Wedemeyer, but not for the limited command in Burma and Yunnan that he had earlier envisaged.

Roosevelt now informed the Generalissimo that he was recalling General Stilwell, but to absolve him of the charges which Chiang hurled regarding tactics in the Burma campaign, the President stated that the important decision in that area, namely, the attack in north instead of south Burma, was made by Churchill and himself. He also revealed that, subject to Chiang's approval, he was appointing General Wedemeyer to be the Generalissimo's Chief-of-Staff and was making him commander of all U.S. forces in the China theater. What had previously been the China-Burma-India theater would be separated into two areas as far as the U.S. interests were concerned: Burma-India, and China; the forces in India-Burma would be commanded by General Daniel Sutton.[51]

The appointment of General Wedemeyer eliminated the Stilwell-Chiang personality problem, but it by no means settled the outstanding differences between Washington and Chungking. Hurley naively believed that the only issue between the President and the Generalissimo was Stilwell and that he had ironed out details for an American to take the command that Roosevelt had suggested in July. He liked the Generalissimo, trusted him, and Chiang reciprocated the feeling; Hurley had as yet no adequate understanding of the frightful conditions in China and, unlike

[50] Roosevelt to Hurley, Oct. 14, 1944; and Hurley to Roosevelt, Oct. 15, 1944, *ibid.*

[51] Roosevelt to Chiang Kai-shek, Oct. 19, 1944, *ibid.* Shortly after the removal of Stilwell, Hurley wired the President that in view of last ditch attempts by Republicans to use the dismissal in the campaign, if he wished he (Roosevelt) could say to the press that much of the responsibility for the action lay with former Secretary of War Hurley, a good Republican (Patrick J. Hurley to Roosevelt, Nov. 1, 1944, Roosevelt Papers).

other American officials, asked few difficult or embarrassing questions. They dined together frequently and spent long hours in discussion during the first month of the Hurley mission. Their personal relationship probably made Hurley far too sanguine about the prospects of success, for he clearly did not see the distinction between what Chiang said he would do in principle and what he was actually prepared to carry out, in view of his desire to retain power and prestige. Certainly it became clear after the Wedemeyer appointment that on one major issue— cooperation with the Communists—there was considerable difference of opinion. And this was a problem with which Hurley was to grapple throughout the succeeding year.

# VII

## The Hopeful Broker:
## Negotiations in China,
## October 1944 to February 1945

Hurley remained optimistic about the prospects of a settlement of the difficulties in China. He did not see that Chiang presided over a mire of disillusionment in the areas he controlled or that he had lost the confidence of a large segment of the Chinese people. The President's envoy had not perceived the depth of the issue separating Stilwell and Chiang and therefore did not see Chiang as antagonistic to compromise. Moreover, he had been schooled in American politics where the two major political parties accepted the same basic premise and where accommodation was traditional. With proper prodding, the Kuomintang and the CCP, like Democrats and Republicans, could iron out their differences and proceed with the military effort against Japan.

The hostility between these two Chinese forces had been partially and temporarily submerged in 1937. In September of that year the Communists announced that they were abandoning their policy of trying to overthrow the Kuomintang, and that they were reorganizing their army as the National Revolutionary Army and placing it under the direction of the National Government; they were anxious to make a common effort against Japan. Chiang Kai-shek immediately accepted the Communist's offer in pursuit of the objective of defeating Japan. The Communist guerrillas in central China became the New Fourth Army, and even prior to the CCP announcement, the Communist Army was renamed the Eighth Route Army of the Government.

But unity on this basis was more apparent than real. The CCP decided at the time of its statement in September that it would maintain its independent leadership in the Red Army and in Communist guerrilla units; "Communists," Mao Tse-tung wrote, "are not permitted to show any vacillation in principle on this issue."[1] Moreover, the Communists refused to accept any Kuomintang cadres in the Eighth Route Army and restored the system of political commissars. The Communists, said Mao, would pursue a policy of "independence and autonomy in the United Front"; in the furtherance of their ultimate objective to achieve power in China, they would refuse to allow the United Front to hamstring them and would use the war against Japan to expand their influence and control.

Because the Communists did not depart from their major goal and because the Generalissimo knew full well their intentions, friction was not long in coming. Charges and countercharges were hurled, with each side indicating that the other was interested only in wiping out its opponent. Then in August 1938 the Kuomintang headquarters at Hankow-Wuchang outlawed three Communist-sponsored mass organizations, while in November Mao Tse-tung pointed out that "the central task and the supreme form of a revolution is the seizure of political power by force of arms and the solution of problems by war"; further, he pointed out, political power grows "out of the barrel of a gun." In December 1938, Communist and Nationalist forces clashed in Hopei; in 1939 and 1940, the Communists attacked and defeated a government force in Hopei. In 1939, the government began a blockade of the Communist areas, and, in 1940, after the Communist New Fourth Army expanded Communist control outward from the area around Nanking, the two sides fought a number of intense battles. In January 1941, the Nationalist forces attacked and destroyed a large segment of the New Fourth Army and ordered its dissolution. Following the outbreak, relations between the two

[1] Tang Tsou, *America's Failure in China, 1941–1950* (Chicago, 1963), p. 129.

forces remained hostile, with sporadic fighting occurring, but with neither willing or able to take the offensive to destroy the other because of the Japanese. During the period prior to Pearl Harbor, American policy makers scrupulously avoided giving advice on this internal matter.

After the United States entered the war, it hoped to prevent a further deterioration between the two sides, for it feared civil war. Thus American officials urged Chiang Kai-shek to refrain from further attacks on the Communists and to work toward greater unity; and Americans on numerous occasions talked with Chou En-lai in Chungking concerning the settlement of CCP-Kuomintang differences. Negotiations between the Nationalists and Communists took place in the spring of 1944, independent of American prodding, though not with satisfactory results.

Vice President Henry Wallace in his mission to Chungking in 1944 admonished Chiang to settle the differences with the Communists in the furtherance of the "prosecution of the war," though he did not prescribe a specific method. To convince Chiang of the benign quality of the CCP, Wallace informed him of Stalin's recent comments to Ambassador Averell Harriman that the Chinese Communists were nothing but "margarine Communists." The Generalissimo was not impressed by Wallace's line of argument, but he did agree to attempt to resolve his conflict with the CCP by political means and to permit President Roosevelt to mediate the dispute.[2] After August 1944 the United States, through the efforts of Hurley, began implementing a more direct approach to achieve a settlement by suggesting a unified command and a coalition government.

Compelling reasons existed for attempting to promote unity in the fall of 1944. There was grave and imminent danger of China's defeat by Japan, a contingency which could prolong the Pacific war and would undoubtedly prove extremely costly to the United States in lives and money. The Japanese were driving closer to

[2] *Ibid.*, pp. 163–164.

Kunming; they threatened to destroy Chengtu, site of an American air base in the north; Chungking might soon fall. Clearly the
situation demanded a determined effort by all Chinese forces
available. In Hurley's view, unity was a military necessity, but
as he was to learn, cooperation between Communists and Nationalists proved easier to advocate than to accomplish.

In September and October each side revealed to Hurley its
interest in discussions leading to unification. Shortly after his
arrival in Chungking, General Chu Teh, military leader of the
Communists, wrote him that the Communists were carrying on a
valiant struggle against Japan but that they, as well as the Kuomintang, should receive American aid to make them even more
effective. Later, Lin Tsu-han and Tung Pi-wu, Communist representatives at Chungking, requested the opening of discussions
with the American envoy, and in October met with Hurley three
times. Similarly, Chiang and his representatives indicated their
readiness to reach an accord with the Communists and held talks
with the American envoy toward this end.[3]

In the meantime, the American embassy prepared a memorandum for Hurley's guidance on the matter. It stated that if and
when talks were opened with the Communists, Hurley should
apprise them of the views of the United States and the Soviet
Union toward the Chinese Communists, and urge the Communists to mute their propaganda and stress the urgency of reach-
ing a settlement with the government. If they were interested,
the memo continued, the American general could inform them
that, provided he got the Generalissimo's concurrence, he would
put forward a proposal for settlement and use his good office to
bring the two sides together.[4] Subsequently, Hurley drew up a
five-point basis for agreement, which included the following: the

[3] Chu Teh to Hurley, Sept. 10, 1944; and Hurley to Roosevelt, Oct. 13,
1944, Hurley Papers; Lin Tsu-han and Tung Pi-wu to Hurley, Oct. 21, 1944,
F.R., 1944, VI, 655.

[4] Document prepared in the Embassy in China, Oct. 17, 1944, F.R., 1944,
VI, 650–651.

Kuomintang and the Communists would work to unify military forces to defeat Japan; the two sides would acknowledge the Generalissimo as Chinese President and military leader; both parties would support democratic principles and those of Sun Yat-sen; the Communist party would be legalized; and only one army would exist in China with equal treatment for all.[5] Chiang agreed to the proposal; the Communist representatives consented; and Hurley began mediating the conflict.

Although both sides accepted Hurley's five points as a basis for talks, events proved that they were still far apart. Discussions with Communist leaders in Chungking proved that they were unwilling to commit their army to Chiang's command without satisfactory guarantees, which he would not provide. And, they wanted abolition of one-party rule and the formation of a coalition government, which the Generalissimo felt he could not permit. More specifically, what the Communists desired was a full and meaningful participation in the government and freedom to continue as a party seeking support in all parts of China. Chiang could not agree, because he could only lose. Short of attaining these concessions, the Communists wanted full recognition of the governments they had established, and supplies for their army. From the Generalissimo's point of view, to grant such concessions was equally dangerous. His position was, therefore, that the Communists "surrender" their army by submitting it to Nationalist control; and this was equivalent to asking them to concede. In reality the one base for agreement was hatred of Japan and the desire to defeat the Japanese forces in China. Hurley recognized the differences but not their depth, and he believed the hatred of Japan sufficient to overcome the mutual suspicions. He therefore informed Roosevelt that he was optimistic about a settlement, as he found the two sides equally interested in unity and in the future of China as a democratic state.[6]

After talks with both Kuomintang and Communist representa-

[5] Draft by Hurley, Oct. 28, 1944, *ibid.*, 659.
[6] Hurley to Roosevelt, Oct. 19, 1944, Hurley Papers.

tives in Chungking, Hurley in late October prepared to travel to Yenan, the Communist "capital," to confer with Mao Tse-tung and other high-ranking Communist officials. He was responding to invitations by the Communists proffered him upon his arrival in Chungking in September and a suggestion by John Davies, second Secretary of the U.S. embassy, temporarily residing in that province. Davies wrote him that his personal visit was needed because "you can take significant information and proposals back to the President vitally affecting the war and future balance of power in Asia and the Pacific, if you will visit Yenan." [7] Hurley also realized that the talks on unification could only succeed if he could meet personally with Communist officials charged with making policy.

On November 7, he boarded a plane along with his interpreter and a couple of advisers and flew to Yenan, where he was warmly greeted by Colonel David Barrett, head of the U.S. Army observer group there, and by numerous Communist officials, including Mao Tse-tung and Chou En-lai. The American Army observer group had been sent to Yenan during the summer of 1944, following the visit of Vice President Wallace in Chungking; it was accompanied by Foreign Service officers John S. Service and Raymond Ludden. The United States had advocated the sending of such a mission since the beginning of the year in the hope that it would assist in gathering information about the Japanese position and the movement of their troops in north China, as well as provide more knowledge of the CCP. Chiang had successfully resisted the move until Wallace pressed him on it.

As Theodore White, correspondent for *Time* and *Life* describes the meeting, the Communist delegation drove up to Hurley's plane, which landed in a rough pasture, in an old ambulance used as their official car. Then, as they ran to meet him, Hurley, bedecked in full military regalia with ribbons and medals abounding, stepped off the plane and emitted a fierce Indian war cry, to

[7] Chu Teh to Hurley, Sept. 10, 1944, *ibid.*, and Davies to Hurley, Oct. 27, 1944, *F.R., 1944*, VI, 659.

the astonishment of his hosts. He was wearing, said Colonel Barrett, "every campaign ribbon but Shay's Rebellion." After greetings were exchanged, the Communists and Hurley's party crammed into Mao's ambulance and went bouncing off to Hurley's lodgings, Hurley "entertaining" them all the while with tales of the Old West. "That evening," White reports, "the Communists gave an enormous banquet in honor of the November revolution in Russia, and Hurley was the star guest, though he baffled the Communists with an occasional bellowed yahoo." [8]

Interestingly, according to Hurley's account, the Communists were very much impressed by his trip to Yenan, mainly because of the great risk involved. "They expressed great admiration that I had come into Yenan at a time when it was necessary for my plane to be covered by fighter escort. This seemed to be of great significance to them. In opening our first formal meeting, Chairman Mao Tse-tung stated that our meeting was so important that I had risked my life to come to see him. That fact, he stated, impressed him with the earnestness of our desire to see all Chinese military forces united to defeat Japan and to prevent civil war in China." [9]

As the U.S. envoy prepared to begin discussions with his hosts, Theodore White, who had recently spent considerable time with Chairman Mao came to him to suggest that the talks held little hope of success. Mao did not believe that Chiang Kai-shek had any interest in unification and was only willing to hold conversations on the topic because of pressure from the United States; Chiang, White said, wanted to delay as long as possible, so that the Japanese could be defeated and then he could turn his armies against the Communists. White's comments in effect reaffirmed the deep suspicion held by the Communists toward the Generalissimo and again invoked the barriers which Hurley had to hurdle. Hurley remained optimistic, however, and mentioned the talk

[8] Theodore White and Annalee Jacoby, *Thunder Out of China* (New York, 1946), p. 253.
[9] Hurley to Secretary of State, Jan. 31, 1945, Hurley Papers.

with White only in a brief note to Washington, stating that White's whole conversation was against the mission with which he was charged.[10]

Hurley then opened his conversations with the Communists on November 8, discussions which were conducted in a free give and take atmosphere. "For two days and two nights," Hurley wrote, "we argued, agreed, disagreed, denied and admitted in the most strenuous but most friendly fashion."[11] Beginning the remarks, the American general stated that he had come to Yenan as an agent of the President of the United States, and with the consent of Chiang Kai-shek, to assist in working out a plan of unification leading to the early defeat of Japan. Japan was the enemy of democracy in China; both Chiang and Mao had expressed deep concern for democracy and for the future of China, and it seemed to him that a basis for understanding existed. Notably, Hurley also stated that the United States had no wish for future control over China nor did she care to dictate to China her ideologies or economic policies. Avowing his belief that the Generalissimo wished unification of military forces, he then put forward the five-point program earlier discussed in Chungking; he did so with the comment that the proposals constituted a basis for discussion and not a "take it or leave it proposition."[12]

The conference broke up at about noon on the 8th, resuming that same afternoon. In the second session, Chairman Mao responded to Hurley's earlier comments and to the proposals he presented. In a passionate monologue he condemned Chiang's attempt to retain his dictatorship, stating that what China needed was democracy, but in order to get democracy, the Generalissimo would have to agree to sweeping governmental reorganization; unity, he said, was dependent in large part on democracy. He also criticized the Kuomintang armies as corrupt, cowardly, and

[10] Theodore White interview with Mao Tse-tung, Nov. 2, 1944, *ibid.,* Memorandum by Hurley, Nov. 8, 1944, *F.R., 1944,* VI, 673–674.

[11] Hurley to Secretary of State, Jan. 31, 1945, Hurley Papers.

[12] Memorandum of conversation, Nov. 8, 1944, *F.R., 1944,* VI, 674–677.

unable and unwilling for the most part to resist Japan. The Communists, by contrast, were efficient, honest, and waged successful campaigns against the Japanese.[13] Now, for the first time, Hurley negotiated with a true ideologue and began to see the depth of Kuomintang-Communist animosity; he replied that he "did not know that the feeling was so deeply engrafted as it appeared to be this afternoon"—that the feeling seemed so deep as to make even discussing it seem unwarranted.[14]

Probably Hurley at this point saw his task in better perspective and temporarily his hopes undoubtedly lessened. Nevertheless, he continued the talks with the Communists and managed to hammer out alternate proposals to those he had brought from Chungking. These proposals, consisting of five separate points, called for the unification of all military forces in China, the creation of a coalition government containing all anti-Japanese forces and parties and promoting democratic reform, a United National Military Council with central authority in military matters by the coalition government, with supplies from foreign governments to be equally distributed, and the legalization of the Communist party as well as all other anti-Japanese parties.[15] Also included was a statement that the Coalition National Government would pursue policies designed to promote progress and the establishment of the principles embodied in the American Bill of Rights. The Communists, obviously pleased with the new points, signed the agreement. Decidedly vague, the plan avoided comment on how the coalition would work and clearly did nothing to diminish the differences between the two parties. Hurley, however, regained his enthusiasm and returned to Chungking, hoping to persuade Chiang Kai-shek to accept the plan or a modification of it; he believed he had established the basis for Chinese unity.

When Hurley returned to the Chinese capital, he had a heavy cold, and he spent the remainder of that day and the next in bed.

[13] Memorandum of conversation, Nov. 8, 1944, *ibid.*, 678–687.
[14] *Ibid.*, 684.
[15] *Ibid.*, 687–688.

In the meantime he sent a signed copy of the proposals to Foreign Minister Dr. T. V. Soong and other members of the Chinese government, requesting that it be translated and given to the Generalissimo. Soong and Dr. Wang Shih-chieh, Minister of Information, then called on Hurley during his second day of confinement. Soong promptly informed Hurley that the Communists had duped him and that the National Government would "never grant what the Communists have requested." Rejecting Soong's comments about the defects as "trivial," Hurley maintained "that the offer made by the Communists did outline at least a basis upon which to construct a settlement."[16] He then approached Chiang with the plan, but reported to Washington, "Drs. Soong and Wang saw the Generalissimo before I did. They had convinced him that a settlement on the basis suggested by the Communists was impractical."[17] Nevertheless, Hurley urged the Generalissimo to accept; he emphasized that the Communists were ready to recognize Chiang's leadership and that unity was a military necessity. To the Generalissimo's response that the agreement would ultimately amount to giving the government to the Communists, Hurley said he disagreed. "I am talking to him and his advisors almost constantly," Hurley wrote to Roosevelt, "and I may be able to convince them that a reasonable agreement with the Communists is necessary. Chiang Kai-shek asserts that he desires to unite the military forces of China and give the Communists representation in the government."[18] But, Hurley later reported, "my arguments were ineffective as were also the arguments of General Chou En-lai, Vice Chairman of the Central Committee of the Communist Party, who had accompanied me from Yenan to Chungking."[19]

In view of later charges and countercharges involving Hurley and the Chinese revolution, the envoy's position here is most in-

[16] Hurley to Secretary of State, Jan. 31, 1945, Hurley Papers.
[17] *Ibid.*
[18] Hurley to Roosevelt, Nov. 16, 1944, *F.R., 1944,* VI, 699.
[19] Hurley to Secretary of State, Jan. 31, 1945, Hurley Papers.

teresting. He did not side irrevocably with the Generalissimo nor did he adopt a blind anti-Communist position; he tried to convince Chiang to accept a coalition government, a plan favorable to the CCP. Since he spoke so frequently of the need for military unification, and for haste in accomplishing it, it seems apparent that his main interest was military and that long-range Chinese political considerations were not of much concern. Indeed, the conclusion is that Hurley was not averse to the Communist proposals because he did not think they had sufficient strength to attain power, and even if they did succeed at some future date, he would not object, in part because he did not understand their true ideological nature and in part because, in his view, postwar Chinese domestic affairs were not the business of the United States.

Hurley could not convince the Generalissimo, and the government responded to the Communist proposals with a set of counterproposals. Therein, Chiang agreed to incorporate, after reorganization, the Communist army into his own, provide them equal treatment, legalize the Communist party, grant the Communists a spot on the National Military Council, and carry out the principles of Sun Yat-sen to establish a truly democratic state. In return, he expected the Communists to support the National government in the war effort and in the postwar period, and to give control of all of their troops to the government immediately.[20] Though it was now apparent to the U.S. envoy that the two sides were worlds apart, and though he recognized the defects of the proposals, he tried to convince the Communists to accept a revised form of Chiang's counteroffer just as he had attempted to secure the Generalissimo's consent to the Communist proposals. He did not, however, author the proposals, as the government stated. "Dr. Wang stated, in a meeting, that the three-point counterproposal of the government was prepared by me and that it represented my idea of a fair compromise. To this

[20] First counterdraft by Chinese government representatives, Nov. 15, 1944, *F.R., 1944*, VI, 697–698, and second and third counterdrafts, Nov. 17, 1944, *ibid.*, 703–704, 706–707.

statement I replied publicly that there was not one word of the counterproposal that I considered mine and that I had not presented it as my idea of an equitable compromise." [21]

In the meantime, discussions were being concluded in Moscow which colored the American view of the dispute in China. At the Teheran Conference in 1943, the Soviet Union had agreed to enter the war in the Far East once Germany had been defeated. In October 1944, Prime Minister Churchill traveled to Russia to discuss this matter and others related to the war. The United States suggested the participation in the talks of American officials General John R. Deane and Ambassador Harriman, hoping to use the occasion to secure a commitment from the Russians as to a more exact manner and time of their intervention against Japan. In the ensuing conference, Stalin and his generals made such a commitment. They informed the British and Americans that Russia at that time had thirty divisions on the Manchurian and Trans-Baikal fronts, but that she hoped to have about sixty before launching an attack on Japan. It would be necessary to move certain divisions from the European front and stockpile supplies and equipment prior to entering the Far Eastern conflict; this would take about three months.

On the matter of the Soviet intervention, Stalin informed his Western guests that Russia might have to push deep into China to defeat the Japanese—perhaps as far south as the Great Wall or beyond. Russia could not limit itself to the Pacific region but would have to move into Manchuria from different directions and at the same time would strike blows at Kalyon and Peking. The major battles, in Stalin's view, would be fought, not in Manchuria, but in China proper. The talks concluded with Stalin's implied suggestion that an allied arrangement would be necessary, spelling out the terms under which she would begin these military moves. [22] Thus the stage was set for the Yalta Conference of the following February.

As a result of these talks, President Roosevelt undoubtedly saw

[21] Hurley to Secretary of State, Jan. 31, 1945, Hurley Papers.
[22] Herbert Feis, *The China Tangle* (Princeton, 1953), pp. 226–231.

a greater urgency for promoting a settlement of political differences in China. Even though evidence was lacking of a close relationship between the CCP and the Russians, American officials expected that, once Soviet troops intervened in China, they would work closely with the Communists, and the CCP would be in a much-strengthened position vis-a-vis the Kuomintang. Thus the President stressed the need for early unification in a note to Hurley on November 18, stating that it would be well for him to prod Chiang with a hint of Russian intervention. "I wish you would tell the Generalissimo from me in confidence," Roosevelt wrote, "that a working arrangement between the Generalissimo and the North China forces will greatly expedite the objective of throwing the Japanese out of China from my point of view and also that of the Russians. I cannot tell you more at this time but he will have to take my word for it. You can emphasize the word 'Russians' to him." [23] Militarily it was no longer so important to achieve cooperation of the two forces in China, for the Soviet Union held the balance against Japan. Political considerations were far more significant. On December 15, Ambassador Averell Harriman informed Roosevelt of his views resulting from a recent talk with Stalin: "With regard to the negotiations between the Generalissimo and the Communists, Stalin made no comment. If no arrangement is made before the Soviets attack the Japanese, I believe that it must be assumed that the Soviets will back the Communists in the north and turn over to them the administration of the Chinese territory liberated by the Red army. Then the situation will be progressively difficult for Chiang." [24]

Perhaps because of Roosevelt's hint of Russian entrance into the war, and in any event because his own survival compelled him to avoid antagonizing the United States, Chiang Kai-shek felt compelled to continue negotiating with the Communists, and he responded to the CCP proposals with the plan mentioned above. He also proposed sending his brother-in-law T. V. Soong

[23] Roosevelt to Hurley, Nov. 18, 1944, *F.R., 1944,* VI, 703.
[24] Harriman to Roosevelt, Dec. 15, 1944, *ibid.,* 737–738.

to confer in Moscow with Russian officials, and the Russians indicated a readiness to treat with the Chinese—at the end of February.[25] Hurley, who was named Ambassador to China on November 17, replacing Clarence Gauss, continued his efforts toward unity, still concerned primarily about the military consequences of the lack of political cohesion. Even though he may have inferred from Roosevelt's note of November 18 that Russia would enter the Far Eastern War, he did not know of Stalin's commitment to this effect, nor did he have any idea when it would occur. Moreover, isolated as he was in Chungking, he did not see the large picture and did not realize that success in the Pacific campaign made China less important militarily.

On November 21, Hurley met with both Kuomintang and CCP officials. T. V. Soong called on him to request continued and additional support for Chiang's government, hinting that this, rather than unification with the Communists, was the way to win the war. Chou En-lai, then in Chungking, met with him to receive the three-point proposal proffered by the government. Thereupon Chou returned to Yenan to report to Mao Tse-tung. After conferring with the party chairman, on December 8, Chou wrote to Hurley, informing him that in view of Chiang's counterproposals there seemed to be no common basis for further discussion, that he would not return to Chungking, and that the Communists planned to publish their earlier five-point proposal to bring public pressure to bear on the government.[26]

The Communists had ample reason to reject the government proposals. In the first place, Chiang's vague promises to promote democratic processes within his government meant little, even to him; he had been indicating for the past sixteen years that he would "soon" end the one-party tutelage and institute a constitution. In the second, the offer of representation on the National Military Council, while sounding like a concession, signified nothing, since the Generalissimo as chairman made nearly all of

[25] Hurley to Stettinius, Dec. 24, 1944, *ibid.*, 745–749.
[26] Chou En-lai to Hurley, Dec. 8, 1944, *ibid.*, 723–724.

the key decisions himself. To ask the Communists to turn over their armies, which had grown tremendously in strength, in return for nothing but the good faith of the Kuomintang, was requesting far more than they would grant, especially in view of the fact that the United States was urging the Chinese Nationalists to create a real coalition government.[27]

Trying desperately to keep the talks alive, Hurley asked Chou not to publish the proposals, and informed the Communists that as a result of frequent conferences with government officials he was certain that the Kuomintang wanted continued negotiations.[28] In fact, Hurley had held several lengthy meetings with Chiang Kai-shek in which he had implored the Generalissimo to allow the unification effort to continue. It was Hurley's view that the five-point proposal of the Communists was not given proper treatment by the government and, as he told Roosevelt, "I have stated to him [Chiang Kai-shek] that he and his government have failed to take advantage of the opportunities offered by the Communist Party for a settlement." During these meetings, Chiang assured the U.S. envoy that he would make a settlement with the Communists his first order of business, and he asked him to again use his good offices in the discussions. On the basis of the discussions with Chiang, Hurley made his new appeal to the CCP.[29]

In his reply to Hurley, Chou En-lai agreed not to publish the five points until the U.S. Ambassador granted his consent, but stated that the CCP was greatly surprised that the Kuomintang had rejected them out of hand. Rejection, he believed, represented a general lack of sincerity on the part of the government. The major problem with the negotiations was the unwillingness of the government to reject one-party rule and accept the idea of a coalition government; the CCP did not see as acceptable the recent changes in personnel made by Chiang in his administration

[27] Tang Tsou, pp. 293–294.
[28] Hurley to Chou En-lai, Dec. 11, 1944, *F.R., 1944*, VI, 732–733.
[29] Hurley to Roosevelt, Dec. 12, 1944, *ibid.*, 733–734.

1. Secretary and Mrs. Hurley, New York, December 13, 1930

2. Meeting to consider Philippine independence, September 1, 1931 (*left to right:* Acting President of the Philippine Senate Sergio Osmena, Speaker Manuel Roxas, Secretary of War Hurley, Governor General of the Philippine Islands Dwight F. Davis, and Major General John L. Hines, U.S. Army)

3. Prime Minister Peter Fraser, General Hurley, and Secretary of State Cordell Hull, Washington, D.C., August 1942

4. General Joseph W. Stilwell and General Hurley, Chungking, No-vember 12, 1943

5. General Chu Teh, General Hurley, and Mao Tse-tung, Yenan, November 7, 1944

6. T. V. Soong, General Albert C. Wedemeyer, Generalissimo Chiang Kai-shek, and General Hurley, November 1944

7. Mao's chief of staff, Mao Tse-tung, Lin Tsu-han, General Hurley, General Chu Teh, Chou En-lai, and Col. David Barrett, Yenan, November 7, 1944

8. General Hurley, Chungking, 1945

and only the inclusion of all parties in the national government would suffice.[30]

Recognizing in this letter tacit approval of a continuation of negotiations, Hurley wrote to Mao Tse-tung and Chou En-lai thanking them for the communication of December 16 and for not closing the door to settlement. He reiterated his earlier statement that the Kuomintang was also willing to continue discussions and suggested that Chou travel to Chungking as soon as possible. Mao replied on December 24 that Chou was very busy preparing for an important conference, and in any event the Kuomintang had not yet shown sufficient sincerity to warrant further talks on the five-point proposal; his suggestion was that a conference be held in Yenan.[31] Also on December 24, in an interesting dispatch, Hurley summarized his activities to that date to the Secretary of State. He stated that it was his understanding that his instructions upon coming to China were five-fold: to prevent the collapse of the government; to sustain Chiang Kai-shek as President and Generalissimo of the armies; to harmonize relations between the Generalissimo and the American commander; to prevent the economic collapse of China; and to unify the military forces against Japan. In his view, U.S.-Chinese military relations were now operating on a satisfactory basis, particularly since Stilwell's recall. And Chiang had made significant changes in his government in order to make its operation more effective and to begin liberalization as a step toward democracy: he had relieved General Ho Ying-chin of his dual duties of Chief of Staff and Minister of War, keeping him as Chief of Staff but appointing General Chen Cheng as War Minister; he had appointed O. K. Yui as Minister of Finance replacing H. H. Kung; and in the one other significant appointment, he had named Dr. Wang Shih-chieh as Minister of Information.

On the matter of unity in China, Hurley said he believed he

[30] Chou En-lai to Hurley, Dec. 16, 1944, *ibid.*, 739–740.

[31] Hurley to Mao Tse-tung and Chou En-lai, Dec. 20, 1944, *ibid.*, 744–745; and Mao to Hurley, Dec. 24, 1944, *ibid.*, 745.

was making progress. He stated that he had succeeded in contacting the Communists and had begun discussions toward effecting an agreement to coordinate military forces in China and then mentioned the proposals and counterproposals proffered by each side, particularly citing the five-point plan; in his opinion the Kuomintang "then had an opportunity to make a settlement with the Communists. They neglected or did not coose to do so." Since then, Hurley stated: "I have persuaded Chiang Kai-shek and others in the National Government that in order to unite the military forces of China and prevent civil conflict it will be necessary for him and the Kuomintang and the National Government to make liberal political concessions to the Communist Party and to give them adequate representation in the National Government."[32] This he believed Chiang would now be willing to do, if he could avoid the use of the term "coalition government."

What Hurley apparently did not see was that not only was the term repugnant to Chiang, but so also was the basic idea of a coalition. The Generalissimo believed that agreeing to a coalition would eventually lead to Communist control of the government; he would grant Communist representation only if such representation had no directing influence. In any case, he believed the Communist's avowals regarding democratic principles were nothing but a "ruse." Chiang, moreover, recognized the growing political power of the CCP and correctly saw that its devotion to the goal of achieving power, its virility, its skill and appeal would lead to a diminution of his control.

While the U.S. Ambassador thought he was making significant headway on unity, he saw formidable opposition to his actions. Some of this opposition came from "die hards" in the CCP and the Kuomintang, but most of it came from foreigners in China, mainly the British, the French, and the Dutch, the imperialists who hoped to re-establish their colonies in Southeast Asia and to keep China weak and divided. Others, like some American

[32] Hurley to Secretary of State, Dec. 24, 1944, *ibid.*, 745–749.

military and diplomatic officials, believed that Chiang's government would fall, that it had lost the support of the people, and that therefore there was no point in seeking unity under the Generalissimo; it would be better to deal with the CCP. Hurley said he was not impressed by the arguments of the opposition, but presented them, in any case, for the use of the Secretary.[33] Clearly, Hurley was still of the opinion that the Communists did not have sufficient strength to gain power and that efforts for unification under Chiang should continue.

Hurley's hopes for continued dialogue between the CCP and the Kuomintang received a severe setback, however, on December 28. Hardening their position, the Communists, in a letter transmitted from Chou En-lai to Hurley, said they were not willing to continue negotiations until the government released all political prisoners, withdrew Kuomintang forces then surrounding the Shensi-Kansu-Ninghsia border and those attacking the New Fourth Army, abolished all repressive regulations restricting people's freedom, and ended all secret service activity. Once these requirements were met, then preparations could be made for establishing a coalition government.[34] In view of the fact that only two weeks earlier the CCP had indicated its decision not to publish the five-point proposals, the message reflected a determined obstinancy which puzzled the U.S. Ambassador.

Not long thereafter Hurley learned the reason for the Communist position. General Robert McClure, Chief of Staff for General Wedemeyer, advanced a military proposal for U.S. cooperation with the Communists to strike the Japanese in Communist-held territory. More specifically, the plan called for placing U.S. airborne units in Communist territory; such units would attack railways and bridges, and would organize and lead CCP guerrilla attacks on Japanese installations. The Communists would also be used to build airfields, as guides, to do intelligence work, and to transport supplies. McClure approached Hurley with the sug-

[33] *Ibid.*

[34] Chou En-lai to Hurley, Dec. 28, 1944, *ibid.*, 755.

gestion in mid-December and received his tentative approval—approval, however, conditioned on assurances that the CCP would not be informed of the plan beforehand, for it could make them intractable in the negotiations then under way. Hurley also thought that the Generalissimo should approve before anything further was done. Subsequently, McClure discussed the idea with T. V. Soong and with General Chen Cheng, Chinese Minister of War, on December 19, but not with Chiang. Enthused to the point of imprudence, McClure then used the occasion of a trip by Colonel Barrett to Yenan to send along his own emissary, Lt. Willis Bird of Strategic Services, to find out possible CCP reaction to such a scheme. Bird made no commitment to the Communists, but thereafter they knew the plan was in the wind.[35]

When Hurley learned that the proposal had been communicated to the Communists, he was furious, and he informed Washington that he saw in it not only the source of the recent CCP intransigence, but also a plot to subvert his efforts. Already upset about the position of the "imperialist" powers and the American foreign service officers, he saw it as an effort to by-pass him and arm the Communists.[36] Since he learned at about the same time of a secret attempt by Mao Tse-tung and Chou En-lai to arrange a trip to Washington and of other attempts by the CCP to by-pass him to achieve their ends, it probably also marked a turning point in his attitude toward the Communists. The Communists were attempting through the Foreign Service officers to use a rumored Kuomintang-Japanese accommodation to try to secure U.S. aid, but refused to share knowledge of the alleged "deal" with Hurley because they knew he would not believe it and feared the scheme would die aborning.[37] In other words, the

[35] Wedemeyer to Marshall, Jan. 27, 1945, Hurley Papers; and Memorandum of conversation, Dec. 19, 1944, *F.R., 1944*, VI, 741–743.

[36] Hurley to Roosevelt, Jan. 14, 1945, Hurley Papers.

[37] Secret information regarding the interconnections between the Japanese puppets and Chungking, n.d.; and Chu Teh to Wedemeyer, Jan. 23, 1945, Hurley Papers. Hurley learned about the proposed trip to Washington of Mao and Chou on Jan. 10. He reported it to Roosevelt on Jan. 14. Richard L.

Communists, eager to procure American supplies and even more eager to drive a wedge between the United States and the Kuomintang, continued to fling charges against the government and now proposed to by-pass Hurley and go directly to the United States. Hurley was henceforth much more alert to the true aims of the CCP and much less flexible about the matter of unification under Chiang Kai-shek.

There were many in China who thought the U.S. Ambassador had long been too inflexible. During 1943 and 1944, a group of Foreign Service officers had been assigned to assist General Stilwell as political advisers: John Davies, John K. Emmerson, Raymond Ludden, and John S. Service. Originally sent only to help the commanding general, they found their duties enlarged to include intelligence work and political reporting from various parts of China, later including Yenan; and their proper function in relation to the U.S. embassy was never more than vaguely defined. These were strong-willed, highly sensitive, and intelligent men, who formed varying opinions on the Chinese political climate and who filled the mails with reports about the Kuomintang-CCP conflict—reports over which the head of the U.S. diplomatic team had very little control.[38] Though he often agreed with the reports, Clarence Gauss, before resigning, had expressed his displeasure with the system: "Davies did not so inform me," Gauss wrote, "but I am told reliably that he intends to 'offer the services' of the Foreign Service group to Stilwell's successor." He went on to state that the relief of Stilwell offered a chance to hammer out a more thorough understanding about these Foreign Service officers, "their duties, relative position, and relation to Embassy. I do not believe there is any occasion to designate political advisors to Army Headquarters in countries where we have Diplomatic Missions."[39] Hurley found their "relationship" to the

Evans to Wedemeyer for Joseph Dickey, Jan. 10, 1945, Hurley Papers. Hurley to President Roosevelt, Jan. 14, 1945, *F.R., 1945*, VII, 172–177.

[38] See Feis, pp. 256–260.

[39] Gauss to Secretary of State, Oct. 31, 1944, *F.R., 1944*, VI, 663–664.

Embassy exasperating, but the content of their reports often more so.

Others often agreed on the content of the reports. In 1944, Stanley K. Hornbeck, former chief of the Far Eastern Division and now political adviser, wrote in regard to one of John Service's messages: "Seldom if ever have I seen any document prepared by a responsible officer of the Department or of the Foreign Service, of no matter what age or length of experience, expressive of such complete self-assurance on the part of the author that he knew the facts, all of the facts . . . and that he could prescribe the remedy. . . . Never before have I encountered so sweeping a charge that almost everything . . . is wrong with China." He went on to say that he considered the dispatch presumptuous, immature, and somewhat irresponsible. Then he said, "I turned to refresh my knowledge of its author."[40] Ambassador Gauss had long been critical of Chiang, of conditions in China, and was pessimistic about the Generalissimo's future, but his reports had never inspired the reaction in Hornbeck triggered by Service's self-assurance.

In the fall of 1944, Davies and Service did most of the commenting on the political situation, and, though their views are examined in more detail in the next chapter, it is pertinent to point out here that their dispatches contained several salient themes. They believed the Communists exceedingly strong miltarily and assured of control at least in north China in the postwar period; they considered the CCP an efficient, honest, and "committed" organization which not only promised, but effected, reforms and which, as a result, elicited the support and respect of great numbers of Chinese; they saw the Communists as active and effective in fighting the Japanese. By contrast, they believed Chiang's government corrupt, inefficient, and often unsolicitous of the interests of the Chinese people; they believed that he was losing support because he had not brought about expected re-

[40] Hornbeck to Secretary of State, July 27, 1944, Hornbeck Papers, Hoover Institution, Stanford University.

forms; they saw the Generalissimo as unable to effectively fight the Japanese and unwilling, as long as the United States continued to support only him, to work out a solution with the Communists. They therefore counseled "realism" in dealing with China; the United States "must not indefinitely underwrite a politically bankrupt regime"; the United States "must make a determined effort to capture politically the Chinese Communists rather than allow them to go by default wholly to the Russians." [41] The United States, in other words, should support Chiang Kai-shek but should be very flexible and should not rule out military aid to the CCP. This would be advantageous militarily and, in the long run, politically.

Hurley, who believed his assignment dictated working for unity through the Generalissimo, could not view with equanimity proposals advocating this kind of "flexibility." Particularly was he annoyed at suggestions involving arming of the Communists, for he thought such proposals could only make the CCP more intransigent. Moreover, situated as he was in Chungking, he thought Chiang's power and prestige considerable and believed the Foreign Service officers' views mistaken because of their own narrow perspective. Optimistic about Chiang's future, and his own eventual success as a mediator, he especially resented such "precipitous" reports as that sent to Washington by Davies on December 12. Davies wrote: "The negotiations looking to an agreement between the Generalissimo and the Chinese Communists have failed . . . it is time that we unequivocally told Chiang Kai-shek that we will work with and, within our discretion, supply whatever Chinese forces we believe can contribute most to the war against Japan." [42] Such reports represented defeatism and, in his view, accounted in part for the impasse of late December.

In fact, the negotiations may well have had no chance of suc-

[41] Memorandum by Davies, Nov. 15, 1944, *F.R., 1944*, VI, 696; see also memorandum and reports from Davies and Service on Communist question, *ibid.*, 517–757.
[42] Memorandum by Davies, Dec. 12, 1944, *ibid.*, 734–735.

cess, though Hurley obviously thought they did. The Foreign Service officers may have been correct in their assessment of the strength of the Communists and the weaknesses of the National government. However, they can be sharply criticized for their frequent attempts at by-passing the Ambassador and their unwillingness to be strictly bound by the policy then being pursued. Specifically, Davies' gratuitous and unapproved comments were illustrative of the undefined relationship that had frustrated Gauss and now perplexed Hurley as chief of the China mission. But both procedural and substantive issues separated the Ambassador and his team.

Determined to get the talks moving again, Hurley, in mid-January, informed President Roosevelt of a "grand plan" to "force" unification in China. The President in his forthcoming meeting with Churchill and Stalin should get Russian and British adherence to immediate unity of military forces in China and a postwar, "free, democratic China." When this was done, Hurley believed, it would be possible to present a specific and comprehensive scheme for achieving the desired ends in China. He would then offer a meeting with President Roosevelt to both Chiang and Mao, on the condition that they first reach an agreement—an agreement which would be promulgated by the President. Once again, however, the agreement was the difficult part, even had the President assented to the proposal—which he did not do. Hurley then contacted Mao once more, informing him that Chiang was willing to organize a war cabinet to allow Communist representation and would be considerably more liberal than before on a number of important questions. Accordingly, the CCP agreed to have Chou En-lai return to Chungking on January 24 to reopen the negotiations. Hurley worked closely with both sides in the ensuing conferences.[43]

The Kuomintang representative, Wang Shih-chieh, opened with the suggestion that an American officer under Chiang Kai-shek

[43] Hurley to the President, Jan. 14, 1945, Department of State, File 893.00/1-1049; Hurley to Mao, Jan. 20, 1945, Hurley Papers.

be placed in charge of Communist armies, that a troika arrangement, including a Communist, be set up to advise the Generalissimo on matters relating to CCP armies, and that a war cabinet
of seven to nine men be established which would include representatives of all political parties in China, Communists included.
The only thing really new in the proposal was the suggestion of
an American commander of CCP troops, but he was to be responsible to the Generalissimo, and thus the Communists would be
tied indirectly to Chiang. This they would not permit. Chou rejected the government plan, again stating that only a democrati-
cally controlled coalition government would provide a satisfactory
vehicle under which to subordinate Communist armies.[44]

Chiang would not countenance the latter but did state that in
May he would begin preparing for the abolition of one-party rule
and call a constitutional convention, the purpose of which would
be to involve all segments of Chinese society in the government.
To the Communists, these were hollow promises, and in any event
to all concerned, including Hurley, seemed irrelevant, for they
did not provide the early military unity that was considered so
badly needed. The Communists on their part advocated the holding of a large conference involving important non-Kuomintang,
non-CCP individuals. Hurley liked the idea and pushed the government hard in this direction. Indeed, evidence indicates that
the U.S. Ambassador was growing very impatient with the Kuomintang; he remained convinced that the five-point program of
the previous November was a satisfactory basis for settlement and
that the government could have afforded to make the necessary
concessions then. It was even more urgent now that agreement
be reached; again settlement was within the capability of the government, but it neglected to take the requisite steps.[45]

Perhaps because it was aware of Hurley's displeasure, the gov-

[44] Hurley to Stettinius, Feb. 18, 1945, Hurley Papers.

[45] *Ibid.;* see also U.S. Department of State, *United States Relations with
China* with Special Reference to the Period 1944–1949, pp. 80–81, hereafter
cited as *United States Relations with China.*

ernment moved slightly toward accommodation with its rival, by agreeing to the consultative conference idea. In a proposal submitted on February 3, it advocated the holding of a conference involving all parties and some nonpartisan leaders, the purpose of which would be to consider ways to end one-party rule and create constitutional government, the way to establish a common future political program, and the manner of participation of parties other than the Kuomintang in the national government. Chou En-lai liked the plan, and other CCP officials approved; Hurley was delighted but saw that the problem of military unity was not solved and that there was not much hope the consultative conference would work to create early unification. He believed civil war perhaps temporarily averted, but little else. Further gains would require patience, but, he reported, "it is most difficult to be patient at a time when the unified military forces of China are so desperately needed in our war effort." [46]

The U.S. Ambassador was rapidly losing patience with both sides. Chiang Kai-shek quickly expressed his displeasure with some of the proposals as put forth in the consultative conference plan and countered with a new five-point plan. [47] The Communists again suggested that the government agree to the four points they proffered in December, and attempted, behind Hurley's back, to secure a loan from the United States; General Chu Teh asked Wedemeyer, who revealed the scheme to Hurley, secretly, for twenty million dollars. [48] Both sides resorted to name calling, each accusing the other of bad faith.

Through mid-February, Hurley had worked hard to prevent civil war, to get the two sides together, and he took some satisfaction from achieving the latter, even though the most recent round of discussions was no more fruitful than previous ones. As he prepared to travel to Washington, the U.S. Ambassador clearly recognized his lack of success.

[46] *United States Relations with China,* p. 86.
[47] Hurley to Stettinius, Feb. 18, 1945, Hurley Papers.
[48] *Ibid.;* and Chu Teh to Wedemeyer, Feb. 16, 1945, Hurley Papers.

Success, to Hurley, meant the achievement of a plan for the unification of Chinese fighting forces. This had to be preceded by a political accommodation, but politics was not his main concern. Even though interpreting his instructions as a directive to seek unification through Chiang Kai-shek, evidence indicates that Hurley was not working to prevent the Communists from achieving power. He did not see the CCP as a truly Communist organization. Molotov had assured him that the Soviet Union would not support the Chinese Communists, that indeed they were not true Communists. Moreover, because of his limited view from Chungking and the personal assurances from Chiang, he did not believe the CCP could ever achieve dominance in any case.

While Hurley placed lesser importance on long-range political accommodation, except as a prelude for military unification, President Roosevelt and Averell Harriman and some other policy makers became more concerned about an arrangement to guarantee the postwar political situation and less about the immediate military problem. Roosevelt secured a commitment from Stalin to enter the Far Eastern war and knew that Russian participation would make the CCP more truculent and the position of Chiang more precarious unless an agreement were reached quickly. The military benefits of unity in China were lessening because of the success of the Pacific campaign. It also seems true that projected Russian entrance made it essential, in Roosevelt's view, that the United States not aid the Communists in late 1944 and 1945 as suggested by the Foreign Service officers, because to do so would only make them harder for Chiang to deal with and would serve only limited military purpose. This is why Roosevelt supported Hurley even though he received plenty of contrary advice through the State Department.

# VIII

## Consultation in Washington

As ambassador, Hurley was head of the diplomatic team in China, but the military command, the coterie of political and economic advisers, the fluid politico-military situation, and his own personality soon placed him in the unenviable position of responsibility for a delicate diplomatic negotiation without full support of his subordinates. The situation had long proved exasperating to him, as his comments of December and January about the Foreign Service officers and their advice on arming the CCP well demonstrate. While in Washington for consultation, he confronted a further challenge to his authority which he believed he could not brook. During his absence from Chungking, and without his knowledge, the Embassy had prepared a lengthy dispatch on political conditions in China and sent it to the State Department where it was being evaluated when the Ambassador arrived for a conference on March 4.

Largely the work of Ludden and Service, who had been detailed to the American Military Observer Section at Yenan, but approved and signed by the Chargé d'affaires George Atcheson, the telegram contained several salient arguments. It stated that the attempt to achieve unity in China through diplomatic and persuasive means was correct and necessary, but that the U.S. commitment to rebuild Chiang's armies, the offer of increased aid through the War Production Board, the cessation of Japanese offensives, and the assurances that the United States seemed to be giving him as the only capable leader in China, made Chiang unwilling to compromise to effect unity. Moreover, the CCP recognized U.S. support for the Generalissimo for what it was and, for reasons of self-protection, were expanding their armies and their control of territory nominally held by the Kuomintang; they were also talking of seeking aid from the Soviet Union. The result of all this would be accelerated civil conflict, bringing chaos in China and ultimately danger to American interests.

Averring that military necessity should be considered the basis of American policy, the note continued with some pertinent recommendations. The first step would be to inform the Generalissimo that the United States was prepared to equip and cooperate with the Communists and any other group that could be of assistance in fighting Japan. The United States would continue to assist the central government and would apprise it of all such moves and would also urge the Communists, as a condition attendant to arming them, not to expand their control to other areas of China. In order to facilitate coordination of command, the United States should urge the creation of a war cabinet with Communist representation and the inclusion of CCP armies into the armies of the central government under the command of U.S. officers designated by Chiang with Wedemeyer's advice.

The result of this move, it was expected, would be to end the deadlock and promote eventual unity in China. Pressures for unity existed from various liberal groups, and action by the United States would encourage them to speak up and force Chiang to compromise and "put his own house in order." The Generalissimo, in other words, needed to be told, not asked, regarding U.S. aid to the CCP, and this would force him to terms quicker than anything else. Moreover, through this procedure the United States could "expect to obtain the cooperation of all forces of China in the war; to hold the Communists to our side instead of throwing them into the arms of the Soviet Union, which is inevitable in the event the USSR enters the war against Japan." [1]

The telegram was another episode in the continuing feud between Hurley and his staff in Chungking. When he assumed his

[1] The Chargé in China to the Secretary of State, Feb. 28, 1945, *F.R., 1945*, VII, 242–246.

assignment, he began with a strong prejudice against the State Department and the Foreign Service, partly because of his knowledge of the President's own contempt for it. As George Atcheson later put it, it was "a fixed idea with him that there were officers in the Foreign Service and American military officers who were in opposition to him." [2] For some time after he became Ambassador he refused to share with his staff any knowledge of his negotiations with the Chinese Communists and sent no reports to the State Department; he communicated directly with the President. It was only the strong protests of the Foreign Service officers that finally impelled him to share his information with them and with the Department. At that point, then, he began advising Washington of the disloyalty of the American officers and of their inability to comprehend U.S. policy.[3]

He had serious quarrels with several American officials. At a cocktail party he exchanged bitter words with General McClure, Wedemeyer's Chief of Staff and, livid with rage, challenged him to a fist fight. Fortunately, friends intervened before the two men actually struck any blows, but not before American prestige was severely compromised; Chinese officials witnessed the entire affair.[4] He argued passionately with John Davies, as the latter bid him and Wedemeyer goodby just prior to Davies' departure from Chungking, from which he was being transferred at Hurley's instance; he accused the Foreign Service officer of being a Communist. While Davies, tears in his eyes, begged the Ambassador not to damage his career, Hurley roared at the top of his lungs that he was going to have him thrown out of the State Department.[5] This Hurley did not attempt to do, only because of the intervention of General Wedemeyer. Though their relationship

[2] The Acting Political Adviser in Japan to the Secretary of State, Dec. 8, 1945, *F.R., 1945,* VII, 733.

[3] *Ibid.,* 734.

[4] Albert C. Wedemeyer, *Wedemeyer Reports!* (New York, 1958), pp. 317–318.

[5] *Ibid.,* p. 319.

was generally good, he also at one point had a violent quarrel with Wedemeyer while living in the latter's house; he refused to speak to the general for days, which, as Wedemeyer relates it, proved embarrassing, because they had to sit together at meals. Hurley, later quite contrite, apologized for his behavior.[6]

Life in Chungking undoubtedly contributed to his attitude. He was sixty-one years of age when he arrived in China; he had had some recent history of ill-health, and he was often sick, or thought he was. His teeth periodically gave him trouble and occasionally kept him awake nights. His eyes were deteriorating, and his reluctance to wear his glasses, though he increasingly depended on them, contributed to splitting, searing headaches. He could not read lengthy documents or books, except with great difficulty. Then there was the Chungking weather, the damp penetrating cold and the scorching stifling heat, and the isolation of the place which drove one of his predecessors, Nelson T. Johnson, to request a transfer, and imbued another, Clarence Gauss, with increased hostility and bitterness toward the Chinese. Japanese bombing attacks, which enforced long periods in dank bomb-shelters, added another dimension to the misery. Never one to submerge his feelings for long in the best of circumstances, the mercurial-tempered Hurley reacted with violent outbursts; he roared commands; he hurled profane charges; and he threatened to fire his ablest people.[7]

The U.S. officials in China responded with obvious contempt—for his personality, his ability, and his approach to China's problems. The embassy staff referred to him as "Colonel Blimp," and they accused him of "crass stupidity." One official said he was a "bungler"; he was ignorant of China and was "a stuffed shirt playing at being a great man." It was widely whispered that he "enjoyed the respect of neither party" in the negotiations in China. The staff saw him as "50 percent bull or more"; they re-

[6] *Ibid.*, pp. 312–313.

[7] See also Theodore White and Annalee Jacoby, *Thunder Out of China* (New York, 1946), pp. 248–251.

ferred to him, as the Chinese did, as the "Big Wind" and a "paper tiger."[8] They snickered as he gave them lectures on U.S. policy larded with quotations from the Declaration of Independence and the Gettysburg Address. More importantly, they believed it his policy to grant "blank check" support of Chiang and to prevent any serious political reports recommending contrary action; they informed the Department of declining morale as a result of the restrictions placed on their activities.[9] For these reasons, they felt constrained to wait until he left Chungking to send in their recommendations of February 28.

Hurley was incensed when he learned of the contents of the

[8] Sol Adler to H. D. White, Feb. 12, 1945, Morgenthau Diary, Roosevelt Presidential Library, Hyde Park, New York.

[9] Memorandum by the Deputy Director of the Office of Far Eastern Affairs, Apr. 28, 1945, *F.R., 1945*, VII, 348–350. Hurley also carried on a running feud with foreign journalists in China who, he claimed (correctly), were prejudicial to the CCP in their reporting; he cooperated with Chiang in censoring their work and prevented their further access to Communist-held areas. In August, he developed a plan to counter the pro-CCP reporting: he urged the State Department to authorize Henry Luce to travel to China and report on conditions. This the Department refused to do because it feared charges of favoritism and felt it would create a bad precedent. Critics of Chiang's government and the U.S. ambassador deplored Hurley's moves as reflecting a cavalier attitude toward freedom of the press, while in later years Hurley and his right-wing friends saw the State Department refusal as indication of a pro-communist conspiracy. Both sides clouded the issue. There was precious little freedom of press in Nationalist China, and Hurley knew it, though he professed otherwise; nor were wartime compromises of basic freedoms terribly unusual in many countries. The U.S. envoy could hardly be condemned for supporting a further restriction in view of his belief in the need to support Chiang out of military necessity. On the other hand, the State Department decision was made on the basis stated to Hurley, with no hint of "conspiracy"; and most reporters' opinions were established by factors intrinsic to conditions in Nationalist and Communist China. A better ground for criticism of Hurley is that he opposed the reporters and wanted to counter their work, in large measure because those writers were critical of *Hurley* and made his job more difficult (see Hurley to Joseph Martin, Jr., July 2, 1945, Hurley Papers; *F.R., 1945*, VII, 142–143 and 147–148; see also Kenneth Shewmaker, *Americans and Chinese Communists, 1927–1945: A Persuading Encounter* [Ithaca, 1971], for an excellent discussion of the views of the journalists and influences upon them).

message. Although the Ambassador reacted very strongly indeed, evidence indicates he was not filled with the kind of bitterness he later expressed when he stated he was "called on the carpet with a full array of the pro-Communists in the State Department as my judges and questioners to defend the American policy in China against every official of the American Embassy in China."[10] He informed Chief of the Far Eastern Division John Carter Vincent that he considered the sending of the note a disloyal act by the Embassy which was acting "behind his back," that the matter of arming the Communists had already been settled, and that in any event, he was carrying out the policy of the President. Regarding his charge that the Embassy went "behind his back," the Ambassador was correct, for Ludden's and Service's thesis had long been known, and Atcheson agreed with it, but the Chargé also knew that, if he raised the issue while Hurley was still in Chungking, an angry exchange would occur. In any case, Vincent and others in the Division replied that U.S. policy needed to be reevaluated in the light of current conditions in China and that the Foreign Service officers were simply doing their job; indeed, the Far Eastern Division was in agreement with the message.[11] Hurley refused to accept the argument and now prepared to make changes in the Embassy personnel.

At Hurley's insistence, Atcheson was transferred to another post; Service, who had returned to Yenan at the request of General Gross, was also reassigned and returned to the United States. This was accomplished by the Ambassador through Secretary of War Stimson who transferred Service from General Wedemeyer's staff to that of the Embassy and therefore to Hurley's jurisdiction. The other Foreign Service officers previously assigned as political advisers were removed as well, thus eliminating a source of great friction as far as Hurley was concerned. It was now abundantly clear that, insofar as he supported anyone,

[10] *Military Situation in the Far East,* p. 3256.

[11] Memorandum by the Director of the Office of Far Eastern Affairs (Ballantine), Mar. 6, 1945, *F.R., 1945,* VII, 260–261.

President Roosevelt supported his ambassador against the State Department and, temporarily at least, allowed him virtually full rein; the United States would not arm the Communists and would continue to seek unity through cooperation with Chiang's government.

Relative to the administration of the Embassy in China and the conduct of CCP-Kuomintang negotiations, Hurley had achieved a clear victory over Davies, Service, Ludden, Atcheson, *et al.* Yet they persisted whenever possible in advocating a more "flexible" posture and insisted, along with others in the State Department, that the Hurley approach was fundamentally in error.[12] The Ambassador on his part remained convinced he was correct; he knew that perhaps the United States could "force" Chiang to compromise with the Communists but that it possessed no means of "forcing" the Communists to reach an agreement with Chiang. In view of Hurley's charges upon his resignation and the postwar furor that ensued relative to the Ambassador and the officers, further evaluation of the substance of their respective positions is essential.

Throughout 1944 and 1945, Service, Ludden, and Davies proffered suggestions similar to those of the February memo. One of these was that the United States needed to be concerned about Russian intentions in Asia, because "they are bound to affect our own plans in the same area." [13] Another was that, while the CCP may once have been tied closely to Moscow, during the war nationalism modified its outlook. A third was that the CCP was the most dynamic force in China, while the Kuomintang was slipping. In October 1944, Service wrote that the Communists waged effective war against Japan, because in the area under their control they had the support of the people by virtue of their effecting "an economic, political, and social revolution"—a revolution which improved their economic condition and gave them "democratic self-government, political consciousness, and a sense of their

12 Herbert Feis, *The China Tangle* (Princeton, 1953), p. 273.
13 *United States Relations with China*, p. 564.

rights." In frequent dispatches Davies and Service portrayed the Kuomintang as incapable of governing effectively, as led by power-hungry men who were interested only in their own positions, as displaying "suicidal" tendencies.[14]

A fourth theme was that the Communists were either "backsliders" or "democrats." "The Chinese Communists are backsliders," wrote John Davies on November 7, 1944. "They still acclaim the infallibility of Marxian dogma and call themselves Communists. But they have become indulgent of human frailty and confess that China's Communist solution can be attained only through prolonged evolutionary rather than revolutionary conversion. . . . Yenan is no Marxist New Jerusalem. The saints and prophets of Chinese Communism . . . lust after the strange gods of class compromise and party coalition."[15] Service stated: the Chinese Communist Party aims at eventual socialism . . . not through a violent revolution, but through a long and orderly process of democracy and controlled economic development. . . . Since they believe in democracy, they advocate multi-party participation in politics."[16]

The fifth theme was that civil war would probably occur in China, and that this would hamper the war effort and perhaps throw the CCP into the arms of the Soviet Union. The United States should therefore do all in its power to bring unity to China; to do so meant to encourage "reform" and revitalization of the Kuomintang so that it would be a force in a new coalition government. If the United States could not do this, it should cooperate with the CCP to assist in the war against Japan and to insure the continued friendship of that force for the United States in the event the Soviet Union entered the war.[17]

This is not to suggest that there were not in fact degrees of difference between the two most prominent reporters with regard

[14] *Ibid.*, pp. 566–570.
[15] Memorandum by Davies, Nov. 7, 1944, *F.R., 1944*, VI, 669–670.
[16] Report by Service, Aug. 3, 1944, *ibid.*, 565.
[17] *United States Relations with China*, pp. 573–576.

to the Kuomintang-Communist question, Davies and Service. It appears clear that Davies was more cautious in his evaluation of the Communists as "democrats" and more circumspect in his comments about their relationship with the Soviet Union. Though he did in fact refer to the CCP as comprised of "backsliders" and as democratic, and while he is not always consistent, this was not his main point. In other words, he did not advise America's working with the Communists primarily because of a similarity of political philosophy. The central thrust of his argument was that the United States should assume a *realpolitik* orientation. In one of his first reports from Yenan he wrote that the United States should continue to give Chiang nominal support: "But we must be realistic. We must avoid committing in China the type of error committed by the British in Europe. We must not indefinitely underwrite a politically bankrupt regime. And, if the Russians are going to enter the Pacific War, we must make a determined effort to capture politically the Chinese Communists rather than allow them to go by default wholly to the Russians. Furthermore, we must fully understand that by reason of our recognition of the Chiang Kai-shek Government as now constituted we are committed to a steadily decaying regime and severely restricted in working out military and political cooperation with the Chinese Communists."[18] He went on to say that a coalition government was most desirable. However, "if Chiang and the Communists are irreconcilable, then we shall have to decide which faction we are going to support."[19] Then, he said, "if the Russians enter North China and Manchuria, we obviously cannot hope to win the Communists entirely over to us, but we can through control of supplies and postwar aid expect to exert considerable influence in the direction of Chinese nationalism and independence from Soviet control."[20]

[18] Memorandum by the Second Secretary of Embassy in China, Nov. 15, 1944, *F.R., 1944*, VI, 696.
[19] *Ibid.*
[20] *Ibid.*, 697.

Further, on the CCP relationship with the Soviet Union and especially with respect to Stalin's view of the Chinese Communists, Davies wrote: "However Marshal Stalin may describe the Chinese Communists to his American visitors, he can scarcely be unaware of the fact that the Communists are a considerably more stalwart and self-sufficient force than any European underground or partisan movement." [21] Stalin would not indefinitely support Chiang; he was not averse to acting "realistically." "By our unwillingness and inability to engage in *realpolitik*," Davies cautioned, "the Kremlin may well believe, we stand to lose that which we seek—the quickest possible defeat of Japan and a united, strong and independent China. And the Soviet Union may stand to gain if it chooses to seize the opportunity, a satellite North China." [22]

Service, on the other hand, did not in his reports place major emphasis on realism, but rather gave vent to his disillusionment with the Kuomintang and his admiration for the CCP. In report after report, Service advised that the Communists were advancing democracy. "The Communist political program is democracy"; "The Communist political program is simply democracy"; "whatever the exact nature of this improvement, it must be—in the broadest sense of the term as serving the interests of the people— toward democracy"; [23] "the Kuomintang, as it is today—is weak, incompetent and uncooperative. . . . The situation as far as the Chinese Communists are concerned is just the opposite"; "The Communists have used their influence in a democratic way and to further democratic ends"; [24] and so forth, and so on. Service also went overboard in his belief in CCP trust and friendship

[21] Memorandum by the Second Secretary of Embassy in China, Jan. 4, 1945, *F.R., 1945*, VII, 156.

[22] *Ibid.*, 157.

[23] U.S. Senate, Committee on Foreign Relations, *State Department Loyalty Investigation*, Senate Report 2108, 81st Cong., 2nd Sess., 1950, pp. 1361–1365, hereafter referred to as *State Department Loyalty Investigation*.

[24] Report by the Second Secretary of Embassy in China, Sept. 10, 1944, *F.R., 1944*, VI, 623.

toward the United States, if only American policy did not alienate the Communists. "The Communists," he wrote, "are also friendly toward America"; they wanted "American friendship and support"; they needed American "good will" and "economic assistance." [25] Because of their "democratic" orientation and because of what he believed to be a very loose association with Russia, Service felt that the Communists would establish a close relationship with the United States, in the event American policy proved sagacious.

Ironically, there were points of agreement between Hurley and the Foreign Service officers, but in most cases they came to different conclusions even after starting with the same assumptions. They agreed that the Soviet Union was important to a final settlement of the East Asian problem—but they differed as to the role that power would play. Hurley had talked with Stalin in 1942 and believed that the Marshal liked, trusted, and confided in him. Stalin had assured him that Russia had no aggressive designs on China and sought only to promote Communism in the Soviet Union.[26] Later, during his stopover in Moscow on his way to Chungking in August 1944, Molotov had informed him that the Chinese Communists were not in fact Communists and that no support for them would be forthcoming from the Soviet Union; Russia would continue to recognize Chiang Kai-shek.[27] This position Soviet leaders reaffirmed in their conversations with Hurley in April 1945. Molotov recited the Russian position during the Sian kidnapping of 1936, averring that the Soviet Union counseled Chiang's release in the face of a more belligerent stand by many CCP leaders. Following that event, they gave Chiang Kai-shek's government vast amounts of aid, only curtailing the

[25] Memorandum by Service, June 6, 1945, F.R., 1945, VII, 403–405. See also State Department Loyalty Investigation, p. 1978, and also F.R., 1944, VI, 520–640, for Service's reports of August and September. See Tang Tsou, America's Failure in China, 1941–1950 (Chicago, 1963), pp. 208–210, for a more complete discussion of this question.

[26] See Hurley to Roosevelt, Nov. 20, 1943, Hurley Papers.

[27] F.R., 1944, VI, 253–256.

assistance upon the Nazi invasion of the Soviet Union. In response to Hurley's query, Stalin said he considered Chiang "selfless" and a "patriot" and said that he would continue to support the Nationalist government; Russia would also sign an agreement with the Generalissimo, as stipulated in the Yalta accords.[28]

The Foreign Service officers, by contrast, and especially Davies, believed that while Stalin was very generous with words his actual policy would be far different. The Soviet Union would seek to "capture" the CCP and dominate East Asia if the opportunity presented itself. Thus they believed that the United States should win the friendship of the Communists to prevent their falling prey to Moscow. Because of Stalin's statements disavowing the CCP, which he accepted as Soviet policy, Hurley, on the other hand, believed that the Communists could not possibly prevail; they could not hope to defeat Chiang without Russian support.[29]

Hurley and the two officers were in accord in that they both saw the Chinese Communists as something less than Communists. Davies saw them as opportunists who had altered ideology to fit the Chinese experience and who were truly interested in gradualism. Service, who like Davies apparently knew little of their ideological base, believed that, because the Communists had widespread support in the region they controlled, they were "democrats." He also believed that their democracy was American in "form and spirit" and that this, along with their interest in and need for postwar economic collaboration with the United States, established a base for a natural friendship.[30] Apparently unaware of the prewar Russian orientation of the CCP and the shifts and changes to fit the Soviet line made in the early 1940's and assuming that the Communists viewed the history of U.S.-Far Eastern involvement as the United States did, Service frequently invoked

[28] Memorandum of conversation on situation in China, Apr. 15, 1945, Hurley Papers.

[29] See Tang Tsou, pp. 179–180; and *United States Relations with China*, pp. 564, 565, 573.

[30] U.S. Senate, Judiciary Committee, Hearings on *The Institute of Pacific Relations*, pp. 5423–5424; and Tang Tsou, pp. 204–209.

the specter of CCP-U.S. kinship and cooperation as a lever to change policy.

That Service and Davies were only partially correct in their assessment of the CCP appears obvious. They were right in that the Communists had effected reforms in the areas they controlled, that they provided efficient administration, that they had the support of the peasants, that they had great military strength and fought furiously against the Japanese. They did not see, however, that as ardent Communists, the CCP could only view the United States—the major capitalist power—as their enemy. Moreover, they failed either to see or to assign enough importance to the fact that neither Mao nor Chou ever denied that he was a devoted revolutionary. On this latter point, it is interesting to note that there were observers in China in the thirties and forties who would have shared the officers' views and held that the CCP was not a revolutionary party. But even then, there were also many who recognized the Marxist-Leninist commitment of the Chinese Communists. James Bertram, a Western journalist, came to this conclusion in 1939; radical American journalist Agnes Smedley's writing reveals her belief that the Communists were true Marxist revolutionaries; Freda Utley, a former British Communist in the early forties, rejected the notion that they were agrarian reformers or democrats; Edgar Snow believed it erroneous to see the CCP as anything but a committed Marxist organization. All of these individuals had close contact with the Chinese Communists and, though some were more perspicacious than others, they all provided information and ideas that might have been tapped. They had come to a fairly realistic appraisal as to the nature of the CCP.[31] Interestingly, the American ambassador to China from 1930–1941, Nelson T. Johnson, concluded that "the Chinese Communists are no more democratic than Trotsky or Stalin Communists."[32] As historian Tang Tsou points out, Service apparently

[31] Kenneth Shewmaker, "The 'Agrarian Reformer' Myth," *China Quarterly*, (April-June 1968), 66–81.

[32] Nelson T. Johnson to F. B. Sayre, Mar. 11, 1941, Nelson T. Johnson Papers, in possession of Mrs. Nelson T. Johnson, Washington, D.C.

did not see that the CCP permitted elections or "democracy" in territory it controlled only to secure popular support of its pre-determined actions and that it allowed no opposition party to evolve, a basic constituent of true democracy.[33]

Hurley's view of the CCP is best revealed in his frequent reference to that group as "so-called Communists." In one of his first reports to the President, in November 1944, Hurley stated: "I am convinced that Chiang Kai-shek is personally anxious for a settlement with the so-called Communists."[34] He repeated the phrase many times later. In December of 1944 he stated that he saw "very little difference, if any, between the avowed principles of the National Government and the avowed principles of the Chinese Communist Party."[35] He saw the CCP as attempting to achieve a government "of the people, for the people, and by the people." Early in 1945 he also stated: "the Communists are not in fact Communists, they are striving for democratic principles; and the one party, one-man personal government of the Kuomintang is not in fact fascist."[36] At a news conference in Washington while there for consultation, he reported that the Chinese Communists were not real Communists and that they, like the Kuomintang, sought democracy in that country. In testifying before Congress at a later date he said that when he went to Yenan he saw open shops, exchange of money, and the profit motive very much in operation; he therefore concluded: "When anybody tells me that this is Communism, I know that they are mistaken."[37] He further stated that "the only difference between Oklahoma Republicans and the Chinese Communists was that the Oklahoma Republicans were not armed."[38]

Like the Foreign Service officers, Hurley also misjudged the CCP. He did not understand that in observing private enter-

---

[33] Tang Tsou, p. 208.
[34] Hurley to Roosevelt, Nov. 16, 1944, *F.R., 1944*, VI, 699.
[35] Hurley to Secretary of State, Dec. 24, 1944, *ibid.*, 748.
[36] *United States Relations with China*, p. 86.
[37] *Military Situation in Far East*, p. 2896.
[38] *Ibid.*, pp. 2420–2421, 2903.

prise in Yenan he saw what Mao considered the bourgeois-democratic phase of the revolution, antecedent to the socialist phase. Moreover, he did not understand Mao's true intent in striving for a coalition government, that the aim was a Communist state and only for "democracy" in a strictly circumscribed sense of the word. Hurley also failed to understand that in subscribing to Sun Yat-sen's principles, the CCP was thinking only of the bourgeois-democratic phase of the revolution, not the socialist phase.[39] The CCP and the Kuomintang actually had nothing in common except a common enemy. And recent scholarship has pointed out that the Communists were anxious for the Sino-Japanese war, for therein they saw a chance to expand their influence and eventually to gain power.[40]

In sum, the U.S. Ambassador and the officers thought reconcilable two irreconcilable forces. The Communists would not make a deal with the Kuomintang which placed them permanently in a subordinate position or endangered their power; for all their wartime posturing, they had not abandoned their ultimate aims, control of China. Chiang Kai-shek, on the other hand, was too insecure to make a bargain; he realized that if he concluded an agreement it could wreck his power base. Hurley, however, believed, because of lack of Soviet support and because the CCP was not truly Communist, that the Communists could be brought into the government. But because, in his view, they had less strength than the Kuomintang, the quickest way to do this was through continuation of the negotiations then under way. The Foreign Service officers believed also that the Communists could be brought into the government, but because in their view it was the strong, dynamic, and even "democratic" force in China and because there was danger that Russia would "capture" the CCP, the United States should pressure Chiang, support the Communists, and thus win them to the United States.

[39] Tang Tsou, pp. 184–192.
[40] Charles Fitzgerald, *The Birth of Communist China* (New York, 1966), pp. 80–84.

It was also on this trip to Washington that Hurley learned about Yalta. According to Don Lohbeck, an authorized biographer of Hurley, and according to Hurley's own later account of the episode, Hurley arrived in the United States and went first to the State Department where he received no satisfaction whatever—denial even that any agreement had been made regarding China. He then went to President Roosevelt who also denied that there was such an agreement. Hurley, however, explained that he excused the President for his reply, for he found Roosevelt in ill health and said that he believed the President was telling him the truth—that he did not know of any secret protocol dealing with China that would compromise her territorial integrity. Hurley continued to meet with the President, finally convincing Roosevelt to further examine the accord and also to let him see it. The Ambassador ultimately viewed the document, saw the section in question, and purportedly was extremely shocked and dismayed at what had been done. He then showed it to Roosevelt, who, upon reflection, also became upset that China's territorial integrity had been violated and began to reconsider it, ultimately suggesting to Hurley that he visit London and Moscow on his way back to China to try to ameliorate the effects of the agreement and to secure commitment on the part of those powers to Chiang Kai-shek. Hurley later stated: "American diplomats surrendered the territorial integrity and political independence of China, surrendered the principles of the Atlantic Charter, and wrote the blueprint for Communist conquest of China in secret agreement at Yalta. . . . Your diplomats and mine surrendered in secret every principle for which we said we were fighting. They talk about Stalin breaking his agreements, gentlemen. He never had to break one. We cowardly surrendered to him everything that he had signed and we did it in secret. President Roosevelt was already a sick man at Yalta." [41]

The secret protocol that supposedly was so shocking to Hurley

[41] *Military Situation in the Far East,* pp. 2837–2839 and 2884–2888; and Lohbeck, *Patrick J. Hurley* (Chicago, 1956), pp. 367–368.

dealt with the clarification of conditions under which the Soviet Union would enter the war against Japan. Port Arthur was to be leased to the Soviet Union as a naval base, the port of Dairen was to be internationalized, the Chinese Eastern Railway was to be operated jointly by Russia and China, the Kurile Islands and the southern half of Sakhalin Island were to go to Russia, and the status quo was to be maintained in Outer Mongolia. The segment pertaining to China is the most significant for critics.

Hurley's own criticism of the agreement and his account of what transpired would ring much truer if we did not have the logic of history and his own personal papers to negate it. In the first place, he was not so shocked at the agreement as he would like posterity to believe. Hurley was enough of a military man and then a diplomat to realize that the Soviet Union would not enter the war in the Far East without receiving something in return. What she would receive would undoubtedly be concessions somewhere in the Far East. Anyone who knew of the Teheran Conference, and Hurley did, would also know that the United States hoped to bring Russia into the war against Japan.[42] Hurley himself had conversed with Stalin on the matter in 1942.[43] Moreover, Hurley had discussed with Chiang Kai-shek, who certainly knew of possible Russian intervention against Japan, various contingencies prior to going to Washington in February 1945. A later message to President Truman is revealing: "Before my last visit to Washington [he wrote], and before I had been informed by the President of the Yalta decisions pertaining to China, including particularly the all-important prelude, the Gen-

[42] Hurley was a personal "adviser" of Roosevelt at Teheran, and, although he did not appear officially in the conference room, he knew what transpired. See Hurley to Orlando Ward, Jan. 11, 1952, Hurley Papers.

[43] In Hurley's words, "It was during this conference that Marshal Stalin did say that he would join with the United States at an appropriate time in the war against Japan." Hurley also suggested to Roosevelt that he believed the United States should get a written commitment from Stalin to this effect. See Hurley to Orlando Ward, Jan. 11, 1952; and Hurley to the President, Nov. 15, 1942, *ibid.*

eralissimo had discussed with me China's position on the same problems decided upon at Yalta and had given me his attitude relating to them. . . . Since my return we have continued to discuss the problems that would be involved in promoting future friendship and peace with Russia. Without referring to the Yalta decision as such, all of the problems decided, except number one of the prelude, have been raised by the Generalissimo and discussed fully with me. I am convinced that he will agree to every word of the requirements but will take exception to the use of two words, "pre-eminent" and "lease." [44]

Evidence suggests, in addition, that Hurley was little disturbed by violation of China's territory, as what he was interested in, in 1944 and 1945, was a commitment by Russia to support Chiang. He would have been willing to see China surrender even more if surrender would enhance the prospect of Sino-Soviet agreement. It is clear that Chiang's government felt the same way, as T. V. Soong, in negotiating with Stalin, expressed in July 1945 a willingness to go beyond Yalta in return for assurances from Russia. Truman informed the Chinese that the United States expected China to adhere to the letter of Yalta. [45]

The statements that Hurley made, to the effect that President Roosevelt did not know the implications of the secret protocol and was himself chagrined to learn of its true nature, are even more implausible. Such statements seemingly stem from Hurley's notion of his own importance and provide him a way to fling conspiracy charges, yet exonerate Roosevelt whom he liked personally and who seemed to reciprocate the feeling—even to the extent of trusting Hurley with major tasks. Roosevelt had possession of his faculties at Yalta and knew full well what kind of agreement he concluded. [46] Military advisors told him that it was important to get the Russians into the war in the Far East, and

[44] Hurley to President Harry S. Truman, May 10, 1945, *ibid.*

[45] President Truman to Hurley, July 24, 1945, *ibid.*

[46] No evidence has yet been produced to substantiate the charge that Roosevelt was mentally enfeebled at Yalta.

the President worked systematically to effect such intervention; he knew of the agreement's specifications as far as China was concerned.

Roosevelt was not much more disturbed or concerned about the question of violation of the Open Door policy. First, the President was a pragmatist and would never have been willing to sacrifice effective accord on the altar of principle. Moreover, he realized that there was nothing particularly sacrosanct about the Open Door as it pertained to China's territorial and administrative integrity, and he must have known that the United States had been retreating from its policy, enunciated in the circular of July 1900, almost since its inception, for example, in the Root-Takahira agreement, the Bryan note of 1915, the Lansing-Ishii agreement, and so on. Certainly the President knew of Japanese aggression in China in the 1930's, during which period he expressed little concern for China's territorial integrity.

However, Roosevelt did send Hurley back to China via London and Moscow, a move which Hurley later stated was made to change the secret agreement because Roosevelt had realized his error and worried about violation of the Open Door. If such was not the case, and there is nothing in the Hurley Papers to prove that it was, or was not, then why did the President send the Ambassador on this circuitous route? The answer seems clear. He undoubtedly sent him first to London to get diplomatic support, and then to Moscow because he was now beginning to worry about the Russians and their intentions for the postwar era. Much to alarm him had occurred in Eastern Europe, and he was growing increasingly suspicious: Communist-dominated governments were installed in Romania and Bulgaria; Russia had begun to exert greater influence on Hungary; and it had made obstructionist moves on the reorganization of the Provisional Government of Poland. What he needed was another statement from Stalin reinforcing the Marshal's earlier ones about unity in China and support for Chiang Kai-shek. On April 13, after the death of Roosevelt, Hurley informed the Secretary of State: "It was the President's suggestion that I undertake to obtain cooperation from the British and Soviet Governments for the American policy to support the National Government of China." [47] Had he been commissioned to change the accords, it seems strange that he did not say so here—in his first major communication after the death of the President.

Hurley carried out his assignment with prudence and some skill, never once mentioning to anyone altering the terms of the agreement. In London, from April 4 to 8, he conversed with Prime Minister Winston Churchill, first about British aims in Asia in the postwar era, and secondly about British support for American Far Eastern policy. Churchill agreed that Great Britain would continue to support American policy—that is, supporting the Chiang Kai-shek government as the government of China, but at the same time working for compromise between the two political factions in that country so as to achieve unity. Hurley informed the President of his conversations with the British.[48]

Hurley then moved on from London to Moscow, arriving in the Russian capital in mid-April, where he began discussions with Stalin as instructed. The American Ambassador informed Stalin that the United States hoped to see China establish "a free, united government" and was working toward that end with the support of the British. To promote such a program, Hurley stated further, the United States decided "to support the National Government of China under the leadership of Chiang Kai-shek." In reporting his conversation to Washington, Hurley stated: "Stalin stated frankly that the Soviet Government would support the policy. He added that he would be glad to cooperate with the United States in achieving the unification of the military forces in China. He spoke favorably of Chiang Kai-shek and said that while there had been corruption among certain officials of the National Government of China, he knew that Chiang Kai-shek was self-less, a patriot and that the Soviet Union had in times past befriended him. . . . He [Stalin] wished us to know that we would have his complete support in immediate action for the unifica-

[47] Hurley to the Secretary of State, Apr. 13, 1945, Hurley Papers.
[48] Hurley to the President, Apr. 13, 1945, *ibid.*

tion of the armed forces of China with full recognition of the
National Government under the leadership of Chiang Kai-shek." [49]
Hurley had thus accomplished his mission; he had secured renewed commitments by the British and the Russians to the American course in China. It seems certain that Hurley reasoned, as
did Roosevelt, that the Yalta secret agreement would of itself not
be onerous to anyone if Soviet-Chinese agreement could be
reached; the United States sought to promote such agreement.
Ambassador Averell Harriman later testified: "At no time did he
[Hurley] indicate to me that President Roosevelt was disturbed
about the understanding reached at Yalta or that he desired that
the understanding be ameliorated." [50]

While discussing with Stalin the prospects for Russian support
of American policy in China and of Chinese political and military unity, Hurley also spoke of a related subject, the secret
provisions and the manner and time for conveying them to
Chiang Kai-shek. Historians dealing with the Yalta Conference
point out that the reason for the delay in revealing the agreement to Chiang was that news often leaked from the Chinese
Nationalists to the Japanese and that Stalin advised waiting, for
he feared that if the Japanese learned of pending Soviet entrance
into the war they would attack before Russia was ready. This
may have been true in February, but evidence contradicts the
view that continued delay was Russian-inspired. In the conversation between Hurley and Stalin of April 15, 1945, Hurley asked
the Marshal when he thought would be the proper time to tell
the Chinese. Stalin replied that Hurley could pick the time, even
though there was danger of gossiping and the Japanese finding
out. Hurley, however, suggested it might be better to wait; and
Stalin agreed. [51] In reporting the conversation later, the U.S. Ambassador stated: "Stalin said he would give me carte blanche and

[49] Hurley to the Secretary of State, Apr. 17, 1945, *ibid.*
[50] *Military Situation in the Far East,* p. 3335.
[51] Memorandum of a conversation between A. Harriman, Hurley, Stalin,
and Molotov, Apr. 15, 1945, Hurley Papers.

let me use my own judgment as to when and how to present the subject. However, both Harriman and I were of the opinion that it would be best to delay the presentation because of the possibility of leakage which in turn might bring undesirable results." [52] In view of his postwar attacks on the matter of secrecy, Hurley's position is most interesting. The exchange supports the view that the American Ambassador subscribed to the policy made at Yalta—that he was as firmly committed to secrecy as anyone, even after it apparently was no longer necessary.[53]

After leaving Moscow, Hurley returned to Chungking, where he renewed his efforts to bring the two Chinese sides together. He had a vote of confidence from Roosevelt and, after his death, confirmation from Truman. Moreover, he had secured the transfer of the disputatious and "disloyal" Foreign Service officers. It was not enough.

[52] Hurley to President Truman, May 10, 1945, *F.R., 1945*, VII, 867.

[53] Hurley indicated later that he fully understood the need for secrecy in wartime. Speaking of the conference with Stalin in 1942, he wrote: "Marshal Stalin pointed out to me definitely in Moscow that a leak of information concerning any commitments by him in regard to Japan might result in bringing the Japanese military force down upon his rear on the Pacific-Asiatic front while he was still engaged in a death struggle with Germany and the axis powers on the European front. It should be kept in mind that at that time Russia was our ally" (Hurley to Bernard Noble, June 4, 1954, *ibid.*).

# IX

## The CCP, the Kuomintang, and the Russians

After he returned to Chungking, Hurley commented on political conditions in China and the state of the CCP-Kuomintang talks, as well on the part he expected Russia to have in the final outcome. In late June and July he again played the mediator in China's internal conflict as negotiations resumed—a role he filled until his departure for Washington for consultation on September 22.

As before, one matter that was to dog his steps was the suggestion on arming the Communists, and on arrival in China he found General Wedemeyer considering two memoranda written in the Far Eastern Division of the State Department authorizing such a move. Summarized briefly, the memoranda, the main elements of which Wedemeyer had discussed unenthusiastically with the Division of Chinese affairs in Washington, made the point that when American forces landed on the China coast north of Shanghai they would likely come in contact with Chinese Communist troops. In the event the U.S. military could be aided by these Communist forces, they should be supplied with American arms and ammunition. These recommendations were thus more restrictive than others advanced from time to time, including those of the Embassy on February 28.[1] Nonetheless, angered at what he considered surreptitious action by those who did not

[1] Memorandum by the Chief of the Division of Chinese Affairs, Mar. 1, 1945, Department of State, File 893.00/3-145, and Memorandum of conversation by the Chief of the Division of Chinese Affairs, Mar. 12, 1945, Department of State, File 893.00/3-1245.

understand the President's policy, Hurley again informed Washington that there could be no talk of arming the CCP prior to the successful conclusion of an agreement between it and the Kuomintang. If the Communists expected to receive U.S. support, they would make "extravagant" demands on Chiang Kai-shek's government, and there could be no settlement. On the other hand, since Stalin and Churchill had given him assurances that they supported U.S. policy, Hurley believed a continuation of his efforts could bring the talks to fruition.[2]

In response to Hurley's comments, Acting Secretary Joseph Grew sent to Chungking a new directive which was drafted in the Far Eastern Division and which did not correspond with the President's policy as conceived by the Ambassador. It proved another in a series of documents convincing Hurley that the State Department, and more particularly the Far Eastern Division, was either disloyal to the President, who along with the Ambassador had already determined U.S. China policy, or was unapprised as to that policy. In retrospect it seems unjust to condemn either the Department or Hurley for the mistrust and misunderstanding that developed. President Roosevelt indicated on several occasions his annoyance with State Department procedures and in his frequent use of private emissaries often avoided normal diplomatic channels. Hurley said that the President told him in August 1944 that "he could not get the lower regular State Department officials to decide anything, that he could not ever get prompt reports through the State Department."[3] As Stanley Hornbeck later told George Sokolsky: "F.D.R. did not like Mr. Hull and he looked with disfavor and suspicion upon the Department of State and the Foreign Service; and often, when he could, he by-passed either Hull or the Department or both."[4] Hurley was Roosevelt's personal representative and, even con-

[2] To the Secretary of State, Apr. (n.d.), 1945, Hurley Papers.

[3] Hurley to Truman, Aug. 25, 1945 (unsent), *ibid.*

[4] Hornbeck to Sokolsky, Feb. 16, 1952, Hornbeck Papers, Hoover Institution, Stanford University.

sidering nuances of meaning applied to directives given him by
the President and Hurley's later exaggeration of their close relationship on China policy, Roosevelt did give him sets of instructions. It seems clear that he did not at the same time hammer out
with the State Department the basic points related to Hurley's
instructions or, for that matter, all the elements of the U.S. position. "There was," said Stanley Hornbeck, "all the way along,
administrative confusion."[5] The fact that during the war the
United States had three Secretaries of State dealing with China,
one of them perhaps the most cautious in the annals of the Department and another perhaps one of the weakest and most inef-
fectual, did not help matters.

The Acting Secretary's directive began by stating the U.S. objective to secure the defeat of Japan and establish China as a
stable postwar power in Asia, and then went on to a three-point
discussion of how this could be achieved. First, the United States
hoped to promote a Chinese government, broadly based, which
would bring unity and the able discharging of international and
internal obligations. To effect such a condition the United States
would continue to support Chiang Kai-shek's government—at
least temporarily. At the same time, the United States should
maintain sufficient flexibility so as to cooperate with other leadership that could better achieve unity, peace, and security in Asia.
Second, the United States should do all possible to assist China
to build an integrated economy and to help her promote trade
with other peace-loving nations. Third, militarily the United States
sought the early defeat of Japan and the full mobilization of
Chinese forces to this end, but as to postwar military support, the
United States would not commit itself until Chiang's government
made greater progress toward unity and popular support. The
note concluded significantly: "I feel, and am confident you will
agree, that while retaining fixity of purpose as to our fundamental objectives, it is most important that we maintain complete

[5] *Ibid.*

flexibility, repeat flexibility with regard to the means of achieving them and that we make it entirely clear to the Generalissimo and his Government that our support of them is not of the 'Blank Check' variety." [6]

The Ambassador's annoyance with the document was unconcealed. He related his feelings to General Wedemeyer and then proceeded to draft an angry response to the Secretary of State, which he did not send. Hurley believed that he had done a satisfactory job, in keeping with his original directive, to prevent the collapse of the National government and by working toward unity in facilitating Kuomintang-Communist discussions. And the proof of this was that China still carried on effective resistance. Regarding the Chinese government, he realized that there were defects, that corruption existed, and that rampant inflation and reactionary elements made its existence precarious. Yet it was his belief that his original instructions stated, not that he was "to support the National Government if you find it ideal, but to prevent the collapse of that Government." This he was doing, and he had received no counterinstructions from the President, nor, until the present, from the State Department. If Washington planned to change U.S. policy or abandon it, that would be another matter, and he wanted, "to be informed to that effect." To him it seemed absurd to suggest that policy would remain the same and then suggest "flexibility" and imply arming the Communists in the same communication; that could only result in changing policy. Moreover, in his view the United States "could not have a military policy separate from its diplomatic. That would not be flexibility but confusion and failure." [7] The fact is that the State Department never specified exactly what it meant by flexibility, so, as far as the means to achieve U.S. objectives were concerned, the same vagueness prevailed. If indeed the Kuomintang and CCP were irreconcilable forces, and, in retrospect they seem to have been, then it is also difficult to see what

[6] Grew to Hurley, May 7, 1945, Hurley Papers.
[7] Hurley to the Secretary of State, May 8, 1945 (unsent), *ibid.*

"flexibility" would have produced in the way of unification in any event.

Meanwhile, the Ambassador remained hopeful that Chiang would promulgate reforms and that the establishment of constitutional government would encourage the Communists to work more amicably with the Kuomintang. After the convening of the Sixth Plenary Session of the Kuomintang Congress in May, Hurley reported his view of the achievements of the session and the prospects arising from it. The Kuomintang had decided to close its party headquarters in the army and in the schools; local councils based on free elections would be created in all parts of free China; the government would legalize political parties, implying the inclusion of the CCP; agrarian reforms would be undertaken; and a national assembly would be convened in November.[8] In spite of some misgivings Hurley held about antiliberal Kuomintang elements, he believed all signs were that the Generalissimo realized the need for a broader-based government and was responding to the Ambassador's exhortations and subtle U.S. pressure.

Hurley's assessment was again too optimistic. There had been some activity in the winter of 1945, as Chiang had offered to hold a Political Consultative Conference to deal with ways to move toward constitutional government; and the Communists, who wanted a National Affairs Conference, accepted. The Generalissimo, however, followed this with a speech on March 1 in which he called for the convening of the National Assembly whose main task would be to adopt a new constitution. Since the delegates to the National Assembly had been elected in 1936, and the Kuomintang would control the assembly and the constitution making, the Communists furiously denounced the move; they wanted a coalition government. Notwithstanding the "reforms" described by Hurley, the prospects for an accommodation were not brightened until the Chinese government began direct discussions with the Soviet Union.

[8] *United States Relations with China*, pp. 100–101.

While Hurley refused to deal with Chiang in the manner suggested by certain State Department personnel, he was not averse
to applying some pressure to achieve reform. One of China's most
pressing problems was economic, and, more particularly, the
dwindling purchasing power of her currency. Japanese control
of vast areas of the country and physical devastation in China's
cities and countryside significantly reduced her productive capacity and taxable base, while at the same time vast sums of money
were being spent in expanding the U.S. military commitment
there. The result was burgeoning inflation, which caused untold
suffering and hardship for countless numbers of Chinese and
threatened to bring revolt in the army, and domestic support of
the war to a grinding halt. T. V. Soong, one of the ablest economic minds in China, went to Washington in April and proposed
that the U.S. Treasury authorize China to use 200 million dollars
left over from a U.S. loan of 1942 to buy gold in the United
States, which would then in turn be used to buy up Chinese
paper currency. The sale of gold in China would reduce the supply of paper and therefore lessen inflationary pressures. Since
Secretary of the Treasury Morgenthau had promised in 1943
that China could use the funds to purchase gold, he was committed to permitting the deal, though he received strong opposition from members of his own department. What many Treasury
and State Department officials preferred was the establishment
within China of a dollar currency stabilization fund.[9] Hurley also
thought creation of such a fund the most prudent way of dealing
with the problem.

When informed of the Soong proposal and Morgenthau's concurrence, Hurley reacted strongly. He believed that there was
"little evidence" to support the claim that the sale of gold would
end inflation unless thoroughgoing reforms were carried out. What
he believed would happen was that the government would sell
gold below the open market price, and certain privileged Chinese
would make exorbitant profits. In fact at the end of May, the

[9] See discussion in *F.R., 1945*, VII, 1067–1104; Herbert Feis, *The China
Tangle* (Princeton, 1953), pp. 299–302.

commercial price of gold was more than double the Chinese treasury price and those who had the ability to buy from the government made more than 100 percent. This, Hurley saw as demoralizing. What was needed was a stabilization fund, but apparently the United States had not concluded the deal contingent upon China's establishing such a fund; it had only urged that one be created. Hurley stated that reform could be effected only through pressure. "If you wanted a stabilization fund to be instituted [he informed Morgenthau] you should have made that a condition precedent on which you would supply the dollars gold 200 million to China. Then you would have been in a position to trade or not to trade. Now you ask me to advise you what my reaction is to your reiteration of your suggestion that China constitute dollars 500 million fund for combating inflation and stabilizing currency. No one has more respect for the power of suggestion than I. In this instance, however, I would have relied on the power of dollars gold 200 million." [10]

Oversensitive and embarrassed because he had forgotten his earlier commitment to Soong, Morgenthau was furious when he received Hurley's blunt remarks, and he asked the State Department to chastise the Ambassador. This the Department refused to do, but it did inform Hurley that the matter had been decided only after full consideration of all the factors. Actually, the State Department agreed fully with Hurley's views, and Paul McGuire of the Division of Financial Affairs stated: "I cannot see that either the Ambassador or the Department have any apologies to make to Mr. Morgenthau. . . . The real thing that obviously hurt Mr. Morgenthau's feelings was Ambassador Hurley's pointing out that his opinion on the stabilization fund was not asked until after the gold was gone, so that all our bargaining power was gone." [11]

In any case, to criticize Hurley for granting Chiang Kai-shek a

[10] Hurley to the Secretary of the Treasury, June 6, 1945, Hurley Papers.

[11] Paul McGuire to the Director of the Office of Financial and Development Policy, June 12, 1945, *F.R., 1945*, VII, 1103; Memorandum by R. Borden Reams to the Assistant Secretary of State, June 8, 1945, *F.R., 1945*,

blank check, as Foreign Service officers had long been doing, as : the Communist-controlled press in China was now beginning to do after his return to Chungking, and as did his postwar adversaries in the United States, seems a bit unfair in the light of the gold deal. Clearly the Ambassador was disposed toward the National government and, increasingly, after the CCP began attacking him in their press, did he adopt an anti-Communist position. But, as Morgenthau's action indicates, many of the most important U.S. policies constituting unconditional support for Chiang originated entirely independent of the Ambassador.

Whether the CCP truly believed that Hurley sided with the Kuomintang, or whether it criticized him only as a tactic to impel him toward a more "objective" posture, in June the CCP did attack him and the Kuomintang leadership in vehement terms. Nevertheless in response to government suggestions, made on the urging of the Ambassador, the Communists agreed in late June to resume negotiations. The government had created a seven-man committee to negotiate with the Communists and had communicated with Mao Tse-tung and Chou En-lai, requesting that members of the CCP and this committee reopen talks toward unification. The Communists had replied in a "defiant" tone and, in broadcasts, had castigated the government for its failures, but by late June they had assented to the proposal. Hurley did not see this willingness to talk as an end of the conflict; he had heard plenty of fruitless discussions up to that point; but he did think the situation "definitely improved." [12]

Consistent with the stated position, members of the seven-man committee then came to Hurley for his assistance in reopening the discussions. Hurley informed them that he did not deem it proper at that time for him to formulate a basis for discussion, that the committee should review the terms batted back and

---

VII, 1102; Acting Secretary of State to the Ambassador in China, June 9, 1945, F.R., 1945, VII, 1103.

[12] United States Relations with China, p. 102.

forth over the previous six months and come up with a formula. Then he would provide his plane to fly the negotiators to Yenan and would join in the conversations if both sides wished it.[13]

Representatives of the CCP also approached the Ambassador. General Wang Jo-fei, pre-eminent Communist official in Chungking, and Hurley had a lengthy conversation on June 28. Angered by critical reports of his action in the Communist press, Hurley began the discussion with an extended statement summarizing his efforts in behalf of unity—how he was responsible for the five-point proposal of the previous year, how he had kept the talks going in the face of much adversity, how he had in fact done more to promote a "just settlement" than any other man. He also made plain to General Wang that he considered himself the best friend of the Communists in Chungking and they should realize this fact; it was he who had made possible Communist representation at the San Francisco conference.[14] On this latter point, Hurley had, during his trip to Washington, urged the President to permit a delegate of the Communists to join the regular Chinese delegation at the upcoming UN conference, arguing that to do so could do no harm, would create good will with the CCP, and would indicate to the world a growing spirit of solidarity in China. The President agreed.

Hurley made plain in his conference with Wang that he still believed in the efficacy of the five-point proposal as a basis of settlement. The four points, which the CCP demanded in December be met prior to agreement to the five points, had already partially been accepted in fact by the government; it had withdrawn many troops from the north, and it was permitting a degree of freedom of speech and press. In response to Wang's avowal that the CCP still wished complete agreement on the four points precedent to further negotiations, and that the Ambassador should convince Chiang of the need for such agreement, Hurley said it

[13] *Ibid.*, pp. 102–103.
[14] *Ibid.*, pp. 103–104.

was his belief and that of others that if this occurred the Communists "would not enter into any agreement at all." On the other hand by agreeing to the five points they could become a part of the government and thus help deal with outstanding difficulties.[15] Subsequently, the committee of seven flew to Yenan where it conferred with the CCP and then returned to Chungking on July 5 with a new set of Communist proposals. The proposals constituted harsher terms, as the Communists demanded the calling off of the National Assembly scheduled to open on November 12 and the holding of a political conference at which the Chinese Communists, the Kuomintang, and the so-called Democratic League would all be represented; all parties would be equal. Hurley speculated that the CCP did not at that time want serious negotiations and were awaiting the outcome of talks then under way in Moscow between T. V. Soong and Stalin. Communist action would be dependent on the revealed position of the Soviet Union.[16]

Hurley had long been of the view that the Soviet Union held the key to successful Kuomintang-CCP negotiations. For this reason he had suggested to Roosevelt the importance of getting assurances from the Russians on his trip to Chungking in September of 1944; he stopped in Moscow in April 1945 for reassurance; and, further, he was zealous in attempting to promote friendly Kuomintang-Soviet relations. Some policy makers thought this a backwards approach and, more importantly, feared an unnecessary U.S. intervention in Sino-Soviet affairs. The State Department, acting in response to one of the Ambassador's telegrams of early February, a message in which Hurley advised of discussions with Soong and Chiang preparatory to a proposed visit by Soong to Moscow, cautioned him in a note of February 6 against excessive zeal. Signed by Acting Secretary Grew, but drafted in the Division of Chinese Affairs, the message stated that the

15 *Ibid.*, pp. 104–105; see also p. 99.
16 *Ibid.*, p. 105.

United States "should not permit the Chinese Government to gain the impression that we are prepared to assume responsibility as 'advisor' to it in its relations with the U.S.S.R." In any case, the document advised, the most satisfactory course would be for Chiang to reach agreement with the Communists, for this would greatly strengthen his position in dealing with the Soviet Union.[17] The Department was basing its advice on knowledge of the fact that Chiang Kai-shek had in the summer of 1944 requested through Henry Wallace that the United States assume the role of advisor or mediator in China's dealings with the Soviet Union, but that Wallace, supported by the President, had turned him down. Obviously, the fear was that excessive involvement could leave the United States responsible and thus open to charges by Chiang in the event of future Sino-Soviet trouble.

Though the message was reasonable and not contradictory to the President's directive to Hurley, he saw in it a lack of understanding of the importance of his efforts at establishing a favorable Soviet "commitment" toward Chiang's government and even a desire to see Chiang fall rather than use U.S. influence. Extremely sensitive, he also saw it as an attack on himself. He quickly drafted an angry reply, which he did not send until June, reiterating his views on the tremendous importance of the Soviet Union to a settlement in China and the need for the United States to do more than sit idly by in the Russian-Chinese relationship. "You admonish me," he wrote, "that we are not to act as 'mediator' between China and Russia. That is exactly what we have done and what we are doing." [18] Moreover, he believed he had succeeded in convincing the Generalissimo of the benign nature of Stalin's intentions, and any "progress" made was based on that fact. The State Department, he believed, was "still unaware of the preponderating fact that the attitude of the Soviet Government was and is the paramount factor precedent to any

[17] The Acting Secretary of State to the Ambassador in China, Feb. 6, 1945, Hurley Papers.

[18] Hurley to the Secretary of State, Feb. 12, 1945 (sent June 9, 1945), *ibid.*

agreement between the Chinese Government and the Chinese
Communist Party." [19] These were his views in February, though
clouded by his emotional outpouring.

Reporting to the State Department on his visit to Moscow in
April he stated that Stalin had agreed with the U.S. unification
policy and had agreed to help establish a "free, democratic"
China under the leadership of Chiang Kai-shek; the Soviet dictator would cooperate with the United States to the fullest. "Stalin,"
Hurley wrote, "agreed unqualifiedly to America's policy in China
as outlined to him during the conservation." [20] The Ambassador
reported further that Stalin had been unrestrained in his praise
of Chiang Kai-shek. Hurley, the report indicates, came away from
the conference with few doubts about the Soviet position. [21]
Stalin's comments in April thus made him more sanguine about
the willingness of the CCP ultimately to compromise when they
learned of Stalin's commitment.

Some were not so convinced. George Kennan, Chargé d'Affaires
in Moscow during the absence of Averell Harriman, who left for
Washington immediately after Hurley's Moscow conference,
wired his chief of his misgivings in the Hurley report. He
was troubled that Hurley had portrayed in such glowing
terms Stalin's commitment to U.S. policy in China. Actually there
was nothing to which Stalin would not subscribe in the U.S. position, but to Stalin the words "democracy," "unity," "free" meant
something entirely different. And, "he knows that unification is
feasible in a practical sense only on conditions which are acceptable to the Chinese Communist Party." Moreover, Kennan continued, the United States should not be so dependent on Soviet
acquiescence in its China policy, for that nation probably, in its
strategic interests, would try to reacquire territory once possessed
by the Czars. "Actually I am persuaded," Kennan wrote, "that in

[19] *Ibid.*
[20] Hurley to the Secretary of State, Apr. 17, 1945, *ibid.*
[21] The Chargé in the Soviet Union to the Secretary of State, Apr. 17, 1945,
*F.R., 1945,* VII, 340.

the future Soviet policy respecting China will continue what it has been in the recent past: a fluid, resilient policy directed at the achievement of maximum power with minimum responsibility on portions of the Asiatic continent lying beyond the Soviet border." [22]

Ambassador Harriman's attitude is unclear. Apparently, however, he was influenced somewhat by the communication from Kennan and did comment to State Department officials that Hurley's account was "too optimistic," that Stalin would continue to support the National government of China only while in the Russian interest, and that Hurley perhaps should be cautioned about raising Chiang's hopes based on Stalin's assurances. Harriman's comments were not as strong as Kennan's and seem to have been made more in a cautionary vein. In any event, Secretary Stettinius wired Hurley on April 23 to be careful. The Soviet Union would, for the present, he warned, defer to the United States in Asia, but once she got involved in the Far Eastern war, if unity had not been achieved, she would cooperate with whatever side seemed best to serve her interests. Consequently it was very important that Chiang be informed of the urgency of political and military unification.[23] Hurley realized that Stalin's endorsement could be temporary and that time was of the essence in unifying China, but he believed that both sides had to be committed to this purpose.[24]

Because officials in Washington, despite Hurley's account, were not convinced of Stalin's intentions, they determined in early May that it would be necessary to get reassurances from the Soviet dictator on the Yalta accords. Stalin had agreed at Yalta to write an agreement with Chiang Kai-shek and to support unification of all Chinese forces under the National government. The matter seemed of great import now, because the war in Europe had

[22] The Chargé in the Soviet Union to the Secretary of State, Apr. 23, 1945, *ibid.*, p. 343; *United States Relations with China*, pp. 96–97.

[23] *United States Relations with China*, p. 98.

[24] Draft of Message to Secretary of State, April (n.d.), 1945, Hurley Papers.

ended in early May and the Russians were preparing to enter the Far Eastern war, and because Stalin's intentions were suspect as a result of his actions in eastern Europe. President Truman and the State Department, like Hurley, were clearly convinced that the progression of events in China was dependent on the Soviet Union, and both believed it essential to get Soviet concurrence in U.S. policy. But they arrived at the same destination over different routes. Washington feared that Russia would enter the Asian war full force, occupy strategic positions in Manchuria, and then eventually aid the Chinese Communists. Consequently, it was essential to get an agreement between the Kuomintang and the CCP at the earliest possible date, to prepare for a stable postwar China. Hurley had no such fears; he thought he had already received plenty of assurance from Stalin regarding his intentions and was convinced the Marshal would support Chiang and the National government.

In any event the President and the State Department determined that it was essential to send Harry Hopkins to Moscow, and only after the completion of his mission would Hurley be permitted to inform Chiang of the Yalta accords—the thought being that Yalta would be much more palatable to Chiang if Stalin promised to support him. On May 10, Hurley had wired President Truman that he and Chiang had already discussed most of the terms of Yalta and that the Generalissimo seemed willing to accept them; moreover, continued secrecy seemed pointless, since Chiang seemed to know of the terms and certainly knew of the imminence of Russian entrance into the war. The Ambassador believed he should be authorized to reveal the Yalta document.[25] As events transpired, Hurley was not authorized to apprise Chiang fully until June 15.

In the meantime, Harry Hopkins went packing off to Moscow

[25] Hurley to Truman, May 10, 1945, *ibid.;* see also Hurley to the Secretary of State, May 7, 1945. One of the reasons often cited for delay in telling Chiang of Yalta was the fear of leaks to the Japanese. This was a partial reason for Washington's decision to wait, but by mid-May everyone knew that Russia would enter the war, including Japan.

loaded with some pointed questions for Stalin. In conferences lasting from May 26 to June 6, Hopkins and Harriman queried the Marshal on topics ranging from Poland to his view of the date of Japanese surrender, to Soviet entrance into the Far Eastern war and the prospects for unification in China. On the latter points, Stalin said he thought he would be prepared to join the United States in the Asian war by August 8 and that he would conclude an agreement with the Chinese government in July. He also said he believed unity important to China, that Russia had no territorial claims in China, that Chiang was the best and ablest of Chinese leaders, and that he would support the Open Door.[26] Hopkins was ecstatic; Harriman was "very encouraged;" both believed that Stalin would support Chiang Kai-shek and U.S. policy.[27]

President Truman was similarly delighted at the results of the talks, and in early June he sent Hurley an interesting message revealing his confidence in future prospects: "Stalin has made to us a categorical statement that he will do everything he can to promote unification under the leadership of Chiang Kai-shek. That this leadership should continue after the war. That he wants a unified, stable China and wants China to control all of Manchuria as a part of a United China. That he has no territorial claims against China, and that he will respect Chinese sovereignty in all areas his troops enter to fight the Japanese. That he will welcome representatives of the Generalissimo to be with his troops in Manchuria in order to facilitate the organization of Chinese administration in Manchuria. That he agrees with America's 'Open Door' policy in China."[28]

Hurley must have drawn exquisite pleasure from the message. It amounted to a restatement, slightly more detailed, of what

[26] Memorandum of conversation by Charles E. Bohlen, May 28, 1945, *F.R.*, *1945*, VII, 887–891; Feis, pp. 309–311.

[27] See Robert Sherwood, *Roosevelt and Hopkins* (New York, 1948), pp. 902–903; and Feis, p. 311.

[28] Truman to Hurley, June 9, 1945, Hurley Papers.

Stalin had been telling him since 1943. He had frequently informed Chiang of his view of Stalin's intentions; he had frequently
informed Washington; he had been predicating his action in
China in part on these intentions. Officials in Washington had
viewed his comments with obvious disbelief and cautioned him
about undue optimism. Now, apparently all had come over to
his point of view. Harriman wrote to him on June 5: "For your
private information UJ has reaffirmed to Harry and me what he
told us when you were in Moscow. . . . Harry joins in good luck
to you." [29] What seems most significant here is that, in the final
analysis, important U.S. policy makers, including Hurley, proved
to be wrong in accepting Stalin's word. Hurley was wrong first,
but in judging actions resulting from his assessment of Russian
intentions it is important to note that many other officials ultimately came to the same conclusions, based not on his advice,
but on a common source—Stalin's comments. In retrospect, it
appears that Stalin, when his forces entered Manchuria in 1945,
could no more completely abandon the Communists than the
United States could the Kuomintang (though for somewhat different reasons), and, in the event conditions favorable to the CCP
developed in north China, the Soviet Union would in fact provide positive assistance. In the context of their time, however,
Stalin's remarks seemed essentially believable.

Encouraged by recent developments, Hurley again in early
July informed the State Department that he thought Soviet attitudes toward the CCP were essentially the same as they were the
previous September and that the Harriman-Hopkins talks in Moscow confirmed this. As yet, however, the Chinese Communists
were not certain that Russia would not support them; only the
signing of a Sino-Soviet treaty would convince them. Then, if the
National government were generous enough to make some important concessions, a CCP-government agreement could be
reached. The Communist strength was exaggerated; their num-

[29] Harriman to Hurley, June 5, 1945, *ibid.*

bers overestimated; their support overemphasized. They could hold out only temporarily, pending the outcome of the Soong mission in Moscow.[30]

After Hopkins returned from the Soviet Union, President Truman and Acting Secretary of State Grew conferred with T. V. Soong, apprising him of the results of Hopkins' mission and the substance of the Yalta Far Eastern Agreement. They first gave him this information by providing him with a copy of the communication to Hurley of June 9 and then discussed the important points with him. Soong thereupon departed for Chungking, where he stopped for consultation prior to journeying to Moscow for a round of talks with Stalin early in July. While there, he discussed with Hurley the same subjects recently covered in Washington.

Meanwhile Hurley was cooling his heels waiting to inform Chiang Kai-shek of the terms of Yalta. The message from the Secretary on June 9 instructed him to wait until June 15. The Ambassador was annoyed, as he wrote Stettinius: "I do not know what importance is attached to the date of June 15th since we now know that most of the subject matter has already been presented to the Generalissimo, but I want you to know that I am following instructions regarding date of presentation." [31] Particularly disturbing to him was the fact that the Russian ambassador had discussed with Chiang the terms of Soviet entrance into the war but had not mentioned Stalin's commitment to Hopkins. On June 15, Hurley presented Truman's message to Chiang and discussed Yalta with him; significant by its absence in his report of these discussions, in view of the Ambassador's later charges relative to the Yalta agreements, was any mention of Chiang's reaction.[32] The reason for this was clear; as Hurley knew, Chiang had already been informed.

[30] *United States Relations with China*, p. 99.

[31] Hurley to the Secretary of State, June 13, 1945, Hurley Papers; see also Feis, p. 314.

[32] Hurley to the Secretary of State, June 15, 1945, Hurley Papers.

However, Chiang did have some important questions relative to the agreements. He wanted to know if the United States would participate jointly in the use of Port Arthur as a naval base; if so, he would suggest this to Stalin and would also request the inclusion of Great Britain in the agreement. He also wished to inquire if the United States would not like to become party to the prospective Chinese agreement with the Soviet Union; if so, the benefits would be obvious: it would make certain compliance by all parties with the terms and help insure peace in Asia. The Generalissimo also requested expression of the U.S. view of the prospect of including the United States in decisions concerning transfer of Sakhalin Island and the Kuriles. Hurley sent the queries to the Secretary of State without comment, though later he suggested that he strongly assented to the proposals.[33] The response from Acting Secretary Grew, passed along upon instructions from the President, was that the United States would adhere to the terms of Yalta, specifying lease of Port Arthur to Russia, that the United States "could not very well agree to participate" in its joint use, and that the United States would not be party to a Sino-Soviet agreement. In any case it would seem "doubtful that the Soviet Union would consent to a tripartite or multilateral pact, since the purpose of such a pact would be to regulate Sino-Soviet relations."[34]

Disappointed in the U.S. reply, Soong conferred again with Chiang and Hurley and then set off for Moscow. There Stalin proved pretty rough on the Chinese emissary. He immediately made exorbitant demands for Chinese territory and concessions in return for a Russian friendship treaty. He asked that the Soviet Union be granted control of Chinese railroads in Manchuria, the right to build a Soviet naval base at Dairen, and the creation of a military zone in adjacent areas—concessions which, if granted, would have given Russia virtually complete control over Manchuria. Moreover, he demanded Chinese recognition of Mongolian

[33] *Ibid.*
[34] Secretary of State to Hurley, June 18, 1945, *ibid.*

independence. Instructed by the Generalissimo to reject these demands as excessive, Soong replied with a set of proposals under the terms of which China would retain control of Manchuria. These Stalin rejected, though he did scale down his demands slightly, and promised more categorical support of Chiang in his struggle with the Communists. This is where negotiations stood in mid-July as Soong returned to Chungking for further consultation.

Harriman, cognizant of the course of the talks and impressed with the truculence of Stalin, advised the Secretary of State to support Soong, so as to avoid Chinese concessions in excess of the intent of Yalta. He feared Soong would ultimately wilt under Russian pressure.[35] At the same time, President Truman sent a warning to Chiang on July 24: "I asked that you carry out the Yalta Agreement, but I had not asked that you make any concessions in excess of that agreement." [36] Perhaps as important an outcome of Stalin's hard bargaining with Soong was Harriman's renewed skepticism about Russian policies vis-à-vis the future course of civil conflict in China.

Back in Chungking, Soong expressed his displeasure with the Soviet dictator. He informed Hurley he was a broken man, that Stalin had been very rude and hard on him. "After having related this to me," Hurley wrote, "Soong went into another one of his paroxysms. He raised unlimited hell in two languages. Stalin had really hit Soong in the solar plexus." [37] Stalin had toasted the Generalissimo's son, Chiang Ching-kuo, as the heir apparent in China; this, Hurley believed, hurt Soong deeply and put him in a depressed mood for the duration of the mission. Actually, however, what the Chinese envoy was most concerned about was the opprobrium he would receive at home after negotiating an unpopular treaty with Russia. He did not want to return to Moscow

---

[35] Memorandum by A. Harriman, July 18, 1945, *F.R.*, *1945*, VII, 944–948; Harriman to the Secretary of State, July 28, 1945, *ibid.*, 950–951; Feis, pp. 316–320.

[36] Truman to Hurley, July 24, 1945, Hurley Papers.

[37] Hurley to Secretary of State, July 25, 1945 (unsent), *ibid.*

to sign such a treaty. Chiang Kai-shek himself should go. Or, if the Generalissimo refused, Dr. Wang Shih-chieh, present Minister of Information, could be made foreign secretary, and he could consummate the arrangement. Soong also informed the U.S. Ambassador that he considered Yalta a very bad agreement, that indeed Britain was taking no responsibility for that accord, and the United States should support China more fully in the Sino-Soviet talks. Attempting to reassure him, Hurley said that the United States was China's best friend and then defended Yalta: "I again called his attention to the fact that if he concluded the treaty on the basis of the Yalta decisions people would think it was his treaty and the whole world, including China, would praise him."[38] Hurley came away from this conversation convinced that Soong "did not give a damn what happened to China; that he himself looked out for T. V. Soong."[39]

Soong returned to Moscow in early August, accompanied by Wang Shih-chieh as foreign minister, and renewed discussions with Stalin. The Marshal, Soong found, was just as difficult to deal with as before. He insisted on the concessions previously demanded and now sought complete control of the Kwantung peninsula and the port of Dairen. Thereupon, Ambassador Harriman, who had been urging U.S. support for the Chinese and who had recently returned from the Potsdam conference with a directive from Secretary James Byrnes to do so, entered the picture. He frequently reminded Stalin of the Open Door and of the U.S. view of the term "pre-eminent position" of the Soviet Union and admonished Stalin not to pressure Soong too hard. Partially as a result of Harriman's efforts, the Soviet dictator did compromise slightly.[40]

But the treaty ultimately signed on August 14 nonetheless disturbed Harriman and some in the State Department. One part

[38] Hurley to the Secretary of State, July 24, 1945 (unsent), *ibid.*

[39] *Ibid.* Hurley at one point described Soong as "a devious slippery bastard, as crooked as a corkscrew" (Frank Dorn, *Walkout: With Stilwell in Burma* [New York, 1971], p. 12).

[40] *United States Relations with China*, pp. 118–120; Feis, pp. 342–343.

was the Treaty of Friendship and Alliance, for which the Generalissimo and Soong were willing to sacrifice much. It stated that the two governments would work in friendly collaboration and mutual respect in the postwar period and that each would refrain from interference in the domestic affairs of the other. It also stated that the Soviet Union would give moral and material support in the future "entirely" to the National government. The agreement did not specify in clear enough terms to suit Harriman that Russia would not aid the CCP. Another important part of the agreement specified that China was to remain sovereign in Manchuria, but gave the Soviet Union virtual control over the area by vesting in her joint ownership of the railroads. Also Dairen was to become a "free port," but the pre-eminent position of Russia was guaranteed, as she was to receive free lease of half of the port facilities. And Port Arthur was to be jointly used as a naval base but with its boundaries extended beyond those wished by the United States.[41] Wang Shih-chieh signed the agreement and took it back to Chungking; Soong praised it and flew to the United States.

Reaction to the agreement in Chungking was friendly. Chiang Kai-shek indicated that he was "satisfied" with it, as did other ranking Kuomintang officials. Hurley was delighted. He wrote Washington that the Generalissimo had thanked him for his work in promoting the Sino-Soviet rapprochement, and he said he now thought Chiang had a great chance to exert leadership. He believed that it would not be long until events in China would confirm his view that the agreement would make the Communists more willing to negotiate.[42]

The Communist reaction to the treaty has never accurately been determined. They may have known of Stalin's contemplated moves and that ultimately Russian action would redound in their favor; they may have been caught by surprise. Some recent evidence seems to support the latter. An article by Warren I. Cohen in the *Pacific Historical Review* (August, 1966) is of significance

[41] *United States Relations with China*, pp. 117–118; Feis, pp. 342–343.
[42] *United States Relations With China*, pp. 120–121.

here. Cohen analyzes a captured Chinese Communist document which he procured in the Chinese Nationalist archives—a mimeographed speech given by one Hu Hsi-K'uei, a minor Communist official. Hu stated in this speech that the Communists were caught completely by surprise and were startled and confused by the treaty. Cohen suggests, logically, that Hu spoke for the party.[43] In any event, the CCP for some reason proved more willing to talk unity after the pact was signed.

In the interim, while the Sino-Soviet agreement was being hammered out, numerous reports came from China of the spread of civil conflict. In early June Counselor of the U.S. Embassy Robert L. Smyth and Secretary Arthur Ringwalt reported clashes between government and CCP forces involving as many as six divisions. These allegedly took place in areas of south China, then being evacuated by the Japanese. Later, the CCP newspaper published accounts of fighting, charging the Kuomintang with the main responsibility. General Wedemeyer and other American military officials disputed the reports as greatly over-emphasizing the importance of the clashes, and Hurley appended his own comments to those of Smyth and Ringwalt when sending the message to Washington.[44] Hurley and his military advisers may or may not have been correct in their assessment of the alleged clashes in June. By late July and mid-August, however, there was substantial evidence of conflict for all to see.

Kuomintang-Communist relations grew particularly tense at the war's end. The major question involved the acceptance of Japanese surrender in China. The question was now an urgent

[43] Warren I. Cohen, "American Observers and the Sino-Soviet Friendship Treaty of August, 1945," *Pacific Historical Review*, XXV (Aug., 1966), 347–349. Cohen attempts to refute Charles McLane who suggests that the CCP was not surprised by the Pact. See also Charles B. McLane, *Soviet Policy and the Chinese Communists, 1931–1936* (New York, 1958).

[44] Memorandum of conversation between Hurley, Briggs, Robertson, Smyth, Ringwalt, Biggerstaff, Freeman, June 15, 1945, Hurley Papers. The Ambassador's action spurred some dissension among embassy personnel, and there is little question but that because he looked upon these reports as of the same type as those written earlier by Service and Davies, he began to come to a parting of the ways with Smyth and Ringwalt.

one. At the Potsdam conference the United States had revealed
to its wartime allies that it had a new superweapon which would
shorten the war. And, at the close of the conference, the allies had
issued an ultimatum to Japan advising her to "surrender or else."
When she rejected the ultimatum the United States on August
6 dropped the first atomic bomb on Hiroshima. On August 8, the
Soviet Union, its troops in readiness, hastened to enter the war
against Japan. By the time Japan surrendered on August 14, after
the U.S. atomic attack on Nagasaki, the Soviet Union had already
pushed far into Manchuria. The Chinese Communists had also
begun moving into the vacuum created by Japan, accepting the
Japanese surrender, and taking over Japanese arms.

Under Allied plans laid at Potsdam, Chiang Kai-shek was to disarm and demobilize Japanese troops in China. Pursuant to these
plans, the U.S. War Department sent a directive to General
Wedemeyer for his and Hurley's guidance on the matter. It
stated that the U.S. commander should be exceedingly careful
not to take action which would indicate support of the National
government or American intervention in the Chinese civil war.
But in areas where government troops were not in position and
under authority granted by Chiang Kai-shek, the United States
could act for the National government and accept Japanese surrender.[45] Given the situation in China, these orders were at worst
contradictory and at best vague. They placed the burden of decision on Wedemeyer and Hurley.

When General Chu Teh of the Communists announced de-
fiantly that his troops would deal directly with the Japanese in
areas of "liberated China," Hurley reacted. He informed Secretary
of State Byrnes that CCP capture of Japanese arms would make
civil war inevitable; therefore, it would be well to warn the
Japanese against laying down their arms to anyone but forces of
the National government.[46] Also, he urged Wedemeyer, who

[45] Joint Chiefs of Staff to Wedemeyer, Aug. 10, 1945, *F.R., 1945,* VII,
527–528; Feis, p. 337.
[46] Hurley to Secretary of State, Aug. 12, 1945, Hurley Papers.

agreed with him, to assist Chiang Kai-shek in regaining control in north China, and concurred when Wedemeyer landed U.S. Marines in the Peking-Tientsin area to secure vital strategic points. The Ambassador clearly did what he could to prevent CCP success in its announced aims. All his actions, however, he considered consistent with the instructions from Washington. Hurley believed that when the CCP learned the terms of the Sino-Soviet agreement, it would begin to negotiate in earnest. But if it gained additional arms and thus strengthened its military position, even this accord would not make the Communists more tractable. China in mid-August teetered on the brink of civil war with both Kuomintang and CCP attempting to gain advantage upon Japan's defeat, a condition which forced Hurley to take sides more openly.

Though the Ambassador chose the Kuomintang, he thought events would still make it possible for him to deal with the Communists. Publication of the details of the Sino-Soviet accord on August 24 was the event he anticipated. When he learned of the completion of Soong's negotiations in Moscow in mid-August, Hurley suggested to Chiang that he invite Mao Tse-tung to come to Chungking, confident that the Communist leader would agree. Chiang did this, and after a period of hesitation in which he considered sending Chou En-lai alone, Mao himself agreed. But he feared for his safety unless assured of protection. Hurley, anxious to get the talks moving again, then offered to fly to Yenan in his own plane and join Mao and Chou on the journey—thus giving them his personal assurance against harm. After acknowledging Mao's acceptance of the proposal on August 24, Hurley flew to the Communist capital on August 27.[47] Mao's willingness to accompany Chou to Chungking augured well for success, as it clearly revealed a softening in the CCP position; the Ambassador was pleased at the prospect.

The Communists accorded Hurley a friendly greeting when he

[47] Mao Tse-tung to Wedemeyer, Aug. 24, 1945, and Hurley to Secretary of State, Aug. 16, 1945, *ibid.*

arrived in Yenan, and, on August 28, the Ambassador's party, accompanied by Chou and Mao, returned to Chungking to begin the new round of negotiations. After a brief exchange of cordialities, these discussions began on September 2. There Chiang Kaishek offered to allow moderate CCP representation in the upcoming Peoples Congress and to establish a new government army which would include twelve Communist divisions, under nominal Communist command but with final authority for their disposition resting with the government. At the subsequent meeting on September 3, Mao responded. He wanted authority to disarm the Japanese in parts of China; recognition of CCP "sovereignty" in "liberated areas"; maintenance of the status quo on military positions; CCP nomination of vice-mayors in Tientsin, Peiping, Shanghai, and Tsingtao; forty-eight Communist divisions within the national army under CCP control; the holding of a political consultative conference with adequate CCP representation; and the partitioning of China at the Yangtze River with the Communists in control in the north. Mao did not insist on a coalition government and, in his willingness to accept only partial control of China, revealed a more conciliatory position—a position based on temporary military and diplomatic realities. Nonetheless Chiang rejected his proposals.[48]

Confident now of achieving unity and heartened by his success in renewing the conversations, Hurley failed to recognize the point or points on which settlement might have been predicated. Again, he did not recognize the depth of the issue between the two sides, that they could come to no lasting accommodation— only an expedient one. He played a role in the talks, keeping them going by getting renewed affirmation of principles—espousal of which, he informed Washington, he heard frequently. Principles would not suffice; an agreement to partition China might have. Colonel Ivan Yeaton in Yenan suggested to Hurley

[48] Memorandum of conversation, Chiang Kai-shek and Mao Tse-tung, Sept. 2, 1945; record of points presented by Chou En-lai and Wang Jo-fei, Sept. 3, 1945; and government reply to CCP proposals, Sept. 3, 1945, *ibid.*

that the formation of a loose confederation of territories under control respectively of the CCP, the government, and the warlords, might work.[49] But for the above reasons Hurley did not conceive of this; nor did the State Department advocate it seriously as a solution, even, it might be noted, after Hurley had long since departed and other envoys confronted the problem. Had U.S. policy makers, including Hurley, been more perspicacious, Chiang might have been impelled to compromise (though it is difficult to see how); he would have thus gained a temporary settlement and more time to deal with the CCP. The fact that this "opportunity" was missed, if indeed it could be so considered, meant that the talks would only drone on as they had earlier, while civil conflict spread. And, ultimately, action by Russia in Manchuria and the swinging of the military balance in favor of the Communists would wreck hopes of even a temporary arrangement.

Though the talks bogged down, they were not broken off. Hurley played an important role in preventing complete impasse by admonishing both sides to continue to proffer proposals. As far as compromise by the Communists was concerned, this was largely dependent on the military picture and action by the Soviet Union; Hurley could do little. And inducement of compromise by Chiang was largely taken out of the Ambassador's hands. On September 14, President Truman promised aid to China to expand her military power and achieve peace in China and security in areas formerly occupied by the Japanese. The United States would furnish airplanes and naval vessels, and supply and equip Chinese land forces—but cautioned that this additional aid should not be "diverted" for use in civil war against the Communists or to support undemocratic institutions.[50] Everyone knew Chiang's regime to be undemocratic and knew

[49] Robert Johnson to Hurley, Aug. 27, 1945, *ibid.;* Tang Tsou, *America's Failure in China, 1941–1950* (Chicago, 1963), pp. 320–322.

[50] Memorandum by the Acting Secretary of State to the President, Sept. 13, 1945, *F.R., 1945*, VII, 559–562; see also Feis, pp. 371–373.

how the aid would be used. Again, Washington's policy statement was vague, even contradictory, and seemed to comprise support of Chiang, and lack of it, at the same time. The Generalissimo probably interpreted it as support; certainly he showed no signs of increased willingness to accept Mao's terms. As historians have correctly pointed out, Hurley could not "see the trees for the forest," did not advise pressuring Chiang, and therefore his action amounted to "unconditional support" of the Chinese leader. But it was not Hurley's policy alone to provide this military assistance; it was that of the State, War, and Navy departments, and of the President.

On September 18, both the CCP leaders and the Generalissimo appealed to Hurley to assist them further in making the talks a success. Accordingly, the Ambassador drew up a nine-point proposal as a basis for settlement. The Ambassador again dealt in general terms, as the points clearly indicate. He reported to the Secretary, however, that he believed: "They were attempting to settle too many details. . . . If they could agree on basic overall principles, details could be worked out in accordance with such principles." [51] The points comprised an invoking of Sun Yatsen's principles and a cooperative effort to promote democracy, and also suggested prosecution of criminals and traitors but release of political prisoners. Included also were proposals for incorporation of CCP troops into the national army and creation of a political council with broad representation of political parties in it. After making this latest effort, Hurley informed the Secretary: "The spirit between the negotiators is good. The rapprochement between the two leading parties in China seems to be progressing, and the discussion and rumors of civil war recede as the conference continues." [52]

Meanwhile Hurley prepared to leave China to travel to Washington—a trip he had hoped to make for some time. He was ill (or thought he was) and had long needed medical attention which

51 *United States Relations with China*, p. 107.
52 *Ibid.*

was not available in Chungking. He was physically tired and unquestionably weary of the China "mess." He had been separated from his family, except for brief periods, since 1942, and his financial position was suffering as well. His income had shrunk considerably since the war, but his obligations had not, and his family seemed insensitive to this fact; this worried the Ambassador. He was accustomed to giving careful personal attention to his economic affairs, that is, the administering of his property, and he grew frustrated by his inability to do so properly in China. Moreover, he wished to consult with the President and the State Department about developments in China.

Several specific matters troubled him. Much to his displeasure, he learned in mid-September that John Service and George Atcheson had been assigned to General MacArthur's staff as political advisers. This raised the old issue of conspiracy to thwart his efforts on the part of the Chinese Affairs Division of the State Department, as he thought they hoped to secure the removal of Chiang Kai-shek as China's leader. The Ambassador also read, on September 19, a report in the *News Bulletin* of the U.S. Information Service that cited his own dissatisfaction with the State Department as his reason for going to Washington; the report said that he would not return to China. This he thought must have originated either in the State Department or in the Embassy and was indicative of a move against him. It was humiliating, and would reduce his effectiveness; he hoped to determine its source. He also read several other articles (in the American press), either critical of his efforts or suggesting he would resign.[53] More important, however, was his belief that the European colonial powers were preparing to recover their Asian possessions with the acquiescence of the United States.

On September 11, Hurley drafted a strong statement to Secre-

---

[53] See the *New York Herald-Tribune*, Sept. 22, 1945; *New York Times*, Sept. 5, and 16, 1945; *New York Herald-Tribune*, Sept. 19, 1945; *Washington Post*, Sept. 19, 1945; U.S. Information Service *News Bulletin*, Sept. 19, 1945; see also Hurley to the President, Sept. 16, 1945 (unsent), Hurley Papers.

tary Byrnes about the U.S. position vis-à-vis the imperialist powers. In the Atlantic Charter, Roosevelt had committed the United States to certain ideal policies, among the most important of which was self-determination of nations. Yet the United States at the San Francisco Conference had voted with the British, French, and Dutch on colonial independence. The imperial powers wanted, in Asia, reacquisition of their colonies, a divided China, and a strong rebuilt Japan. For the United States to support them in this was to reject the Atlantic Charter and a basic premise of Roosevelt's Asian policy.[54] Hurley concluded that the State Department with the Chinese Affairs Division in the ascendant position was responsible for the change.

[54] Hurley to Secretary of State, Sept. 11, 1945, Hurley Papers.

# X

## Hurley, the Far East, and European Colonialism

With distrust of the British imbedded in his character by his Irish ancestry and his southwestern heritage, Hurley, soon after his arrival in China, began to suspect the motives of the British officials in the Far East. He quickly arrived at the view that they had assumed the lead in a clandestine attempt with the French and Dutch to promote reacquisition of their colonial possessions in Asia at the expense of the combined war effort against Japan. And they had used U.S. Lend-Lease materials toward this end. The Ambassador's prejudices, his interpretation of Roosevelt's proposed postwar colonial policies, and his cost-accounting mind, led him to react strongly against the imperialist powers.

Indicating deep concern on this matter, President Roosevelt wrote to Hurley on November 16, 1944, requesting to be kept informed on the activities of the Dutch, French, and British missions in regard to Southeast Asia. Shortly thereafter, John Davies informed Hurley that he and Wedemeyer observed what seemed to be attempts on the part of the three European powers to sabotage U.S. war plans. The British, for example, were preparing to drop supplies to the French Army in Indochina, and, in response to a U.S. offer to assist, had replied in the negative. Moreover, a French military organization headed by a General Blaizot, was established at Mountbatten's headquarters and was working closely and secretly with the British.[1] Hurley, in his reply to the President's message, stated that fear of postwar impoverish-

[1] John Davies to Hurley, Nov. 29, 1944, Hurley Papers. The Hurley Papers are the source of the references that follow.

ment made retention of their empires the consuming interest of the three nations. And, as long as opposition to imperialism remained strong, they would display a united front. "You may therefore expect Britain, France, and the Netherlands to disregard the Atlantic Charter and all of the promises made to other nations by which they obtained support in their earlier stages of the war." [2]

Through December, the Ambassador gathered further evidence of the European nations' intentions, and on January 1 sent an "eyes alone" message to the President. In addition to the organizations at Mountbatten's headquarters, the three powers had set up an organization known as the Southeast Asia Confederacy at Kunming, China, the true purpose of which U.S. intelligence had not yet been able to fathom. Hurley did know, however, that a large number of British intelligence and propaganda people operated from Kunming, and that they had requested the placing of some of their members on Wedemeyer's staff. He also learned that they proposed establishing an amphibian air force on a lake south of Kunming, and that planes, jeeps, trucks and other lend lease supplies would be used by the Confederacy for intelligence and propaganda purposes in China and Southeast Asia. These materials would contribute nothing to the war against Japan, and their use by "the imperial powers" would divert hump tonnage from the war effort.

Another organization whose activities Hurley suspected was the British Army Aid Group. The original purpose of the group was to assist escaping British prisoners. And the group also claimed to be rescuing U.S. pilots downed in occupied China. The Ambassador thought differently. Claire Chennault assured him that it had not helped U.S. pilots, and evidence indicated its sole purpose was to promote the postwar position of the British. Led by a Colonel Ride, of the regular British Army, the group was subverting U.S. attempts to promote unity and thus attempting to keep China weak and divided.[3]

[2] Hurley to Roosevelt, Nov. 26, 1944.
[3] Hurley to Roosevelt, Jan. 1, 1945.

Both prior to and subsequent to the dispatching of the above message, Hurley made frequent contacts with the diplomatic personnel of the European nations. Not always given to the discretion of the professional diplomat, he often found himself in emotional exchanges with these representatives. One episode occurred when on November 2, the British Ambassador to China, Sir Horace Seymour, called on him and stated that he believed, "it would be a mistake to try to unify China's military establishments." China had gotten along fairly well as a divided country in the past; he thought it might even be a good idea to promote dissension, because a united China would only "cause trouble" in the Orient. "Success in unification of China," the British Ambassador said, "would in the years to come mean the elimination of imperialism in the Orient and the consequent loss of rule of the Orient by white men." Hurley replied that imperialism was in conflict with the principles for which both Roosevelt and Churchill said the war was being fought and that he "was not of the opinion that the purpose of the war was to establish white imperialism over all the colored races." [4]

In mid-January he informed Achilles Clarac, Counselor of the French Embassy, that he opposed French imperialism and that postwar governments would be established only through the consent of the governed, consonant with the Atlantic Charter, if the United States had its way. When the specific topic of Indochina arose, Clarac stated that France alone would decide its fate, without advice from the Americans. Angered by Clarac's remarks, and impatient for a concrete directive from Washington, Hurley shot off a note to the Secretary of State: "The apparent lack of affirmative American policy on the question of the future status of Indochina will eventually result in the vitiation of what I understand to be among the fundamentals of our war aims as far as that country is concerned." [5]

In London on his way back to Chungking from the United

---

[4] Notes on conference between Hurley and British Ambassador Sir Horace Seymour, Nov. 3, 1944.

[5] Hurley to Secretary of State, Jan. 31, 1945.

States in April, Hurley had an animated conversation with the French Ambassador to Great Britain on the subject of Indochina. The French envoy suggested that the United States was derelict in failing to grant France greater assistance in the liberation of Indochina. Hurley answered that France appeared to be one of the world's "gimme" countries, bankrupt economically and spiritually, and that the United States did not have inexhaustible resources; that the United States' first obligation was to its own forces in the Far East; that his country would use its supplies "to support our own forces in China instead of using them to take back occupied imperialist territories." [6]

Back in Chungking in May, Hurley continued his dialogue with representatives of France, Britain, and the Netherlands. Particularly exasperating to him were the unabashed statements of representatives of those nations magnifying their own importance to the Far Eastern war and the contribution they made through their colonial holdings. The French Ambassador told him that France in particular was contributing heavily to victory in the Far East. The French battleship the *Richelieu* was important in attacks on Sumatra. French were fighting the Japanese in Indochina to free that country from aggression, and the great French effort there prevented Japanese attacks on Yunnan and Kwangsi. If France wished to return to Indochina after the war, that was her business; certainly the Indochinese would not object. "The Indochinese have perfect confidence in France. The real trusteeship is in our heart; that is the mutual confidence between France and the people of Indochina." [7]

Although more restrained in comment to the French Ambassador, Hurley was repelled by his statements. He knew of French collaboration with Japanese forces in Indochina which the Ambassador glossed over without a nod. He also knew that stories

[6] Memorandum of conversation at French Embassy, London, Apr. 7, 1945, with Robert Smyth, Counselor of U.S. Embassy, London, John Allison, U.S. 2nd Secretary, and M. Massigli, French Ambassador.

[7] Hurley to Secretary of State, May 10, 1945.

of the French effectiveness in fighting the Japanese were exaggerated tenfold. Moreover, the mutual confidence between the Indochinese and the French was in his view clear fabrication. Cognizant of French intentions regarding her colony, the U.S. Ambassador continued to petition his superiors for some advice. He asked the Secretary of State if any secret decisions had been made at Yalta on Indochina, saying that if there were he would like to be apprised of them, as the matter was gaining in urgency.[8] Acting Secretary Grew replied: "No Yalta decision relating to Indochina known to Department." [9] Annoyed at the response, Hurley then sent two long letters to President Truman.

In the first of these communications, the Ambassador outlined what he believed was the serious misuse of Lend-Lease aid. The British, he said, provided their embassy in China with a "magnificent" airplane and similarly equipped their personnel around the globe with Lend-Lease funds, while U.S. embassies remained understaffed and poorly equipped. More serious, however, was the fact that the British used American resources to defeat "America's international policies" and to "build their own political and business fences . . . to the detriment of our present and future interests." He was convinced that in international matters "we should not permit Britain to be the tail that wags the dog." In Hurley's view, Lend Lease should be terminated every place except where it directly contributed to the defeat of Japan. The British, Dutch, and French would contend that in their colonial possessions the war was still being fought against the Japanese, but in truth these were simply "mopping up operations," and these three nations were concerned mainly about their Southeast Asian prestige, not about Japan. They were in fact conserving their own resources and "using us as a catspaw in violation of the principles of the Atlantic Charter and of every other principle for which America claims to be fighting." As for Britain's claim that massive U.S. assistance was needed to maintain her Pacific fleet

[8] Hurley to Secretary of State, May 11, 1945.
[9] Grew to Hurley, May 18, 1945.

and to keep her economy from collapsing, all her requests were out of proportion to actual needs and certainly to her wartime contribution. "My own opinion," Hurley wrote, "is that the British economic system is antiquated, decadent, and weak. It must eventually fail if it is not fundamentally renovated . . . having sustained Britain in war . . . it is too much to ask the American taxpayer to continue to burden himself with the weight of an imperialistic, monopolistic, decadent economic system." [10]

In the second letter, he informed Truman that as President he would soon have to make some very critical decisions pertaining to Hong Kong and Indochina, and he proceeded to provide what information he could to assist in making those decisions. Some of the Ambassador's remarks are interesting, in view of speculation on the course of Roosevelt's policy had he lived. Hurley stated that, on March 8, President Roosevelt intimated to him and Wedemeyer and, on March 24, to him alone that he was going to insist that Great Britain return Hong Kong to China. Confirming this, the China Affairs Division informed General Wedemeyer: "It is understood that the attitude of the President with regard to Hong Kong is as follows: Hong Kong should be returned by the British to the Chinese." [11] If Churchill refused to accede to this demand, the President said he would then go over the head of the Prime Minister and appeal to the King and to Parliament. The President believed that if the British would agree to this policy, the Chinese would make Hong Kong a free port; indeed Chiang Kai-shek had so stated. On this latter point, Chiang told Hurley that Roosevelt had brought the subject up at Cairo and, at the same time he committed himself to the return of Hong Kong, he asked the Generalissimo if he would declare it a free port. As Hurley saw the matter, however, there was one obstacle. Churchill had told him in London that Great Britain would surrender Hong Kong "over my dead body." This meant that if Roosevelt's policy were to prevail, the United States would have

[10] Hurley to Truman, May 13, 1945.
[11] Asst. Chief of Staff to Wedemeyer, Feb. 27, 1945.

to take a very firm stand. Hurley further said that while he had a complete verbal understanding of Roosevelt's policy, he had no written directive on Hong Kong. He hoped President Truman would support the policy and formalize it.

Notwithstanding Britain's opposition, Hurley felt that there was an excellent chance that the United States could carry the day on Hong Kong. In Lend Lease the United States had an outstanding diplomatic lever. Churchill had said to Hurley in London that the British policy regarding the postwar world was "to ask nothing and to give up nothing"; to which the U.S. Ambassador replied that it was a little late to adopt that policy and that the United States had made a terrific contribution to Great Britain. Now on the question of Hong Kong, the United States could adopt a trading position with Great Britain. The President should demand an accounting procedure and the immediate return of all unused and used Lend-Lease materials and supplies, including ships, airplanes, automobiles, trucks, pipelines, and so on. Then the United States could indicate its intention to sell these items in the international market. Other supplies that Britain received she should be strictly accountable for, and the President should say that no additional gifts or credit would be granted at U.S. taxpayer expense until Great Britain "shows a more understanding attitude toward the American policy on Hong Kong."

Hurley also included some salient comment on Indochina. He said that, prior to his going to China in 1944, President Roosevelt had discussed Indochina with him, suggesting that he was very displeased by the Vichy French collaboration in Indochina and that he favored setting up a United Nations Trusteeship, which would be entrusted with the tutelage of Indochina until it could establish its independence. But, again, neither he nor Wedemeyer had received a written directive from the President. Indochina was placed in the military jurisdiction of Chiang Kai-shek, which meant that General Wedemeyer made many of the military decisions pertaining to it; the French had little claim to say about events there. Yet the French Ambassador was increasingly insistent in demanding U.S. supplies for French efforts in Indochina, insisting on them "as a matter of right." Hurley believed that the French would use Lend-Lease supplies to re-establish control there.

Hurley said that he had discussed this matter with President Roosevelt in March, stating that he believed the three European nations were cooperating to prevent creation of any trusteeship arrangement. It would be of inestimable value, he had told Roosevelt, to have a written directive on Indochina. Roosevelt replied that at the upcoming San Francisco Conference a trustee- ship arrangement for the colonies would be formalized to pro- vide for a transition period preparatory to independence. After the conference was over Hurley would have his directive. In the Ambassador's view, the conference was a disappointment in this regard, as the U.S. delegation did not align itself against the imperialist nations. It now appeared to Hurley that the United States would not stand in the way of Britain, France, and the Netherlands; and this would be a change from Roosevelt's policy.

The matter was one of urgency, for Lord Louis Mountbatten, British Commander in Southeast Asia, had begun to fly sorties into Indochina (outside his theater) without prior consent of either the Generalissimo or Wedemeyer. Hurley believed that Mount- batten was invading Indochina primarily for the purpose of re- establishing French imperialism—and was doing so with the assistance of U.S. supplies. Just prior to the beginning of the sor- ties, Mountbatten had requested a huge increase in supplies. The United States, Hurley stated, should deny all future requests, as they were made, not in the interest in the war against Japan, but with a view toward recapture of Indochina and Hong Kong.[12]

Acting Secretary Joseph Grew replied to Hurley's telegram on June 10. He stated that, as of April 3, the trusteeship structure had been defined so as to place under it territories taken from the enemy and all other areas voluntarily submitted. This defini-

[12] Hurley to Truman, May 28, 1945.

tion had been confirmed at the San Francisco Conference, though the United States had stressed, and would continue to stress, the importance of providing progressive measures leading either to independence of colonies or self-determination within some kind of federation. In any event, the agreements reached would preclude placing Indochina in the trusteeship structure, unless the French agreed, which was not likely. However, President Truman would at the proper time urge the French government to establish some basic liberties and self-government. Regarding French participation in the war against Japan, Grew made several pertinent comments. The United States believed that it would be beneficial to have French participation but that there should be no long-term commitment of American aid to French forces in Indochina, only such as the United States could afford and not sacrifice elsewhere. No large-scale effort in Indochina involving U.S. forces should be considered. The United States would accept French offers for assistance in the Pacific theater and would aid whatever French forces were so offered, consistent with other American commitments.

On the question of British interest in Hong Kong, Grew wrote: "The President is fully aware of the importance which the Chinese government attaches to the return of this port to its control and considers that arrangements should be made between the British and Chinese governments with whatever help we can give at the proper time to conclude a mutually satisfactory settlement which does not prejudice either the legitimate aspirations of the Chinese people or the particular strategic requirements of the present war against Japan." [13]

Hurley was not pleased with Grew's message, because it revealed what to him seemed a distinct change in U.S. policy from an active anticolonial position to appeasement of the imperialist powers. Precisely what action Roosevelt had in mind, no one has been able to determine. He had worried about the colo-

[13] Grew to Hurley, June 10, 1945.

nial problem for nearly two years; and at Cairo he informed the Chinese, and then at Yalta the Russians, that he favored a temporary trusteeship arrangement for the French colony. But whenever he broached the subject of trusteeships with the British, Churchill refused to listen; he would not, he said, preside over the liquidation of the British Empire, nor, for that matter, permit any plan compromising its position. In private, the President twitted Churchill about adhering to the Atlantic Charter, yet, when the chips were down, he seemed unwilling to risk a rift in the alliance over the issue; preventing the reacquisition of the colonies, in other words, demanded pressure on his allies through a carefully planned strategy, which Roosevelt seemingly never evolved. Whether in the final analysis he could have prevented British and French action vis-à-vis Hong Kong and Indochina cannot be judged. But if Hurley's comments of early 1945 about what the President revealed to him are to be accepted at face value, and there is little reason not to accept them, then the Grew statement did indeed reflect a change in fundamental policy if not in strategy. Certainly for Hurley to inform Truman erroneously of Roosevelt's statements just to serve his own ends would have been such a colossal act of usurped prerogative that the Ambassador could have been quickly discredited—particularly since he cited Wedemeyer as a corroborating witness. However, Hurley and officials in Washington did not view affairs in Southeast Asia from the same perspective. Those responsible for making policy after Roosevelt's death clearly hoped to avoid offending the allies, considering their assistance of significant import in the ultimate defeat of Japan. Moreover, U.S. officials realized the need for postwar cooperation on a wide variety of European matters. Though he did not say so immediately, Hurley came to look upon the policy, as put to him in this most recent message, not as an honest attempt to advance U.S. interests, but as evidence of State Department disloyalty.

Temporarily stilled in his comment to Washington by the above missive, the U.S. Ambassador was still annoyed at the acquies-

cence to French, British, and Dutch control of colonial possessions, and, in August, renewed his reporting. In a note to the
Secretary on August 13 he stated that French Chargé d'Affaires
Jean Daridan had called on the Chinese Acting Minister of Foreign Affairs requesting that China use 5,000 French troops then in
Kunming—French refugee troops who had retreated into China
months before—for occupation of French Indochina. Just prior to
this request the French Chargé visited General Wedemeyer to
urge the United States to support the use of French troops in the
occupation, suggesting even that the United States help transport
them by air. The Chargé stated: "It would have a very bad effect
and might gravely prejudice Sino-French relations should these
French troops not be permitted to proceed to Indochina." Hurley
then noted: "It is obvious from the foregoing that France is ur-
gently desirous of complete re-establishment of her authority in
Indochina at the earliest possible moment, and views with disfavor
having any Chinese troops enter Indochina." [14] Though he disliked the French move, Hurley indicated that he was considering
suggesting to Chiang compliance with the Chargé's request in
the interest of good Sino-French relations. But clearly action of
this kind would bend the wartime agreement under which the
British were to accept the Japanese surrender in South Indochina
(south of the sixteenth parallel) and the forces of Chiang were to
do the same in the north. France wanted, at least in some way, to
participate in acceptance of the surrender and was willing to make
a major issue of it with the Generalissimo's government.

Hurley reported a similar controversy on the question of Hong
Kong. He sent along to President Truman a heated message in
which Chiang revealed his view of British plans. The Generalissimo said that in a message to him of August 11, the President
had indicated that General MacArthur would direct all Japanese
forces, except where the Russians were involved, to surrender to
the Chinese government; MacArthur had complied, stating that

[14] Hurley to Secretary of State, Aug. 13, 1945.

Japanese forces "within China (excluding Manchuria), Formosa, and French Indochina north of 16 degrees north latitude shall surrender to Generalissimo Chiang Kai-shek." Hong Kong, there- fore, was in the area of Chinese jurisdiction for acceptance of Japanese surrender. Nevertheless, Chiang reported he received a message from the British in which was stated: "His Majesty's Government desire that His Excellency the President of the Re- public of China should know at once that His Majesty's Govern- ment are arranging for the despatch of the necessary British forces to re-occupy and restore the administration of Hong Kong. . . ."[15] The message, Chiang believed, indicated lack of desire by the British to act as a member of the United Nations, and an interest in serving exclusively its own interests. The Chinese president suggested, therefore, that the "situation be brought at once to the attention of His Majesty's Government and the Supreme Com- mander of the British Forces and that they be requested to make their arrangements in accordance with your general order. . . ."[16] Hurley did not append any comment to the message, but he ob- viously agreed with Chiang.

The Chinese government sent a similar message to the British, indicating bitterness over the Hong Kong action. The British then replied that they gave plenty of warning on Hong Kong, and that, irrespective of operational theaters, when a sovereign power had the requisite force available it should resume its authority and accept the Japanese surrender "in its own territory." Hurley sent this message to the President along with a new Chinese plan to deal with the question. The Chinese believed that Britain should not accept the Japanese surrender at Hong Kong, as it would set a bad precedent and alter the Potsdam agreement. But the Chi- nese could accept the Japanese surrender in a ceremony in which both the United States and Great Britain would participate; then later the British could reoccupy Hong Kong.[17]

President Truman again refused to thwart his European ally.

[15] Hurley to Secretary of State, Aug. 16, 1945.
[16] *Ibid.*
[17] Hurley to Truman, Aug. 21, 1945.

He told Prime Minister Clement Atlee to go ahead with British plans to take the Japanese surrender, if, as the only condition, coordination were achieved with Chiang Kai-shek's government for further support, through that port, of U.S. troops inland. He then informed the Chinese that this was a military matter, not a political one, and it seemed "reasonable that, where it is practicable to do so, surrender by Japanese forces should be to the authorities of that nation exercising sovereignty in that area."[18] Truman further stated that, in his view, Chiang was not raising questions about British sovereignty. Technically, of course, the President was right. Actually, this was exactly what the Generalissimo was doing, and it was what Hurley had been doing since January.

Pursuant to the President's message, Chiang relented, allowing the British to proceed with their plans. He was acting, he told Truman, "in compliance with your request" and out of desire "to cooperate with you in every way possible," difficult as it was for him to do so. Truman was pleased, informing the Generalissimo that he had "eased a difficult situation."[19] While Chiang relented in this situation, he did not change his view of the British or their European colleagues. He believed that they not only worked to reacquire their possessions in Asia, but were seeking to reduce the effectiveness of his government as well; in his view, they were actually cooperating with the CCP either wittingly or unwittingly. And the Generalissimo pointed to reports like that of Hurley on August 31. The Ambassador informed the Secretary of State that the British, French and Dutch tried to persuade General Wedemeyer to transport their representatives to Shanghai so they could reassert themselves there. Admiral Mountbatten also made "alarmist" reports to Wedemeyer on Annamese agitation, expressing a desire to take over parts of that region and south China.[20]

[18] Truman to Hurley, Aug. 22, 1945.

[19] Chiang Kai-shek to Truman, Aug. 22, 1945, and Truman to Chiang Kai-shek, Aug. 23, 1945.

[20] Hurley to Secretary of State, Aug. 31, 1945.

As a result of his intense feeling against the European powers, and perhaps to encourage more support from the United States, Chiang in early September sent a message to Washington through Hurley, stating that British and other forces were not welcome in China. "I respectfully request," he wrote, "that if and when the American fleet enters any China port it will not be accompanied by any British ships or contingent." [21]

Chiang Kai-shek and Hurley were of one mind on the question of the imperialism of the European powers; and both were annoyed by the recent policy directives of the President and Secretary of State. Chiang acquiesced in them, because he believed he had to, in view of his struggle against the CCP and his need for U.S. aid to rebuild after the Japanese war. Hurley, uncharacteristically, after the June message, simply stopped protesting. But he continued to be distressed that the United States did not stand in the way of Britain, France, and the Netherlands, and he made an issue of this when he arrived in Washington in September.

Many diplomats would have accepted the directive and would have recognized any change as prompted by circumstances associated with prosecution of the war and the rapidly approaching peace. Not Hurley. Already on bad terms with the many Foreign Service officers who had served in China and increasingly convinced that they conspired to obstruct progress toward unity there, the U.S. Ambassador concluded that the different direction on colonial matters was prompted by the State Department.

[21] Hurley to Secretary of State, Sept. 1, 1945.

# XI

## Resignation

While Hurley was in Washington, the politico-military situation in China grew more distressing by the day. China, at the end of the war, represented an advanced stage of devastation and disarray, with her railroads destroyed, her cities bombed, her crops burned, with over 1,000,000 Japanese troops on her soil, hundreds of thousands of puppet forces, and Communist armies in the north ready to secure advantage from the harassed, inefficient, and, at best, partially corrupt, National government. These were problems of the first magnitude, which, if soluble at all, required a concerted effort by the Chinese government and skilled diplomacy by the United States, not to mention the cooperation of the Soviet Union and large amounts of luck.

Since one of Chiang Kai-shek's problems was the securing of governmental control over Chinese territory and acceptance of the Japanese surrender, and because he continued to implore the United States to provide more aid to this end, American policy makers had to arrive at a decision on the continuance of military and economic assistance now that the war had ended. Hurley had informed the Generalissimo that Lend Lease would terminate with the end of the fighting, and it did for all intents and purposes, but on August 17 an exception was made by the President and the Joint Chiefs of Staff so that Chinese forces could participate effectively in the occupation of Japan, Formosa, and Korea. Shortly thereafter, on September 5, the President extended for six months Lend-Lease support, through which China was given stocks of ammunition, airplanes, other equipment reposing in the China-Burma-India area at the termination of the war, and assistance in transporting her troops.

These commitments did not satisfy Chiang. He informed Hurley and Wedemeyer that President Roosevelt had promised him at Cairo to help China equip a ninety-division peacetime army. He wanted the United States to make good on this promise and to establish a permanent military mission in China with General Wedemeyer as its head. Chiang's request threw U.S. officials into a quandary. At length, and after much discussion, it was decided that the United States would equip and supply thirty-nine Chinese divisions, as it had begun to do under military Lend Lease, rather than ninety divisions. And the United States would equip an equivalent-sized Chinese air force and provide river and coastal naval vessels.[1]

In making this commitment, U.S. policy makers were, as always, deeply concerned about political conditions in China and did not want to involve the United States in an open conflict between the government and the Communists. They also hoped to be able to withdraw American forces from the country sometime in the fall. And so the United States reiterated its objectives, democracy, peace, unity, and stability, and, at least for its own use, re-established the guideline that American aid would be forthcoming only so long as it was not used in a "fratricidal war."[2]

Related to the matter of the amount or scope of American assistance was the question of how deeply to involve the United States in the occupation of the northern sectors of China in view of the trouble developing there in late summer. Chinese Communist armies controlled the Shansi-Hopei-Chahar area, parts of Shantung province, and a good many of the communications facilities in northern China, and were rapidly arming themselves with Japanese weapons. In Sinkiang province a group of rebels promulgated a temporary uprising against Chungking's domina-

[1] Herbert Feis, *The China Tangle* (Princeton, 1953), pp. 368–372; Hurley to the Secretary of State, Sept. 2, 1945, and Truman to Chiang Kai-shek, Sept. 13, 1945, Hurley Papers.
[2] Feis, pp. 374–376.

tion. In Manchuria, Soviet troops established nearly complete control, and, though they did not at once make contact with CCP forces, they did set up "democratic unions" to take control of local governments in the area. They also entered Jehol and Hopei. Recognizing the ominous possibilities arising from these facts, Chiang Kai-shek as early as mid-August requested the United States to transport some of his troops to the northern reaches and to send American forces to important spots in north and east China; U.S. Marines then occupied Peiping and Tientsin and railroads and coal mines in the area. Later, pursuant to a request by the Generalissimo on September 10, the United States agreed to land Chinese troops in Manchuria, specifically, to take them to the port of Dairen, which it did in October.

Meanwhile, Russian intransigence in Manchuria in dealing with Nationalist representatives and their cooperation with the CCP posed a very serious problem indeed. The Soviet Union had agreed in the Sino-Soviet Pact to begin withdrawing Soviet troops from Manchuria three weeks after Japan's surrender and to allow the Nationalist government to assume full authority in the region. However, Marshal Malinovsky, in command of Soviet troops in Manchuria, refused in mid-October to allow Chiang's forces to land when they arrived on U.S. vessels. Neither in this confrontation, however, nor in the diplomatic maneuvering previous to it did the United States intercede in behalf of the Nationalist government; it preferred to see the affair as a Sino-Soviet squabble. Instead of unloading Chiang's troops at Dairen, then, U.S. ships, on the request of the Generalissimo, took them to Hulatao where, it was found, the CCP had already established control. The same was found to be true at Yingkow, another possible landing site, and finally the forces had to be landed at Chinwangtao, a port in north China, from which they would then march overland into Manchuria. This made assertion of Nationalist control in the region exceedingly difficult, as CCP troops attacked them during the march, and the Soviet Union refused to assist in any way, thus delaying their arrival in Manchuria. What was happening in Manchuria began to be clear: the Soviet Union, though it had promised to allow Chiang's troops to enter Manchuria and to withdraw Russian forces to the north, was, for reasons of its own, not willing to honor its August agreement; forces of the CCP and the Russians made contact, and the Communists began rapidly to dominate the region; Chiang Kai-shek could not, without a significant effort coupled with U.S. assistance, gain the ascendancy.[3]

In late October and November these conditions in China forced American policy makers to agonize over decisions, decisions of a kind which would have earthshaking consequences. Unfortunately, however, because of the great fear of the danger in either a full-scale commitment to Chiang Kai-shek, which in any event the American people might not have approved, or the complete withdrawal of U.S. troops and economic and military aid, which would make all China a vacuum area, the decisions made constituted a kind of compromise between the two. They also represented a form of conciliation arrived at by the various groups within policy-making circles concerned with the matter—officials of the State, War, and Navy Departments as well as the President. The way the decision was made is significant. In view of the extremely inflamable situation in north China and Manchuria, General Wedemeyer, now back in Chungking, wanted a specific directive on the extent to which to involve U.S. troops, and he requested the War Department to inform the State Department of the seriousness of the situation. When the heads of the War, Navy, and State Departments threw the ball back to Wedemeyer, asking him to further clarify the situation regarding the Chinese government's capabilities to disarm the Japanese and take control in north China, the General replied that Chiang's forces did not have this capability, that his government was inefficient and often corrupt, and that U.S. assistance would be needed. He further stated that the United States could not avoid involvement in China's civil conflict if it attempted to give Chiang this assistance.

[3] Tang Tsou, *America's Failure in China, 1941–1950* (Chicago, 1963), pp. 324–332; Feis, pp. 377–387.

He awaited further word from Washington. Ultimately, after serious discussions in which Secretary of the Navy James Forrestal and Secretary of War Robert Patterson argued for all-out support to Chiang, and thus acceptance of the risks, it was decided that U.S. Marines should be kept in China, that the United States should continue to contemplate transferal of more Kuomintang armies to the north, that a truce should be arranged in those areas from which the Japanese had been removed, and that the United States should continue to work for an accommodation between Nationalist and Communist forces.[4]

Again, quite clearly the fundamental aspects of these decisions suggested that China's crisis was grave, that U.S. officials, though willing to keep the U.S. Marines there for the time being and to consider transporting additional Chinese troops, did not want to get deeply involved in a Chinese civil war. General Wedemeyer said it was impossible not to do so if American troops stayed and hoped to be at all effective in assisting the Nationalist government, and he was right; he wanted either to pull out or to have his directive changed so that he could really affect the situation.[5] This, Washington was not ready to do. In any event, the most significant point was that the decisions inferred that the need to get the CCP and Kuomintang together was greater than ever. To this end, it was again implied that U.S. aid could be used as both a club and a lure.

While these lines of policy were being hammered out in Washington, Secretary of State Byrnes and Secretary of War Patterson contemplated sending Hurley back to China to implement them. Patterson believed that it would be wise to have the U.S. Ambassador again visit Moscow on his way back to China, especially in view of the obstructionist tactics of the Soviet Union in Man-

---

[4] See James Forrestal, *The Forrestal Diaries*, Walter Millis, ed. (New York, 1951), pp. 108–109 and 110–112; Albert C. Wedemeyer, *Wedemeyer Reports!* (New York, 1958), appendix IV; Feis, pp. 404–405.

[5] *United States Relations with China*, pp. 131–132; *Forrestal Diaries*, pp. 110–111.

churia. Byrnes scotched the idea, stating that he should return as quickly as possible to Chungking. It is significant that there was no serious discussion of relieving Hurley, even though his "program" for peace in China depended on the cooperation of the Soviet Union, which now acted increasingly uncooperatively, and on diplomatic support of Chiang Kai-shek. In short, there was no diminution of confidence in Hurley, because it now seemed that he had forecast Russian intentions inaccurately; it seems clear that President Truman, Harry Hopkins, and Averell Harriman held a similar view after Hopkins' visit to Moscow in June. Russian actions in Manchuria and, indeed, on the broader question of policy toward the CCP, in the fall of 1945 represented opportunism of the first order, and even now it is difficult to establish patterns and consistency in their actions. Nor was there any special fear that because Hurley favored Chiang Kai-shek in his negotiations with the Communists that he would be unable to carry out the policy of support for the Nationalists conditioned on the effecting of a political settlement. The President and Byrnes were, in fact, anxious that Hurley resume his work.[6]

Moreover, for some time after Hurley's return from Chungking some considerable optimism prevailed, and there was little real reason to believe at that time that he had not done an adequate job in China. When he arrived in Washington, he had a letter from Chiang Kai-shek, whose "leadership" the administration continued to support, commending him highly to President Truman and strongly advocating his return. The Generalissimo, realizing that circumstances had placed the Ambassador firmly in his corner, said of Hurley, his "wise statesmanship and human qualities have won the respect and affection of the Chinese people who see in him a fitting symbol of America's foreign policy of fair play and justice. . . . I am looking forward to General Hurley's return to China as America's representative."[7] H. H. Kung wrote: "It is no exaggeration to say that seldom has a

[6] *Baltimore Sun*, Nov. 28, 1945; see also *Military Situation in Far East*, Part 4, pp. 2936–2937.

[7] Chiang Kai-shek to Truman, Sept. 18, 1945, Hurley Papers.

foreign diplomat in China so completely won the heart and respect of the Chinese leaders and people as has Ambassador Hurley."[8] Furthermore, in early October reports arrived in Washington of a very favorable trend in the CCP-Kuomintang negotiations. Dr. K. C. Wu, Minister of Information of the Chinese government, conveyed to Hurley through the U.S. Embassy word that the Communists had agreed to accept the government offer alloting them twenty divisions in the National army and that arrangements had been made to organize a political council of 37 members, representing all parties, which would consider and make recommendations on a draft constitution, the proper date for the convening of a peoples congress, and on a policy "for peaceful reconstruction." Shortly thereafter, on October 11, Chou En-lai stated that the only area in which CCP-Kuomintang agreement had not been reached was on the question of control of the liberated areas, especially Hopei, Shantung, and Chahar.[9]

Later, in mid-October, the U.S. Embassy informed Washington that it had learned that a new round of negotiations was to begin in Chungking relative to the Political Consultative Council, liberated areas, and the National Assembly. After the talks were completed the Communist delegates would return to Yenan to make a decision on the proposals and then in early November would return to Chungking to attend a Political Consultative Conference. U.S. officials in Chungking believed that the Communist official there "was definitely much more optimistic than he had previously been with respect to the likelihood of an eventual agreement between the Central Government and the Communists, and had expressed great satisfaction over the announcement in the press that Ambassador Hurley would shortly return to China."[10] Walter Robertson, Chargé d'Affaires of the U.S. Embassy, also informed Secretary Byrnes that everyone looked for-

[8] H. H. Kung to Truman, Sept. 18, 1945, *ibid.*

[9] *United States Relations with China,* pp. 107–108; Walter Robertson to the Secretary of State, Oct. 2, 1945, Hurley Papers.

[10] *United States Relations with China,* p. 109; Robertson to Hurley, Oct. 19, 1945, Hurley Papers.

ward to Hurley's return. He then wrote Hurley: "Chiang Kai-shek paid a tribute to you, saying that you were primarily responsible for the state in which discussions are now. Gratification over your return is also expressed by the Communists." [11] Meanwhile, issues of the *Baltimore Sun*, the *Washington Post*, and the *New York Times* hailed Hurley's previous efforts in China as masterful diplomacy and eagerly anticipated his resumption of his duties.[12]

Hurley, however, had other ideas; he wanted to resign. As early as August 25, he had drafted a letter to the Secretary of State, which he did not send, stating that he wanted to return to the United States, make his report, and then submit his resignation. Shortly after he arrived in Washington, on September 26, he began discussions with the Far Eastern Division of the State Department, with Under Secretary Dean Acheson and with officials of the War Department; on October 9 he visited with Secretary of State Byrnes. In his conversations with both Acheson and Byrnes, the Ambassador said that he would like to quit: his health was bad, he stated—although evidence seems to indicate that he was in better condition than he thought—and the job in China had worn him down; he had gotten the two sides together, but much was yet to be done, and a younger person could do it better.[13]

Besides the reasons mentioned to Acheson and Byrnes, Hurley had other reasons in early October. He thought he had done reasonably good work in China, and, like a pitcher with a five-run lead in the seventh inning, had nothing to lose and everything to gain if he were relieved; he wanted out while he was ahead. Also, as mentioned in an earlier chapter, because his financial position had slipped during the war years, he was anxious, again personally, to manage his business affairs. And he wanted to be with

[11] Robertson to the Secretary of State, Oct. 15, 1945; and Robertson to Hurley, Oct. 16, 1945, Hurley Papers.

[12] *Baltimore Sun*, Oct. 13, 1945; *New York Times*, Oct. 7 and 12, 1945; *Washington Post*, Oct. 13 and 21, 1945.

[13] Wedemeyer, p. 358; Office Diary, 1945; and Hurley to Truman, Aug. 25, 1945 (unsent), Hurley Papers.

his family once more. Moreover, there were some indications that if he did not resign he would be fired, or his influence would be reduced: in September and October he read newspaper speculations of his impending resignation—articles which he believed had been based on "official leaks" from Washington, probably from the State Department; he also learned that, despite his protests, his old "adversaries," George Atcheson and John Service were being sent, as earlier planned, to Tokyo to work as advisors to General MacArthur—thus it seemed to Hurley their views still had great currency in the State Department.

When Hurley first learned of the appointment of Atcheson and Service to the Far Eastern Commission, he urged Chiang to protest to the President on the grounds that it would be inimical to the best interests of China. He then drafted the message upon which the Generalissimo based a protest sent to Washington. In it, he indicated the belief that the Commission would have jurisdiction over all of Asia, including China as well as Japan, and that the two foreign service officers had supported the Communists and favored the overthrow of China's government; their appointment, if the Commission made policy regarding China, could further divide China and foster civil war.[14] Significantly, on this same matter, Walter Robertson wrote the Ambassador on September 27, stating that there was some indication that the Communists were dragging their feet, perhaps in the hope they might receive some sub rosa help from the Russians, and that U.S. policy might change. He then wrote: "We have good reason to believe that the Atcheson and Vincent [as Director of the Office of Far Eastern Affairs] appointments publicized in Chinese press gave them considerable encouragement that our policy might be changed." [15]

[14] Draft of message for Chiang Kai-shek prepared by Hurley, Sept. 16, 1945; see also Aide Memoire by the Chinese Ministry of Foreign Affairs, Sept. 19, 1945; and Robertson to Hurley, Sept. 27, 1945, Hurley Papers. Robertson told Hurley that the Generalissimo's message was "what you would have wished."

[15] Robertson to Hurley, Sept. 27, 1945, *ibid.*

Hurley also believed that the State Department had changed U.S.-Far Eastern policy, in its broader aspects, away from the anti-imperialist course charted by President Roosevelt. Secretary Byrnes refused to accept his arguments; he again assured the Ambassador of the complete support of the Department for his efforts in China, and urged him to take a rest and return to Chungking.[16]

Later, on October 13, Hurley conversed with the President, reiterating the reasons why he hoped to resign. Truman's response was to refuse to accept his resignation and to suggest that he have a good physical check-up at Walter Reed Hospital, take some time resting in the New Mexico sun, and then return to Washington; he would then have a completely different perspective on the whole matter.[17] Undoubtedly flattered by the President's expression of confidence and support, Hurley now began to have second thoughts about quitting. On October 13, Byrnes publicly announced that Hurley would return to Chungking.

Hurley's indecision persisted as he "took the cure" in New Mexico; he did not want to return to China, but he hated to refuse the President, who had made his case so strongly. On October 31, he revealed his more intimate feelings to businessman and friend Warren Grimes. He said he was not ill; he had "accumulated fatigue" and needed some rest. But even so, and even though the President and the Secretary of State wanted him to go back, he "was not anxious to return to China." "My desire," he said, "is to return to my own business. I am undergoing a struggle with . . . myself." "To return to China in my present condition," he continued, "might, perhaps, bring an end to my usefulness quickly." Hurley informed Grimes further that he wished to continue in public life, but that he thought, since he was sixty-two years of age and the war was now over, it would be much better if he devoted his time to business while he thought about different areas where he could be of service to his country.[18]

[16] *Baltimore Sun,* Nov. 28, 1945.
[17] *Military Situation in the Far East,* Part 4, p. 2936; Wedemeyer, p. 358.
[18] Hurley to Grimes, Oct. 31, 1945, Hurley Papers.

Yet most of the reports he received from Chungking in mid-October expressed optimism regarding the CCP-Kuomintang talks, if not always about the military picture; this heartened him and gave him cause to think that he might be able to resume his efforts successfully, without the mental and physical strain previously experienced. At the end of October, however, very disturbing news began to arrive from China which undoubtedly was instrumental in Hurley's ultimate decision. He heard of frequent and bloody clashes between Nationalist and Communist troops. As he wrote his friend Grimes: "Before I left I was of the opinion that we had reduced the strife in China to a conversational basis, by bringing the leaders together. The reports indicate that this is not true." [19] He then read a report sent from the U.S. Embassy on October 31, stating that although Dr. K. C. Wu, the government's Minister of Information, indicated optimism on the talks, Wang Ping-nan, a Communist representative in Chungking, informed U.S. officials that indeed no progress had been made. Wang further stated that it was the CCP view that the government was stalling for time while the United States assisted it in establishing control over areas already liberated by the Communists. The Communists resented the government position and the U.S. assistance in this endeavor. He also referred vaguely to the situation in Manchuria and implied that the Eighth Route Army was already there in some numbers and had made contact with the Russians.[20]

On November 4, Hurley received another report on the situation in which the Embassy indicated that the U.S. Military Attaché believed the threat of widespread civil war was increasing. Evidence of the gravity of the situation was the postponement of the beginning of the Political Consultative Conference while the two sides sought to arrange a truce. The Communists admitted that they were attacking government troops in areas they had liberated and were demanding, as a price for stopping this action,

[19] *Ibid.*
[20] *United States Relations with China*, p. 110; U.S. Embassy in Chungking to Secretary of State, Oct. 31, 1945, paraphrased in Hurley Papers.

that the Generalissimo's forces cease moving troops into north China. To the Embassy, the situation looked "almost hopeless." [21] This report had great impact with Hurley because it was sent in by Walter Robertson, whom he liked and trusted; the Ambassador must have been upset by the news from China.

Perhaps most distressing to Hurley, however, was word from Chungking about Russian activity in Manchuria, activity which revealed a callous disregard for their prior commitments. On October 31, a message was sent from Chungking stating the news that Wang Shih-chieh, the government's Minister of Foreign Affairs had received no cooperation from the Russians in his attempt to get Nationalist troops into Manchuria. Instead, the Russians were delaying their departure from the region, preventing the landing of Chiang's forces at the good ports in Manchuria, and allowing the Communists to take over. Moreover, they permitted CCP attacks on government troops as they attempted to advance northward and into Manchuria. Early in November, Everett Drumright, chief of the Chinese Division of the State Department, informed Hurley of the obstructionist tactics of the Russians.[22] Then, on November 10, Robertson sent another telegram to Washington, a paraphrase of which was sent to Hurley on the 18th, in which he stated that K. C. Wu had informed him that clearly the Communists did not want to reach an agreement and that the Russians were to blame because they had assisted and were assisting the Communists in north China and Manchuria.[23]

At about the same time he read Robertson's report of November 10, Hurley read another message from Chungking which was of great importance. It stated that on October 30 the government had made a six-point proposal to the Communists suggesting that: both sides refrain from attacking the other; the Com-

---

[21] *United States Relations with China,* p. 110.

[22] U.S. Embassy in Chungking to Secretary of State, Oct. 31, 1945, paraphrased in Hurley Papers.

[23] Chargé d'Affaires Robertson to Secretary of State, Nov. 10, 1945, paraphrased in Hurley Papers.

munists remove their troops from along the railways which they were raiding—the railways in north China to be guarded by railway police—while the government would refrain from sending its troops to "those places"; the government would negotiate with the CCP if it found it necessary to move troops along key railways north of Peiping; the two sides would agree on the reorganization of the Communist's troops; and the People's Consultative Conference would be convened at once.[24] The Communist reply, Robertson stated, proved totally unacceptable to the government, and an impasse had been reached. At this point it must have appeared to any initiated observer that a CCP-government accommodation was no closer than it had been in November 1944 and that one of the reasons for the impasse, in view of the Communist's willingness to negotiate in earnest only a month before, was the action in Manchuria and north China of the Soviet Union. Since Hurley's efforts in China were based largely on Soviet assurances, these facts had to give him pause.

In any event, it seems clear that, upon reading these last two messages from Chungking, Hurley gave up hope of seeing any early unification of forces in China and at this juncture again leaned heavily toward resigning. As events transpired, simultaneous to these ominous reports from Chungking, the U.S. Ambassador began reading increasingly critical reports of his role in China. On October 30 and November 2, the *New York Herald Tribune* criticized him for what it alleged was his full-scale support of the Generalissimo, which he had carried out independent of directives from Washington. Other papers, among them the *Detroit News* and the *Buffalo Evening News,* also voiced critical opinions. Then he read articles in the *Herald Tribune* and the *Washington Post* in which it was reported that William Z. Foster, Communist leader in the United States, said in testimony before the House Un-American Activities Committee that he should be removed.[25] Never thickskinned on the matter of personal criti-

24 *United States Relations with China,* p. 111.
25 *Detroit News,* Nov. 7, 1945; *Buffalo Evening News,* Nov. 3, 1945; *New*

cism, Hurley was stung deeply by the articles; as he reflected on the situation in China, he made up his mind. He definitely would resign, removing himself from the China mess; on November 20, he began drafting his letter of resignation.

While the Ambassador was penning his letter to the President, the lines of American policy discussed above were being sketched by the Secretaries of State, War, and Navy, with a view toward stemming the tide in China. They planned on having Hurley implement the policy. However, on November 26, at nine-fifteen A.M., Hurley arrived at Byrnes' office and handed him an envelope containing his letter of resignation. He informed the Secretary that he had heard from Wang Shih-chieh that Byrnes had told him that since the war was over his position would be given to a "deserving Democrat," that he had heard through a U.N. figure that the administration was going to relieve him; he also believed that if he returned to China he would not get the support he needed from the State Department because of differences he had had earlier with individual members of the Department. And related to this, he had just read items from his own reports in the *Chicago Sun* and in the *Daily Worker* (sent him incidentally by Alfred Kohlberg, the indomitable and irrepressible China "lobbyist" whom Hurley did not yet know) which could only have appeared through the connivance of a State Department official.[26]

During the lengthy discussion that followed, the Secretary again refused to accept the resignation, said that he would not give it to the President, told Hurley he would check on his charges, but to be assured he would have the full support of him-

---

York Herald Tribune, Oct. 30, 1945, Nov. 2, 1945, and Nov. 9, 1945; and the *Washington Post*, Nov. 9, 1945. Interestingly, Hurley kept these articles in a clipping book. Particularly did he consider the *Herald-Tribune* criticism significant. In fact, he noted, and kept in his clipping book, a report that the *Herald-Tribune* article of Oct. 30 was reprinted in *Izvestia*.

[26] *Military Situation in the Far East*, Part 4, pp. 2936–2937; *Baltimore Sun*, Nov. 28, 1945.

self, the Department, and the President if he returned to China, and asked the Ambassador to read over the statements of policy then being formulated in the State Department. Hurley then departed, leaving his letter with the Secretary, while he read the items given him by Byrnes. He returned in the afternoon of the 26th, agreed with the Secretary that there had been "no change in policy," and after receiving renewed assurances of support from Byrnes, agreed to return to Chungking as requested—after he delivered a scheduled speech to the National Press Club on the 28th.[27]

On November 27th, Hurley arose, talked on the telephone with Secretary Forrestal about China policy, and went to his office whence he called Byrnes again to discuss with him arrangements relative to his flight back to China. He then began reading the evening paper of the 26th, only to discover in it a report of a speech given in the House of Representatives by Congressman Hugh DeLacy of Washington. The speech was critical of Hurley for his "full-scale" support of the "reactionary" regime of Chiang Kai-shek, stating that U.S. assistance was used to stifle the legitimate democratic aspirations of the Chinese people, and alleged that the Hurley-Wedemeyer program constituted U.S. imperialism and was leading China to civil war. DeLacy further charged that Hurley was responsible for the resignation of Ambassador Clarence Gauss and the "reversal" of President Roosevelt's policies as well as the "purging" of able Chinese hands. Hurley had previously been informed about DeLacy in a letter by one of the Congressman's constituents, a man who wrote that DeLacy was a ne'er-do-well, a former relief recipient, and a former writer for a Communist-leaning newspaper in Seattle, *The New World,* and either a Communist himself or a sympathizer.[28]

Always very sensitive to such criticism, and extremely suspici-

---

[27] *Baltimore Sun,* Nov. 28, 1945.

[28] U.S. Congress, *Congressional Record,* 79th Congress, 1st session, Nov. 26, 1945, pp. 10993–10995; C. Montgomery to Hurley, Nov. 8, 1945, Hurley Papers.

ous about the source of DeLacy's views because of what he had heard about him and in view of his vague knowledge of what had transpired in the *Amerasia* affair, Hurley reacted strongly. He concluded that the speech could only have been based on privileged, confidential, and as yet unpublished information, probably furnished by someone in the State Department with the intention of undermining his effectiveness in China. Whether the speech was based on any secret source is doubtful; DeLacy said later it was not, that he had used only material garnered from the wire services and U.S. news correspondents, and, in retrospect, it seems that he was probably entirely candid, that he could have written such a speech only from the above sources. If one reads the speech carefully, however, it becomes apparent that DeLacy, in his observations about U.S. actions in north China and Manchuria and about the CCP, was either extraordinarily naive or was simply assuming the line then emanating from Moscow, or both. But this clearly does not mean conspiracy, at least not conspiracy originating in the China Affairs Division.[29] Actually, the point is irrelevant to the Ambassador's resignation in any case; what is important is what Hurley thought. And he now firmly believed that notwithstanding Byrnes' assurances to the contrary, this speech was evidence that he would not have Departmental support.

Determined now to go ahead with his earlier plans, the Ambassador called various press headquarters in Washington and at 12:30 P.M. released a statement that he had prepared prior to his latest encounter with the Secretary of State. Addressed to the President, Hurley's letter began with a brief statement of resignation and a review of his previous wartime experience in the Pacific, the Middle East, and in China; then it went on to an accounting of the "reasons" for the action. Hurley said that he had always found objectives clearly defined in the higher echelon of policy-

[29] *Washington Star*, Nov. 28, 1945.

making—but frequently a huge discrepancy between stated objectives and their actual implementation. In the case of China, the principles of the Atlantic Charter were supposed to govern policy, but, in his view, at the level of implementation, the United States was supporting "Communism and imperialism"; he had tried to harmonize relations between various conflicting groups in China, but "the professional foreign service men sided with the Chinese Communist armed party and the imperialist bloc of nations whose policy it was to keep China divided against herself." Major opposition to Hurley's efforts, he said, came from the "career diplomats in the Embassy at Chungking and Far Eastern Division of the State Department." In spite of his recommendations that these men be relieved, they had been retained in supervisory positions and as advisers to General MacArthur in Japan.

The problem with American foreign policy, Hurley continued, was that although principles were established they were not carried out, because policy officials were always "divided against themselves." An example of this was rhetorical support during the war to the Atlantic Charter and, at the same time, support for the imperialist bloc. Simultaneously, "a considerable section of our State Department is endeavoring to support Communism generally as well as specifically in China." Since the discrepancy was mainly the result of State Department action, there should be "a complete reorganization of our policy-making machinery beginning at the lower official levels." Not only were U.S. principles not upheld, but American material interests also suffered: "America has been excluded economically from every part of the world controlled by colonial imperialism and Communist imperialism."

Interspersed with the indictment of America's failures chargeable to the Foreign Service, Hurley included seemingly irrational comments to the effect that the weakness of U.S. foreign policy "backed us into two world wars," that "there is a third world war in the making" and that "we are permitting ourselves to be sucked into a power bloc on the side of colonial imperialism against

Communist imperialism." He then stated that he opposed both; he still was for democracy and free enterprise.[30]

Irrational as it may seem, particularly the latter comments about power blocs, the statement indeed represents a fairly accurate accounting of Hurley's reasons for resigning and, though confusedly written, it is not so puzzling when one understands his thinking. His charge that a discrepancy existed in policy making was based on his correspondence on the question of U.S. action toward Hong Kong and Southeast Asia which revealed that Washington would not pursue the course of action charted by Roosevelt. His view that the United States was supporting the colonial imperialists was predicated on knowledge of support for the French, Dutch, and British, whom he personally despised, in their re-establishment of colonial control; the United States had already squandered a large portion of its resources on these nations, especially the latter, and he wished it stopped. Although Hurley was not a student of international relations or even a professional diplomat with an ear acutely attuned to world affairs, it might be noted that his statement about "being sucked into a power bloc on the side of colonial imperialism against Communist imperialism" was not so unsophisticated as it seemed on the surface; in fact, again if we keep in mind his Southeast Asia frame of reference, it has the ring of foresight. Certainly events of the postwar years were to prove that in the case of Indochina, much to its later chagrin, the United States did the very thing that Hurley feared. In the case of the charges against the Foreign Service officers, Hurley gave full vent to his wrath built up over the previous twelve months. On this matter and in the wording of the resignation, his powerful ego played a very important part. Clearly he recognized that, though he seemed to come close, he had not succeeded in unifying the forces in China; in November the situation grew apparently hopeless after some very hopeful signs in October. In view of his previous troubles with the officers, he

[30] Hurley's letter of resignation was published in *United States Relations with China*, pp. 581-584.

had no nagging doubts about where the blame should lie; he lashed out at the only visible opponents.

Why Hurley chose to exit in such a dramatic manner, however, is a question which elicits speculation. Part of the answer probably lies in his personality—he had "exploded" many times before—and in his personal desire for public attention. He also may have wanted to call public attention to the problem of China. Indeed, in writing Chiang Kai-shek of his action, he stated that he "hesitated long before taking drastic action but, in my opinion, it was the only way in which we could force public definition and approval of the American policy that we had upheld in China." He further stated that he resented the organized defamation that the policy he had followed was his own and not American policy, and that it continued "until the day I took action." Now, he said, perhaps General Marshall could succeed without opposition from other U.S. officials.[31] Notwithstanding the above remarks, one cannot escape the possibility that he may have been thinking the big splash would help him politically—either as a contender for a spot on the Republican ticket in 1948, or more immediately, in the race for a Senate seat in New Mexico in 1946. Certainly his remarks to Warren Grimes revealed that he planned to continue in public service, in some capacity.

To say that leading officials of the administration were shocked, stunned, and incensed is to understate the reaction to Hurley's announcement. Secretary Byrnes, who had only shortly before received assent from Hurley on going back to China, heard of it as he prepared to go to a Cabinet meeting and was "very surprised." President Truman heard it at about the same time, was "astonished," and considered the action "an inexplicable about-face."[32] He reveals in his memoirs that, with or without the letter of resignation, Hurley would have been fired. That the matter would be the major item on the agenda of that afternoon's

[31] Hurley to Chiang Kai-shek, Dec. 8, 1945, Hurley Papers.
[32] Harry S. Truman, *Memoirs: Vol. II, Years of Trial and Hope* (New York, 1958), p. 66; *Baltimore Sun*, Nov. 28, 1945.

Cabinet meeting goes without saying; in fact, the entire session was devoted to the statement and to a possible replacement for Hurley. At length, the President decided, pursuant to a recommendation by Secretary of Agriculture Clinton Anderson, to ask General Marshall, who only recently had resigned as Chief of Staff to go to China. This would have the effect of taking the steam out of Hurley's announcement, at least in the press, and indicate to the Chinese the view of Washington as to the importance and seriousness of the China situation, while at the same time gaining the assistance of one of the U.S.'s best public servants. Marshall agreed and, after several rounds of conferences with the President and the Secretaries of State, War, Navy, and the Chiefs of Staff, departed for Chungking.[33]

Meanwhile, Hurley, who had warmed up with his announcement on the 27th, continued flinging charges. On November 28, in his address to the National Press Club he extolled his own efforts in China, saying that he had made great progress in bringing the Communists and the Chinese government together and that while he was there civil war was averted. Then he reiterated the charge that U.S. policy had been subverted by the Foreign Service officers either because they did not understand what the policy was or because they stood in opposition to it. These same officers, whom he had earlier removed from China, he repeated, were now his supervisors in Washington. Compounding the problem was the fact that while Stalin and Churchill gave him assurance that they supported American policy, British diplomats, bent on imperialistic goals, changed official British policy in a manner not unlike the way in which the U.S. officers altered American policy! [34]

Such dramatic charges naturally evoked strong comment from the press, thus stirring public interest in the Hurley resignation. In a critical vein, the *New York Tribune* and the *New York Times*, respectively, ran editorials to the effect that Hurley's con-

33 Truman, *Years of Trial and Hope,* p. 66; *Forrestal Diaries,* p. 113.
34 Speech by Hurley to National Press Club, Nov. 28, 1945, Hurley Papers.

fused and ambiguous statements tended to prove that he mis-
understood policy as it was formulated in Washington, that he
lacked insight into the situation in China, and that he was impul-
sive and given to impetuous and irrational behavior. Later, the
St. Louis Post Dispatch deplored Hurley's reckless charges as
irresponsible and even un-American. Some, like the Washington
Post and Evening Star were somewhat favorable to Hurley but
demanded an investigation. Numerous other papers across the
country inclined toward defense of the former ambassador and
advocated investigation of the State Department, but clearly part
of the more influential press questioned the integrity of his remarks.[35]

A strong sentiment for investigation of Hurley's remarks was
obviously generated. As a consequence, Congress in early December began making arrangements for a full-scale inquiry. Senator
Kenneth Wherry introduced a resolution calling for the Foreign
Relations Committee to conduct hearings on the charges, and, on
December 5, hearings began; Hurley had another forum. As the
first witness, he began his testimony with a passionate reiteration
of his previous statements, embellished here and there as the
passage of time would have it. He again alleged existence of a
"pro-Communist, pro-imperialist" faction in the State Department which sabotaged American policy in China by advocating
arming the Communists and which "leaked" important information to the press. He singled out George Atcheson, John Service,
John Carter Vincent, John Davies, Fulton Freeman (former third
Secretary of the U.S. Embassy in Chungking), John K. Emmerson
(formerly with the U.S. Embassy in Chungking and then assigned
to the office of the Political Advisor to General MacArthur), and
Arthur Ringwalt (former Second Secretary in Chungking). He
also said that he had earlier called for a strong public statement

[35] See New York Tribune, Nov. 28, 1945; New York Times, Nov. 28, 1945;
St. Louis Post Dispatch, Nov. 28, 1945; Washington Post, Nov. 28, 1945;
Washington Evening Star, Nov. 28, 1945; Detroit Free Press, Nov. 29, 1945;
Newark Star-Ledger, Nov. 28, 1945; and Indianapolis Times, Nov. 28, 1945.

of U.S. policy so everyone would know what it was; he still believed such a course wise and prudent. On this point, and on many others, he clashed angrily with the chairman of the Committee, Tom Connally; his face reddened, and he repeatedly roared at the senator in response to questions. To reinforce his testimony, Hurley also presented the Foreign Relations Committee with a list of thirteen documents, then still classified, which he alleged would prove his case against the State Department.[36] Among these papers were some of his own reports and those of Atcheson, Davies, and Service, many of which contained pungent comment by the Foreign Service officers on the situation in China and did indeed point up differences between themselves and the Ambassador. When the State Department granted access to these to the Committee but refused to make them public for the obvious reason that they would have been extremely embarrassing in view of continuing negotiations in China, Hurley again saw a conspiracy—an attempt to put him at a disadvantage and to discredit him.

Curiously enough, Hurley, as indicated in his testimony, was so busy hunting conspiracies that he blamed everyone for the failure in China but the one party largely responsible for the changed situation in November, the Soviet Union. He informed the committee correctly that the Soviets and the Chinese Communists were vastly different and, in his view, had different goals for China. Then, "Marshal Stalin and Commisar Molotov had been telling me, and throughout the entire period of the vicissitudes through which we passed so far as I know they have kept their word to me, that . . . Russia . . . does not recognize the Chinese armed Communist Party as Communists at all. Russia does not desire civil war in China."[37] Continuing, Hurley stated,

---

[36] Statement by Hurley to the Foreign Relations Committee, Dec. 5, 1945, and unpublished copy of Investigation of Far Eastern Policy, U.S. Senate Committee on Foreign Relations, Dec. 5, 6, 7, 10, 1945, Box 104, Hurley Papers; *San Francisco Chronicle*, Dec. 6, 1945; *Los Angeles Herald Express*, Dec. 6, 1945.

[37] *Military Situation in the Far East*, Part 4, p. 2895; Hurley testimony before Senate Foreign Relations Committee, Dec. 6, 1945, Hurley Papers.

"I have read that the Soviet Union has transgressed certain matters that involve the territorial integrity and the independent sovereignty of China, but frankly I have no evidence that would convince me that that is true. I believe that the United States and Russia are still together on policy in China." [38]

Since it is clear that Hurley did have the Embassy reports of November, spelling out Russian activity in Manchuria and thus did have word of their transgressing of China's territorial integrity from a trusted friend—and he admitted in the testimony the reading of these—his comments are indeed puzzling. To recapitulate, we know that he had as reliable information as he could have wanted on the situation; and there is no reason to believe he regarded it as inaccurate at the time. Only a person completely ignorant of events would fail to see the ominous consequences to negotiations posed by an aggressive Russian policy, either in arming the CCP or in denying the government access to strategic positions in north China; all this Hurley well knew. In a word, it appears that Hurley was less than candid with the committee, but more importantly, with himself. Why he would engage in this self-deception is difficult to assess, but probably the explanation lies in his over-reliance and trust in personal relationships, which characterized his career. He realized Russia's recent activity threatened the success of the U.S. program in China, and this surely was a factor in his resignation, but his personal contacts with Stalin, the importance and warmth of which, incidentally, he vastly overestimated, and the repeated assurances from the Russian dictator would not permit him to believe that Stalin had deliberately deceived him. So the Russians were not to blame, nor was the philosophical position of the CCP, nor the instransigence of the Kuomintang; American and British professional diplomats were.

After Hurley had testified, Secretary Byrnes had his innings. In his presentation he informed the committee of the policy only

[38] *Ibid.*

recently worked out—that the United States would continue to assist the Chinese government in disarming the Japanese but would avoid involvement in China's civil strife; her internal affairs would have to be resolved without the interference of the United States. The United States continued to support the idea of a united, democratic, and stable China, but insuring these conditions was largely a Chinese responsibility. Byrnes also defended the action of the Foreign Service officers in China, whose reports were included in the thirteen documents Hurley presented, stating that it was absolutely essential to allow the officers to express their honest judgment on policy and on political conditions in the countries to which they were assigned. Relative to the allegation that the officers Hurley had had removed from China were placed in new and important positions, the Secretary stated that they were being used and would continue to be used primarily because they were Far Eastern specialists, a rare breed at that time. In the case of Service and Atcheson and their reports of February 28, 1945, and October 10, 1945, there was no disloyalty to the Ambassador, only difference of opinion. Moreover, charges that they had been disloyal to the United States or that other departmental personnel had leaked important information to the American press in an attempt to discredit Hurley were unsubstantiated but were being investigated by the legal adviser to the State Department. (The legal adviser, Green H. Hackworth, submitted a memorandum on March 1, 1946, stating that he found no evidence to support Hurley's allegation.) Byrnes also parried the committee's questions about an agreement at Yalta regarding China, as those provisions were as yet veiled in secrecy.[39]

With the conclusion of Byrnes' testimony, the Foreign Relations Committee decided that further hearings would be held in private executive session. To this, Hurley, who hoped to get as broad publicity for his views as possible and who was now

---

[39] Statement of the Secretary of State before the Senate Foreign Relations Committee, Dec. 7, 1945, Hurley Papers; *Washington Star*, Dec. 7, 1945.

hammering on the evils of secrecy in U.S. diplomacy, would not agree. The result was that the hearings came to an early end, with the credibility of the former Ambassador, whose highly emotional and vague charges against career officers of the State Department remained unsubstantiated, in severe question. Unfortunately, as will be shown, Hurley's activities over the eighteen years that followed were to call it into even greater question, to obscure his work, and to complicate the dispassionate appraisal of his career.

Meanwhile, events in China furnished the backdrop against which Hurley's comments in the late forties and early fifties gained some currency. As Hurley's replacement, General Marshall undertook his mission to China and arrived on December 20, carrying with him plans to effect a "strong, united and democratic" China; his job was to arrange a CCP-government truce and to work out a mode of political unification intended to sustain the current government of Chiang Kai-shek as the basic political unit. On January 10, Marshall got officials of the two sides temporarily to stop fighting, thus effecting a truce which was supervised by three-man teams placed in the areas of greatest conflict. He also applauded the decision agreed to by both sides to convene and broaden the base of the Political Consultative Conference, which met from January 10 through 31, to include all political factions, thereby paving the way for a coalition and constitutional government. Later, in February, Marshall assisted in working out an agreement under which the Communist armies were to be integrated into the national army. All this constituted a hopeful start.

Very soon thereafter, however, fighting began anew, and while Marshall was back in the United States arranging a loan and other aid for the Chinese Government, the entire unification arrangement began to crumble; both politically and militarily each side sought the advantage. Leading Kuomintang officials opposed any military reorganization which might weaken their power and influence and sought to sabotage any political accommodations with them through the Political Consultative Conference. Communist forces, in violation of the cease-fire, occupied additional areas in Manchuria, including on April 18, Changchun. Chiang responded with a full-scale attack on the Communists. Though another truce was arranged in June, it proved only temporary. The Generalissimo from the end of June forward was bent on a military victory over the CCP. The Communists continued to fight while seeking a negotiated settlement on their own terms. Despite pressures, including the embargoing of arms and ammunition, attempted by Marshall on the Chinese government, Chiang confidently continued his drive, while the Communists, themselves confident of ultimate victory, remained intransigent and also continued the fight. By the end of 1946, it was apparent that the Generalissimo's regime continued unreformed, that liberals within China did not have sufficient influence to establish a new government, and that unless something drastic occurred, the situation would further deteriorate. Disgusted with both sides, in December, Marshall returned to the United States; the American effort at mediating the conflict promptly ceased. Upon his return to the United States Marshall became Secretary of State and began, shortly thereafter, to withdraw American forces from China.

As events moved along in China, the so-called "China bloc" in Congress, comprised of conservative Republicans like Senator Styles Bridges and Representatives Walter Judd and John Vorys began to publicize the situation, while fighting for more economic and military aid to Chiang. They achieved only moderate success in the latter, because the administration, after the end of the Marshall mission, came to the conclusion that not only should the United States withdraw from China, but American assistance would not really change things there very much. Constant discussion of the issue, however, did serve to keep it before the American public, which never understood the complexities of the problem, thereby complicating the task of withdrawal. Hurley's charges upon resigning and his subsequent statements, like those he made about the "White Paper," about Yalta, and about the Foreign Service officers, aided in the publicity campaign, though Hurley himself appears never to have focused on specific items with a view to pressuring the administration toward a particular policy. Meanwhile the administration played the game as discreetly as it could by not publically announcing its intentions, and, as a gesture to the "bloc," especially to Walter Judd, agreed in 1947 to send General Wedemeyer to China.

Subsequently, in the summer of 1947, General Albert Wedemeyer was dispatched to China on a mission designed to gather facts and to impress upon the Chinese the need to effect reform in order to receive additional American aid. After a month spent touring China, Wedemeyer observed for the benefit of government officials, that political and economic reform to end inefficiency, nepotism, and repression was a necessity and that the National government could not defeat the Communists through military action alone; he also inferred that U.S. economic assistance would continue only on the condition that these changes were made. Chiang remained undaunted by these remarks. Nevertheless, Wedemeyer, who deeply feared the CCP and the Soviet threat in China, advised large-scale economic assistance to the Chinese government extending over a five-year period and the stationing of a 10,000 man U.S. military advisory force there. Because the administration had already made an economic commitment to Europe, because of the fear that such massive aid to China would do little good in view of the failure on the part of the government to bring reform and would only involve the United States further in China's civil war, and because of the previous reduction in American forces, Wedemeyer's recommendations were rejected, and his report suppressed. Despite the granting of limited assistance to China following the Wedemeyer mission—assistance which was provided in large measure as a political move to insure Congressional support of economic programs for Europe, yet avoid broadening U.S. commitments in China—the situation in China rapidly worsened as the Communists clearly began to win militarily. Eventually, in December 1949, the government was driven ignominiously off the mainland to Taiwan.

Because of attitudes in the United States, disillusionment arising out of the China situation was probably inevitable. Though American policy makers had never at any time in the twentieth century assumed extraordinary responsibility for China, missionaries in China and other people with experience there fostered the myth that the Open Door, in its statement of an ideal in behalf of China's territorial and administrative integrity, made China America's ward. When the Communists won their victory, some of those who saw China in a paternalistic fashion naturally believed the "ward" had rejected the "father," while many blamed the "father" for the loss of a "son." Moreover, President Roosevelt during World War II elevated China to the level of importance for its usefulness in winning the war and to a world status which it did not in fact occupy. While the President did come to realize the lessened importance of China's military contributions, he did not then reduce his rhetoric or significantly alter the American diplomatic effort in China and thus added to the illusions about that country.

The Marshall and Wedemeyer missions, we can now see, tended to dramatize the American failure to "save" China. In 1945 events were moving inexorably toward a showdown between the Kuomintang and the Communists, the outcome of which in retrospect it seems unlikely the United States, with the options available, could have changed. This was all the more true in 1947. Though it was not so apparent at the time, such diplomatic missions, which from the start had an overwhelming chance of failure, would probably have been better unsent because of the effect they would create in failing. Moreover, the suppression of Wedemeyer's recommendations and their subsequent revelation, when the American people were sustained by some hope for the success of his mission, added fuel to the attacks on administration policy. As it turned out, both the missions contributed impetus to acrimonious post-mortems in the United States, debates which were perhaps the more inevitable because attitudes on the China question to a certain extent paralleled differences in point of view on fundamental economic and social questions. Many Republicans and conservative Democrats saw New Deal foreign policy as an extension of the "disastrous" domestic program; others, more pragmatic, whose views of the China matter were at best ambiguous, simply sought to embarrass the administration. In any case, leading Republicans, anxious for a victory in 1948 after a highly successful congressional election in 1946, took up the cry of Democratic neglect of China, urging that more economic and military assistance—though not more troops—be sent to that country. Fed by those with a personal interest in the China "tangle," this criticism soon mushroomed into charges of Democratic betrayal of America's loyal Asian ally.

# XII

## Politics of Frustration
## and Revenge

Immediately following his resignation and his appearance before the Senate Foreign Relations Committee, Hurley was inundated with letters commending him for his action. Moderate critics of New Deal domestic and foreign policy vented their pent-up frustrations by sending congratulatory messages to the former ambassador. Right-wing groups saw in his action proof of their paranoic suspicions, thought of him as an obvious spokesman for their views, and sought to win him to their side. The latter misinterpreted his remarks and obviously did not sufficiently understand the events in China or the Hurley personality to know the basis of them. But it did not matter. Hurley associated himself with members of this group, at first because his anger prevented him from delineating the differences between their views and his, because they flattered him in their communications and, finally, because in view of his intemperate behavior, there was nowhere else to go. In addition, political currents in the United States between 1945 and 1953, which he had a hand in generating, helped sweep him farther to the right.

The period between 1945 and 1953 brought developments both in American foreign relations and in American domestic life which can only be described as cataclysmic. The United States officially abandoned its traditional peacetime isolationism and assumed massive responsibility for preserving world peace. But, as became very clear, the possession of considerable military power, including the monopoly (until 1949) of atomic weapons, did not bring instant success in promoting American foreign policy goals;

in short, there were many world problems which obviously were beyond the competence of the United States to solve. For many, whose expectations were great and who came to assume the omnipotence of the United States, this was hard to grasp. There were also countless numbers of Americans who were impatient with wartime restrictions and economic sacrifices and who looked with suspicion on governmental intrusion in their affairs. The result was that, as world problems multiplied, internal frustrations accumulated, finally manifesting themselves in two ways: in a kind of conservatism which castigated all New Deal and Fair Deal programs, foreign and domestic, and, more vehemently, in a wave of anti-Communist hysteria comparable to the post-World War I Red Scare.

Several specific factors triggered the hysteria of the forties and early fifties, not the least of which was the revelation of Communist infiltration of American government positions. Investigations conducted in 1945 and 1946 indicated numerous Communists in government employ. In March 1945, the *Amerasia Case* occurred. Philip Jaffe, editor of *Amerasia* magazine a monthly Communist-sponsored sheet favorable to the Communists in China, was arrested and convicted on evidence that he had illegally procured American diplomatic documents from individuals in positions of authority. Also implicated, though later cleared of anything other than bad judgment for having contact with Jaffe, was John Service. Between 1947 and 1951, several hundred government employees were dismissed as loyalty risks. In 1948, Whittaker Chambers accused Alger Hiss, a bright and highly respected State Department official of being a Communist and in fact a Soviet agent, who in the thirties had engaged in important espionage work. Hiss denied the allegations, and Chambers came back with "proof." Hiss was then tried for perjury. The ultimate result was his conviction in January 1950. In 1949, Judith Coplan, an employee of the Justice Department, was convicted of giving secrets to a Russian agent. In February of 1950, Dr. Klaus Fuchs, a physicist and British subject who had worked on the atomic bomb, confessed to having given virtually complete information on the bomb to the Soviet Union.

These facts frightened and deeply troubled the American people. World problems, among them Russian domination of eastern Europe, Soviet intransigence in the United Nations, her development of the atomic bomb, attempts to control the eastern Mediterranean, the Communist victory in China, and, finally, the outbreak of the Korean War in 1950, added to and deeply intensified these fears. These developments also convinced many that, in view of the greatness of American power, only the disloyalty of a vast number of officials could produce Communist advance of such threatening proportions. Capitalizing on this sentiment and twisting and molding it for his own purposes was Senator Joseph McCarthy of Wisconsin. In need of an issue to get himself re-elected in 1952, this vulgar and unprincipled small-town bully seized on the idea of an internal Communist threat and rode it until he was discredited by his own Senate colleagues in 1954. After his initial salvo in Wheeling, West Virginia, where he announced that he would expose some two hundred and five Communists in the State Department, he went on, through innuendo and vicious accusation to impugn the loyalty of countless Americans in and out of government. He also gave impetus to one of the most pervasive moods of intolerance ever seen in the United States. On domestic issues this intolerance was apt to sanction labeling as "Communist" any political liberal who supported the New Deal or Fair Deal programs. On foreign policy matters it deemed the wartime and postwar "sellout" of American interests by Democratic administrations responsible for the broad range of complicated and perplexing world problems.

Taking advantage of a tailor-made issue, McCarthy, more specifically, concentrated much of his demagoguery on the American China policy. He quickly alleged that among the Communists he had "discovered" in the Department was a group of men who had shaped American policy in favor of the Chinese Communist party. The most prominent of these were John Carter Vincent, John S.

Service, and the "top espionage agent," Owen Lattimore, of Johns Hopkins University, an editor of *Pacific Affairs* and formerly of the office of War Information, all three of whom were subjected to a battery of reckless charges. That the Wisconsin senator never proved the men to be Communists, let alone espionage agents, or even that they had the determining influence on policy, was secondary to the emotion generated by the charges themselves. Again, Hurley's comments in December 1945 and the theme he reiterated so frequently thereafter laid the groundwork for this mischief.

While Hurley never actually joined the McCarthy camp in the strict sense nor condoned some of the senator's actions, he did his part in setting the national mood, and, through his support of the Republican right and through his own rhetoric developed in his political campaigns of 1946, 1948, and 1952, at least indirectly aided the senator's cause. Moreover, he "did not believe that we should be fighting anyone who is fighting communism."

The Hurley papers on this part of his career are chock-full of right-wing material, including an array of publications ranging from the *Monthly Journal of Spiritual Mobilization* and the *National Republic: A Monthly Magazine of Fundamental Americanism* to the antiflouridation newsletter; most of it was sent him by individuals who saw him as a crusader for their cause—which he, in fact, became, in a kind of spasmodic unplanned way. He carried on a brisk correspondence with Fulton Lewis, Jr., who became one of his best friends, and he appeared on Lewis' television program, and pinch-hit for Lewis occasionally in writing his newspaper column. He also had from George Sokolsky several lengthy letters which he answered warmly and enthusiastically, essentially agreeing with Sokolsky's point of view. He agreed with Walter Judd on China and exchanged letters with him on a number of occasions.

Others with whom he corresponded were Henry Regnery, the publisher, and Robert Welch, who made his fortune in the candy business and achieved fame as a founder of the John Birch Society. To Hurley's credit, however, when Welch wrote him asking for his endorsement of some material particularly critical, almost hysterical, on administration foreign policy, he refused. Also to his great credit, he refused to participate actively in the so-called China Lobby, although he gave the group some of its ammunition. Alfred Kohlberg, wealthy textile importer and former member of the Institute of Pacific Relations, was the group's guiding light who frequently told people: "I am the China Lobby." He wrote Hurley often and sent him all his publications; the Hurley papers contain large quantities of material to and from Kohlberg. Hurley first met Kohlberg in the winter of 1947, and they talked about John Carter Vincent, whose promotion to minister was about to be discussed by the Senate. Hurley apparently provided Kohlberg with some documents that he thought would either incriminate or embarrass Vincent, and informed Kohlberg that while in London in April 1945 he had been told that Vincent was "a secret Russian espionage agent." Kohlberg thanked Hurley for doing his part "to check the slimy traitors who are playing the game of our enemies" and mailed a memo to Senator Arthur Vandenberg of Michigan opposing Vincent's confirmation.[1] Hurley also partially agreed with Kohlberg, at least after 1949 and 1950, always wrote warm, friendly letters to him addressed "Dear Alfred," and on two occasions when people contacted him for material on China, he referred them to the "American China Policy Association." On the other hand, he did not become a formal member of the association, knew almost nothing about its "lobbying" tactics, and in fact did not intend to be a China "lobbyist." "I certainly have never participated in any lobbying," he wrote Kohlberg, "and I am not a member of any lobby. I have, of course condemned the American policy which needlessly lost China and its 450 million citizens as our allies." Later he refused to sign a statement of foreign policy worked out by Kohlberg's

[1] Kohlberg to Hurley, Mar. 14, 1947, and Kohlberg to Hurley, Apr. 10, 1947 (enclosure), Hurley Papers. Unless oherwise noted, the Hurley papers are the source of the references that follow.

group because he did not "have the time" to devote to all the issues advanced in the statement and because all such groups eventually were infiltrated by "undesirables." [2]

The obvious focal point of the "lobby" and of the other most venomous right-wing charges in the late forties and early fifties was America's "failure in China," which at the end of 1949 appeared complete. The charges included the indictment of "disloyal" American State Department officials for their "sellout" of China at Yalta, criticism of General Marshall's attempt to "impose" a coalition government on China, and the failure to provide military support in time of peril for "America's best friend in Asia," Chiang Kai-shek. Although his own efforts had constituted an attempt to achieve unification of China's political forces and in many respects paralleled those of his successor, Hurley added fuel to the fire; as he moved to the right, he gradually joined the chorus of criticism of the Truman-Marshall China policy.

For Hurley personally to attack Marshall, however, required convolutions of some great magnitude and an adroit explanation of his own role in China. Displaying a callous disregard for fact and a boldness perhaps born of opportunism, Hurley nonetheless proved capable of the task. He began informing people that what he had attempted to do was to unify China with a coalition government during the war but that his efforts had to be considered as separate and distinct from Marshall's postwar policies. In a speech to the Chicago Executives Club he stated: "After the War our government continued attempting to force a unification or coalition between the National Government and the Communist Armed Party. That policy which was right during the war was wrong after the war." [3] Later he said: "I resigned as Ambassador rather than stultify myself by going along with a Chinese policy, which I said at the time of my resignation made certain the communist conquest of our ally." [4] Concentrating on the *State De-*

---

[2] To Kohlberg, Mar. 2, 1954 and Oct. 21, 1955.

[3] Address, Oct. 7, 1949.

[4] Hurley to Edward Weeks of the *Atlantic Monthly,* Sept. 28, 1950.

*partment's United States Relations With China,* published in 1949 and known as the *White Paper,* he reiterated this point and said that the Department's effort to portray his own work toward a coalition government constituted an exercise "to disguise my true position in its effort to whitewash those subversives in the State Department who are responsible for the Communist conquest of China." [5] In the late fifties he wrote: "President Truman's press secretary, Charles Ross, has written that General Marshall was 'sent to China to do a specific job.' He did that job. The Yalta secret agreement was made effective. The anti-communist leader of China, America's greatest friend, Chiang Kai-shek was defeated. The Communist armed party was placed in control of China." Interestingly, Hurley then absolved Marshall of blame, saying he was still a general in the army and following orders. "He merely made effective the plan of the pro-communists in the American State Department. As a good soldier, he carried out orders—he did not make the policy." [6]

Hurley's comments were as disingenuous as they were interesting and were designed to obscure a feature of his own efforts that he came to consider unattractive. Obviously Hurley did work to achieve political unification of government and Communist forces in China during the war, and he continued his efforts after the war was over, though he never wished to "impose" a coalition government, which he took to mean forcing the Kuomintang to accept Communist terms. In any case, neither did Marshall. The intention of United States policy, during Marshall's stay in China as during Hurley's, was always to subordinate the Communists to Chiang Kai-shek. Hurley, for over a month after the war ended believed it would be easy to achieve unification or coalition along these lines, because of his belief that the Chinese Communist party would despair of aid from the Soviet Union; it is significant in light of his comments that he continued until he

[5] Hurley to Henry Luce, Aug. 12, 1949.

[6] Address to the New Mexico Chapter of the Public Relations Society of America, Albuquerque, July 31, 1959.

left for Washington to work hard to get a Chinese Communist party-Kuomintang accommodation. Conditions had changed by the time of Marshall's arrival, and a new set of circumstances, among which was greater CCP confidence and power, naturally forced him to employ different tactics than his predecessor, but with the same goal.

Perhaps the more incredible were the former ambassador's postwar fulminations about the Yalta agreement. As shown in an earlier chapter, Hurley was little troubled by the Yalta Far Eastern agreement when it was made; he had had a hand in implementing it, and even at one point had defended it in glowing terms to T. V. Soong; in short, he saw it for what it was, an apparently necessary wartime accommodation with the Soviet Union. Yet, when Yalta became synonymous in the minds of critics of the Roosevelt-Truman foreign policy with conspiracy and "sellout" of American principles, Hurley joined in the criticism. And like many who engage in deception, after a time he apparently came heartily to believe in what he was saying; certainly the emotion he displayed and the language with which he attacked the agreement indicate as much.

He usually began his charges by saying that America's traditional policy in China was to support individual liberty and self-government, a policy which was reaffirmed by President Roosevelt in the Atlantic Charter. The United States had always followed these fundamental principles, until Yalta, when it grossly violated them all. "Every principle for which we claimed we were fighting," he wrote, "was surrendered at Yalta and in subsequent conferences." [7] He also stated: "Our greatest friend in the world— the nation which desires so sincerely to emulate America by adopting our Bill of Rights and by establishing a government of the people, for the people, and by the people, was abandoned by the ally upon which it relied." [8] More than this, and inferring

[7] Address to the Central Labor Union Meeting in Albuquerque, Sept. 1, 1947.
[8] Address at Georgetown University, Mar. 3, 1949.

conspiracy, he wrote: "the student of history and of diplomacy must see in these secret agreements by the United States the blueprint which has been followed by the Communists in the conquest of China." [9]

Because the American commitment at Yalta was considered so unwise, in fact so nearly treasonous, Hurley found it necessary to ascribe blame for the decisions made there. Wishing to absolve Roosevelt, whom he liked personally and who was himself responsible for Hurley's wartime assignments, the former ambassador frequently stated that "President Roosevelt was a sick man at Yalta," implying, of course, that he did not have full command of his faculties. The way Hurley now saw it, the President was duped by his disloyal advisers. "The surrender of China to the Communists in the secret agreement of Yalta was engineered by the officials of the American State Department under the brilliant leadership of a young American, Alger Hiss." [10] State Department officials forced the President's hand. How it came about that American officials would urge such an agreement was a question which also drew Hurley's comment. On Fulton Lewis' radio program, he rejected as a "nebulous statement," Secretary of State Acheson's contention that the Yalta agreement was made in the hope of saving perhaps a million casualties in the event of an invasion of Japan's home islands; it was absurd to suggest such losses would occur or that the deal was made for that reason. The real reason was simply that "the pro-Communists in our State Department agreed to repeal the provision of the Atlantic Charter that provided that the nations 'seek no aggrandizement, territorial or other.' The pro-imperialists in our State Department wanted the colonial imperialists to be given the right to reconquer their colonial empires. . . . Our diplomats gave both Russia and Britain what they desired—the right to expand Communism and the right to re-establish imperialism." [11]

[9] Address at Georgetown University, Mar. 3, 1949.
[10] Hurley to Edward Weeks of the *Atlantic Monthly*, Sept. 28, 1950.
[11] Comment on Fulton Lewis's radio program, Jan. 9, 1950.

At Yalta and afterwards, American diplomats, in Hurley's view, abandoned the Atlantic Charter, a rejection of its ideals that he constantly bemoaned. In nearly every speech he gave—he must have done it one hundred times—he invoked in the same breath Patrick Henry's "Give me liberty or give me death"; Jefferson's words in the Declaration of Independence, "governments deriving their just powers from the consent of the governed"; excerpts from Wilson's fourteen points; and the language of the Atlantic Charter. The charter, Hurley maintained, represented the goals and ideals for which the United States told its soldiers it was fighting, but the Communists and imperialists and "pro-Communists" and "pro-imperialists" in the West, who opposed these ideals, undermined the charter. After Yalta, these officials secured a second major surrender of principles at the San Francisco Conference, where the United States allowed trusteeship arrangements to be established by the colonial powers instead of by the United Nations. Subsequent to San Francisco, U.S. policy makers, in Hurley's view, simply ignored the language of the charter, passing it off as little more than wartime rhetoric.

Responsible for the "sellout" of American principles was a whole coterie of Foreign Service officers, with some of whom he had previously crossed swords in China and in State Department offices in Washington, and whom he had named upon resigning. He could never be more than very vague, however, when it came to indicating exactly how they influenced a change in United States policy. Of those drawing the Hurley wrath, toward none was he more vehement than Dean Acheson, an assistant Secretary of State under Roosevelt, later Secretary under Truman, and the target of much of the hysterical right-wing ranting of the early fifties.

Hurley's personal hatred for Acheson went back to 1944 when he had the bitter row with the Assistant Secretary in the latter's office over comments by Acheson and Eugene Rostow that Hurley's Iranian plan was nothing but "messianic globaloney." This "stuck in Hurley's craw," and, when he resigned as Ambassador, he charged before the Senate hearing which followed that Acheson was responsible for "sabotaging" American policy in the Middle East. Acheson had slighted him and had defended Rostow's belittling of his efforts; Hurley, who was extremely sensitive, fought back with his highly emotional verbal shafts, which incidentally Acheson's testimony soon proved false. The Assistant Secretary indicated he had done nothing, and the facts sustained him, that could be construed as undermining United States Middle East policy and that the Hurley charges were based exclusively on the verbal exchange in Acheson's office.

Though it had no perceptible effect on Acheson, Hurley's attack continued. Joining with the extreme right of the Republican party and some moderates who sought desperately for anything to throw the Democratic party out of the presidency, Hurley blamed Truman's Secretary of State for much that was wrong in American life and all that was frustrating in American foreign policy. When the Alger Hiss case burst upon the scene, Hurley inferred a close official policy-making connection between the Secretary and this former lower-echelon State Department figure, a connection which did not exist but which Acheson's critics seemingly never bothered to explore. The Hiss case reinforced, at least in his own view and in the view of many who corresponded with him, Hurley's contention that State Department officials had long conspired to undermine American ideals; Secretary Acheson aided and abetted this effort. "Even after the conviction of Alger Hiss," Hurley wrote, "the Secretary of State continued to shield him and his associates." [12] On the broader question of U.S. diplomacy, Hurley wrote: "Secretary Acheson . . . is one of the authors, if not the prime mover in the whole system of secret sessions and secret commissions and secret agreements in which the principles of the Atlantic Charter have been surrendered by our diplomats." After the Secretary released the volume *United States Relations with China,* Hurley said that apparently the Secretary had re-

[12] Hurley to Edward Weeks, Sept. 28, 1950.

covered the "five or six suitcases full of State Department docu- ments that were given or sold to the pro-Communist *Amerasia* magazine." [13] Now he wanted to know why the Secretary of State refused to let the public see the "Amerasia papers" and why he did not provide "an explanation of the reasons why the officials arrested by the F.B.I. in the *Amerasia* case were released and white-washed by the State Department." [14]

Interestingly, as the Truman administration moved to thwart Communist expansion around the world, it cut the ground out from under those self-fashioned anti-Communist critics like Hur- ley. But this did not stop Hurley's attacks on Acheson, nor for that matter the more general assault on the administration; the critics merely shifted their front. In the case of his criticism of Acheson, Hurley, who agreed with the "get tough" policy, said that the Secretary was pro-British and pro-imperialist and only with the threat to the imperialist powers and their interests did he urge the United States to adopt a stronger policy.[15] With Hur- ley, Acheson simply could not win. The fact is the Secretary represented many of the things Hurley disliked and distrusted, and, indeed, two more disparate personalities one would have difficulty imagining: Acheson an Easterner, a scholar widely read, articulate, urbane, witty, and skilled in the gentlemanly "craft" of diplomacy; Hurley a Westerner, largely self-educated, poorly read, rough-hewn, flamboyant, and highly volatile. More than this, the two had already "had words." In short, Hurley's attitude, one must conclude, was based largely on personal feel- ings.

Hurley saved some venom for Averell Harriman as well. In characteristic prose, Hurley described Harriman as simply the product of propaganda put out by his own press corps "paid for by money earned by his father"; as a diplomatist he "came up short." "Averell Harriman," Hurley wrote, "was always looking

---

13 Hurley to Fulton Lewis, Jr., June 1, 1950.
14 Comment on White Paper, Aug. 7, 1949.
15 *Ibid.*

after Averell and promoting his own position. He never seemed to fully understand what those around him were talking about. He never understood the principles that we were trying to sustain in the second world war. He claims in his propaganda that he was close to Winston Churchill. Of course he did carry Winston Churchill's portmanteau for him on many occasions." [16] Later he said that Harriman was mentally unable to produce any kind of sophisticated document.

However, while maintaining that Harriman's mental capacity was decidedly deficient, Hurley pointed out that he did play a major role, along with Dean Acheson—though this inconsistency Hurley never explained—in engineering the "sellout" of American ideals. President Roosevelt, Hurley contended, had wanted him (Hurley) to meet with Stalin to arrange the agenda and make other preparations for the Yalta conference, but Harriman considered this his prerogative; he "did not want me to have anything to do with the Yalta conference," and, in fact, refused to inform Stalin of the President's wishes. "In other words, Harriman managed to keep the conference at Yalta in his own hands and in the hands of Mr. Harrimen's close friend, Alger Hiss." The President, Hurley said, on whom the hand of death already lay in February did not know what was done at Yalta. But, "Harriman knew, Alger Hiss knew." [17]

Regarding Harriman's wartime warning published in the White Paper that perhaps Hurley placed too much credence in Russian assurances of continued support of American policy in China, Hurley stated that of course Harriman could say this—and here one can see Hurley's postwar logic—for Harriman knew what few others knew, that he (Harriman) had already sold out to Russia at Yalta. In fact it was his work and the work of Alger Hiss and other State Department officials whereby they had in secret written the blueprint for the Communist conquest of China." [18] So much for Averell Harriman.

[16] Comments on Averell Harriman, n.d.
[17] *Ibid.*
[18] *Ibid.*

One could continue indefinitely the dreary detailing of the Hurley view of contemporary decision makers. The one thing that stands out, of course, in all of this is his attempt to expurgate his record, to vindicate his position, to glamorize himself, but more than this, to destroy the reputation of those who deprecated his diplomatic efforts, no matter how reckless he needed to be in the process. But at the same time there is little reason to believe that he had any nagging doubts about the rectitude of the course he took; though willing to "use" the issues discussed above, he was not unprincipled like Senator McCarthy. He really believed what he said about pro-Communist influence and the "sellout" of American ideals, and, if the charges he hurled seemed more hysterical and more personal as he grew older, it was because the process of repeating them over the years led to adornment and because he accepted without critical evaluation the "evidence" of others who spewed their poison into America's life stream.

Though obviously highly critical, often seeming hysterical in his verbal abuse, there were some elements of the Truman-Acheson foreign policy with which Hurley heartily agreed. He liked the "get tough" policy on which the Truman Doctrine, the Marshall Plan, the Berlin Airlift, and N.A.T.O. were based; he also strongly favored the President's action in intervening in Korea. And he agreed with the nonrecognition of Communist China and the support given to Chiang Kai-shek on Taiwan. He frequently stated in his speeches and in correspondence with friends that he believed "it was about time" the administration awakened to the threat of Communist imperialism, though he often suggested that it did so only after the threat to the interests of the older imperialist powers.

While agreeing with the philosophy of the stronger policy, at the same time he deprecated America's "give-away" practices. Beginning with Lend Lease, the United States, he believed, became the great "give away" nation by dispensing products paid for with taxpayer's money; in so doing it threatened completely to squander its resources and to undermine the American system of free enterprise. "We have reached the point," Hurley wrote, "where our State Department cannot find any solution for any world problem except by spending stupendous sums of American money and giving away American resources." [19] The basic weakness of the American position, he thought, was indicated by "the tendency in diplomacy to assume that the only way to obtain world cooperation is by the lavish giving away of American resources." [20]

Interestingly, however, Hurley claimed to have originated the Point Four program, President Truman's proposal for giving technical and economic assistance to poor and backward nations. The program actually had its birth, Hurley said, after the Teheran Conference when President Roosevelt asked him to develop a plan through which the United Nations could assist underdeveloped states; the result was his Iranian plan which called for the United States to furnish experts in various economic areas to these countries so as to help them to help themselves. The experts would be paid by the nations to which they were assigned to avoid further burdening the already overburdened taxpayer. If one examined the documents, Hurley stated, he would "conclude that the essence of the present Point Four program was devised by me and approved by President Roosevelt. The plan was sabotaged in the American State Department under the leadership of the present Secretary of State, Dean Acheson. The plan was revived almost in its entirety as soon as the give-away statesmen could devise a scheme whereby the plan could drain American production and billions of dollars from the American taxpayer." [21] A major difference between his plan and that of the administration, which Hurley emphasized, was this feature of its funding; Hurley did not want to spend American dollars.

While the philosophy behind Point Four was good, and in essence reflected his own earlier efforts, the reliance on American

[19] Address by Hurley, n.d.
[20] Address to the Lions Club at Albuquerque, Feb. 28, 1946.
[21] Hurley to Ray Tucker, Nov. 20, 1951.

economic power was bad. In fact, in Hurley's view, it reflected a trend in postwar American foreign policy: an attempt to use dollars and force and the atomic bomb to "overcome our mistakes in foreign policy and our surrender of fundamental principles." [22] A much wiser course would have been to work more closely with the United Nations.

Although he was often vague, even at times contradictory, as to what kind of international organization he envisioned, curiously enough, Hurley did not share the open hostility toward internationalism held by many in the Republican right. He concluded early that there was little point in continuing the isolationist rhetoric, for the Unted States could never again be isolationist. In his opinion, lasting peace could be achieved "only by collective action through an organization such as the United Nations." The United Nations provided the "instrumentality through which international law could be made and enforced for the achievement of world peace." The problem was that the United States failed at the San Francisco Conference to help evolve a workable charter for the United Nations; it then helped set up a Council of Foreign Ministers for the purpose of by-passing the world organization. After 1945 and 1946 the United States often continued to by-pass it. In Hurley's view, the result was that "since the death of President Roosevelt, we have been operating in a power bloc on the side of imperialism against communism." [23]

At the same time—as a matter of fact, in one of the same speeches in which he extolled the virtues of international organization—he revealed the contradiction in his position and a fuzzy notion of what the United Nations was all about. He said that it should be the American purpose to make the United Nations "a living, democratic organism, with legal and moral authority and physical strength to insure peace." Recognizing that this could involve the United States in war, as the isolationists argued, he

[22] Address at Georgetown University, Mar. 3, 1949; Address to Lions Club at Albuquerque, Feb. 28, 1946; Address, n.d.
[23] *Ibid.*

opined that perhaps it would, but "at least if it does, we will know why we are getting into war. Heretofore we have entered wars on the judgment of others." Hurley was not devoted to the concept of limited sovereignty; he stated further: "We should evolve a foreign policy that will hereforth give the United States a voice in determining the time, the place and conditions under which we will send materials and our men into combat. If we must fight wars, *let us* determine the cause for which we will fight." [24]

As a good part of the aforementioned would demonstrate, the record of Hurley's actions and intellectual processes between 1945 and 1955 is one of fits of emotion, inconsistency, and "non-think"; it is a period during which he had much to say on all topics, some of it partly of substance, some of it almost completely false; none of it of any effect on United States policy. It is important to examine this period of his life mainly to demonstrate his postwar ideas—in short, to fully explain Hurley. Nothing manifests more clearly his decline as a national figure than his political record in New Mexico between 1946 and 1952. And much of the foregoing material must be seen in the context of his political activity during those years.

Always interested in politics, but never a candidate in a national election, Hurley decided in 1946 to run for the Senate from New Mexico, in part to indulge his interest in remaining in a position of power and prestige, and in part to gain a national forum from which to disseminate his views. Accordingly, he sought and received the Republican nomination and ran against incumbent Democratic Senator Dennis Chavez, the candidate of labor and of the poor Mexican-Americans. Hurley lost, largely because he had not lived in New Mexico long enough to communicate sufficiently with New Mexicans to overcome the natural advantage of the incumbent and because he introduced controversial foreign policy items into the campaign which the voters

[24] Address to the Lions Club at Albuquerque, Feb. 28, 1946.

neither understood nor cared much about. But he lost by only 4,000 votes; and, as a consequence, he believed he should have won, and suggested that he in fact did win, only to have the election "stolen" by fraudulent practices by followers of his opponent. He was never specific as to exactly how the fraud was perpetrated.

In 1948 he had another go at it, this time in a contest against former Secretary of Agriculture Clinton Anderson, a Fair Dealer strongly backed by President Truman. Again, Hurley's familiar foreign-policy theme, that the United States had sold out its principles at Yalta to Communism and imperialism and remained "soft" on Communism, failed to strike a sufficiently responsive chord; again he lost the election; this time by better than 26,000 votes. Now, however, he did not charge fraud, attributing his loss more to the Truman presidential victory and to the "smear" tactics employed by his opponent.

He tried again in 1952, in the meantime having kept his name in the headlines with speeches hither and yon on his favorite topic; he was one of the speakers at the Republican national convention where he recounted his World War II efforts and subsequent frustration caused by those who were disloyal to American ideals. In 1952, however, he was to have more difficulty getting the nomination than in the two previous campaigns. Some state Republicans, reluctant to have a two-time loser as their candidate, argued against supporting Hurley and tried to convince him not to run. Hurley himself even charged that the State Republican chairman, Harry Robins, backed by Governor Ed Mechem, tried to shake him down to the tune of $100,000 in return for support from the Republican organization. This Hurley claims he refused to agree to, instead going to the State convention for support. There, the governor and the state organization put forward a candidate, and an independent Republican also ran, both of whom Hurley beat—easily, as it turned out. However, New Mexico law permitted anyone who received 20 percent of the vote in the convention to continue in the primary, and, consequently, the administration candidate, Wesley Quinn, ran against Hurley. Once again he defeated Quinn, though not without recriminations on both sides.

The general election brought more trouble, and elicited additional charges of conspiracy by Hurley. After Hurley's victory over Quinn in the primary, Governor Mechem promised that he and his administration would support Hurley's candidacy in the general election; Hurley contended throughout, and especially after the election was over, that Mechem failed to honor this commitment, instead supporting Chavez. At any rate, the campaign was bitterly conducted, with Chavez, the Democratic candidate, charging that Hurley was simply a wealthy businessman who did not represent the views of the majority of the New Mexicans, particularly the poor. Because Chavez had the support of labor and specifically that of the Mine, Mill, and Smelter Workers Union, Hurley charged that Communist forces, including help from outside New Mexico, were aligned against him. He also charged that Chavez's candidacy was backed by Jewish money collected nationally with the support of the Anti-Defamation League of New York. This occurred, he said, because of his well-known anti-Zionist position and because of the mistaken notion that he was also anti-Semitic. When the election was over, Hurley had lost again—by some 5,000 votes out of a total vote of 239,911.

Convinced that he could not have lost in what was obviously a Republican year nationally, Hurley immediately alleged that the election had been stolen and promptly contested it. He took his case before the State Supreme Court, and stated that numerous illegal votes had been cast; voter coercion had occurred in many voting districts. The board subsequently investigated the charges, and, on November 29, certified that Chavez had indeed been elected by a majority of 5,071 votes. Hurley then protested vehemently that Governor Mechem and the canvassing board, in association with Chavez, allowed the records to be changed so as to remove all traces of corruption. And on December 8, Hurley demanded a recount in certain precincts.

As a result, the Board conducted a recount in some 218 precincts in twelve different counties which Hurley himself selected. To avoid further charges of fraud, the recount was conducted with representatives of both Hurley and Chavez present, as well as personnel from state district courts. When complete, the recount indicated a gain of 304 votes for Chavez. Still unconvinced, Hurley on December 30, filed a petition of contest with the United States Senate, which established a subcommittee of its Rules and Administration Committee, comprised of Senators Frank Barrett of Wyoming, Charles Potter of Michigan, and Thomas Hennings of Missouri, to investigate.

In a lengthy study, which continued over eight months and involved the expenditure of over $200,000, the committee—or at least two members of the committee—concluded that there were sufficient irregularities to recommend to the Senate voiding the New Mexico Senatorial election. This the committee did in March of 1954, over the strong objection of the third member of the committee, Mr. Hennings, who argued that the investigation had been slapdash and the allegations unproven. In any case, the Senate, with very substantial Republican support—not too surprisingly, since a Republican governor had earlier designated Chavez as the winner—declared by a vote of 53–36 that Chavez should assume his seat. Once again Hurley lost. This time he said it was because White House aides Harry Robins and Isodore Martin and Max Raab convinced the President and other Republicans that the earlier decision by Governor Mechem should stand.[25] The Zionists and Communists had done him in again.

Like his reaction in the China situation, Hurley again saw a conspiracy—this time to prevent him from attaining a forum from which to expound American ideals. Reflecting later on his foray into politics, Hurley stated confidently: "I think that if I had been elected to the Senate and could have had a forum through which

[25] See U.S. Senate, *Hearings before the Subcommittee on Privileges and Elections of the Committee on Rules and Administration*, 83rd Cong., 1st Sess. 1954; and Thomas Hennings' Minority Report of the Committee Investigating the New Mexico elections, Mar. 4, 1954, Hurley Papers.

to reach the American people, I could have prevented the loss of our great ally, China and the Korean, Indonesian (sic) and Indo-China wars." [26] Again he refused to consign blame to the proper source—either to circumstances virtually beyond his control (in China) or his own failure to articulate the issues so as to have enough appeal with the electorate (as in New Mexico). In this period, as earlier, Hurley's ego was a major factor, but so too were fear, suspicion, insecurity, and rage, all of which emerge much more vividly in the postwar Hurley personality.

Perhaps most illustrative of the extent to which Hurley manifested these elements and, in retrospect, took them to the sublime were comments he made on Mrs. Eleanor Roosevelt's television program, in correspondence with the editor of the *Atlantic Monthly*, and in a letter to Senator Everett Dirksen. On Mrs. Roosevelt's program of April 16, 1950, the topic of which was the situation in China with Hurley, Senator Warren Magnuson, Richard Lauterbach, and John King Fairbank as participants, Hurley refused to speak to the current problems and reiterated his thesis about the "sellout" of American ideals at Yalta; he stated again and again that this was the "blueprint" for Communist conquest in China. United States diplomats gave China to the Chinese Communist party "because they were in favor of communism." When asked by Senator Magnuson about who, specifically, was in favor of Communism, Hurley replied: "Mr. Hiss at Yalta and the crowd gave this to . . ." Lauterbach then mentioned the reasons for the Yalta accord and stated that most statesmen, including former Secretary of State Stettinius, saw it as necessary at the time; he asked if Hurley thought Stettinius was a Communist and if he had read the former Secretary's book. To this Hurley replied: "Listen, all the books written now are alibis just like the White Paper." Hurley went on to offer a gratuitous comment explaining why he continued to "fight"; "whenever you do as much for this government, young man, as I have done," he told Lauter-

[26] Hurley to Walter Harrison, May 29, 1956.

figure in regard to previous U.S. China policy, Hurley told the Senator, he thought it best "to give you some data in the event that you wish to make some reference to me while you are in New Mexico." "Please understand, my friend," he continued, "it will be perfectly satisfactory if you do not make any reference, but I feel that I should help to give you a few salient facts in the event you do wish to use them." He then went on to say that Dirksen might well use the following: "There's not much to report on Patrick J. Hurley, not much, that is, except that he has been a coal miner and cowboy in the Southwest. He has served in every grade in the army from private to Major-General. He has been Secretary of War, Ambassador to China, and during World War II the personal representative of President Roosevelt in twenty-one different nations." However, this was a generalization and he would "fill in the facts"; he then proceeded to do so, beginning with a description of his wounds suffered on a "dangerous" mission in Australia.[29]

29 Hurley to Everett Dirksen, Nov. 27, 1951.

# XIII

## An Appraisal

Nineteen sixty-three was the th___ istration. Congress, acting to stim___ acted a tax-reduction bill which i___ into the system. In August, with ___ dent, 200,000 demonstrators marc___ gress discussed a new civil righ___ United States and the Soviet Un___ other nations, signed a treaty w___ clear explosions among the si___ United States announced the sa___ to the Soviet Union. In Nove___ Texas, President Kennedy was ___ Dallas by a former marine an___ Patrick Hurley, long forgotten ___ nence, quietly passed away in ___ New Mexico.

Aside from his speaking eng___ for a time to fill, Hurley devot___ his life to business activity. Th___ still in real property, with se___ majority of his assets: his in___ Company totaled between si___ lars; he also owned real esta___ well as a farm near Tulsa and ___ together were worth approx___ fifties he invested heavily ir___ the Board of Directors of ___

pany, a___ assets i___ alone, r___ the We___ him in ___ vested. ___ for oil ___ other fr___ registrat___ portion ___ sold like___ sum of r___ real esta___ of his de___ his worth___ he joined___

By sev___ be deem___ went hur___ he becam___ tary of W___ envoy fo___ though h___ candidate___ the obvio___ talent wh___ stance, ne___ lives; in ___ his own g___ across the___ inence, it___ intellectua___ ments mu___ factors.

Not the___

bach, "you won't secede." Responding to the question of what the United States should do in 1950 and particularly in the event the Chinese nationalists, inspired by United States encouragement, began bombing the mainland with American planes, all Hurley could manage was a pathetic, "in the first place we should stop making secret diplomacy." [27]

Hurley's exchange with the *Atlantic Monthly* was prompted by an editorial in that magazine of September 1950 averring that Hurley, like the Foreign Service officers, favored a coalition between Chiang Kai-shek and the Communists and that Hurley was just as much to blame as they for pressuring Chiang to compromise with the Chinese Communist party. This threw Hurley into a paroxysm, prompting him to reply that from "the purport of the falsehoods, I am convinced that the writer has access to the so-called Amerasia secret documents that were stolen from the State Department." When the editor wrote back defending the earlier published statement as essentially correct, Hurley, now furious, said the editor's efforts reminded him of an old soldier rhyme:

> "I wish I were a wittle egg
> Away up in a Tree
> I wish I were a wittle egg
> As wotten as could be
> And when the mean ole Sergeant
> Began to shout at me,
> I'd throw my wotten little self
> Wight down and splatter he." [28]

To this the *Atlantic* editor did not respond.

On November 27, 1951, he wrote an incredible unsolicited letter to Senator Everett Dirksen upon hearing that Dirksen would be guest speaker at a Republican party banquet in Albuquerque the following month. Inasmuch as he was a controversial

[27] Comments on Mrs. Roosevelt's television program, Apr. 16, 1950.
[28] Hurley to Edward Weeks, Mar. 6, 1951.

figure in regard to previous U.S. China policy, Hurley told the
Senator, he thought it best "to give you some data in the event
that you wish to make some reference to me while you are in
New Mexico." "Please understand, my friend," he continued, "it
will be perfectly satisfactory if you do not make any reference,
but I feel that I should help to give you a few salient facts in
the event you do wish to use them." He then went on to say that
Dirksen might well use the following: "There's not much to report on Patrick J. Hurley, not much, that is, except that he has
been a coal miner and cowboy in the Southwest. He has served
in every grade in the army from private to Major-General. He
has been Secretary of War, Ambassador to China, and during
World War II the personal representative of President Roosevelt
in twenty-one different nations." However, this was a generalization and he would "fill in the facts"; he then proceeded to do so,
beginning with a description of his wounds suffered on a "dangerous" mission in Australia.[29]

[29] Hurley to Everett Dirksen, Nov. 27, 1951.

# XIII

## An Appraisal

Nineteen sixty-three was the third year of the Kennedy administration. Congress, acting to stimulate the lagging economy, enacted a tax-reduction bill which injected about ten billion dollars into the system. In August, with the encouragement of the President, 200,000 demonstrators marched on Washington, while Congress discussed a new civil rights bill. Meanwhile, in July, the United States and the Soviet Union, promptly joined by some 90 other nations, signed a treaty which banned all atmospheric nuclear explosions among the signatories; and, in October, the United States announced the sale of 250 million bushels of wheat to the Soviet Union. In November, during a political trip to Texas, President Kennedy was gunned down in the streets of Dallas by a former marine and self-styled Marxist. On July 30, Patrick Hurley, long forgotten as a figure of any national prominence, quietly passed away in his sleep at his home in Santa Fe, New Mexico.

Aside from his speaking engagements, which he had continued for a time to fill, Hurley devoted most of the last eleven years of his life to business activity. The preponderance of his wealth was still in real property, with several major equities comprising the majority of his assets: his interest in the Shoreham Investment Company totaled between six and seven hundred thousand dollars; he also owned real estate in Santa Fe and Albuquerque, as well as a farm near Tulsa and a home in Washington, D.C., which together were worth approximately $200,000 more. In the midfifties he invested heavily in uranium and became chairman of the Board of Directors of the United Western Minerals Company, a Delaware Corporation, with offices in Santa Fe, whose assets included 500,000 acres of mineral leases in New Mexico alone, not to mention thousands more in Utah and elsewhere in the West. Perhaps illustrative of the good fortune that followed him in his business career was another project in which he invested. A long-time friend of his invented a simple safety device for oil derricks and asked Hurley to intercede for him with another friend of Hurley's at the U.S. Patent Office for a rapid registration of the invention. In return, Hurley was to get a fixed portion of the royalty from the patent. Hurley agreed; the device sold like lemonade in the desert, and Hurley made a considerable sum of money. These ventures, along with the earnings from his real estate, provided him a bounteous annual income. At the time of his death he was, as he earlier put it, a "modest" millionaire; his worth, however, was considerably less "modest" than when he joined Hoover's Cabinet in 1929.

By several measures of the term, Hurley's life must, of course, be deemed a "success." An extremely poor youth who frequently went hungry and barely had enough clothing to cover his body, he became a prominent lawyer, a millionaire businessman, Secretary of War, friend and confidant of one President and personal envoy for another, United States Ambassador to China, and though he was never nominated for either post, a prospective candidate for both the presidency and vice presidency. To state the obvious, every generation produces thousands of men of great talent who, because of lack of ambition, personality, or circumstance, never ascend such heights, either in their private or public lives; in Hurley's own time many whose abilities far transcended his own quietly lived out their lives in small towns and on farms across the country. In accounting for Hurley's comparative prominence, it is pertinent to note that he was a man not without intellectual talent, unspectacular though it was, whose achievements must be ascribed to a number of other complementary factors.

Not the least significant of Hurley's qualities was his good looks

and attendant facility for making a superb first impression. As a
young man he was six feet two inches in height, with thickly
cropped auburn-colored hair, a prominent nose and chin, and
carried his 180 pounds on a ramrod-straight frame which gave
him the appearance of an army officer right out of West Point.
As he matured he added a mustache, which he kept properly
trimmed and which added an aura of dignity to his presence.
Later, though his hair turned snow white, it did not thin per-
ceptibly, while his age did nothing to alter his posture, and his
weight fluctuated only about ten pounds; if anything he became
more strikingly handsome in his fifties and sixties. He possessed
powerful well-formed hands, which seemed to reinforce his
character, and a resonant voice, which commanded attention the
moment he entered a room. As one who gained some wealth
early, he was also always impeccably dressed, with expensive
well-tailored suits and hats and perfectly polished shoes. At many
social functions after his marriage, the only person more handsome than he was his wife Ruth, the beautiful and charming
daughter of Admiral Henry Wilson who made her own contribution to the Hurley image.

His appearance, combined with his extroverted and gregarious
manner, won him innumerable instantaneous friends and ad-
mirers, not all of whom necessarily remained so. He spoke well,
personally drafting and memorizing most of his formal speeches
so that he could deliver them extemporaneously. He had a wealth
of stories, homilies, and personal sayings to impart, many of
which bore the roots of Oklahoma and the Southwest: he was
especially fond of telling people he was with them "from the
first jump to the end of the trail," or that the "latchstring" at the
Hurleys was always out for them, or that someday they would
"get together in some canyon" to solve this or that problem. To
their astonishment and great amusement and enjoyment, he addressed one of his Russian aides in the winter of 1942 as "Rain
in the Face" and another as "Sitting Bull"; he never missed a
chance to let out an Indian war whoop and, in China, he regaled

Mao Tse-tung and Chou En-lai with tales of his youth in Oklahoma, of his toil in the mines, and on the range.

As with most men who achieve business, professional, or national stature, luck also played an important part in Hurley's career; fortunately for him his luck came in more generous portions than to others. He bought real estate and settled in Tulsa just as the oil boom developed; his friend became principal chief of the Choctaws and appointed him national attorney, a coincidence which led him to Washington and put him in contact with important Congressmen; he met and married a socially prominent girl who was a definite asset in his career; he worked for Hoover in Oklahoma and received for his efforts appointment as Assistant Secretary of War, and, less than a year later, the Secretary died, opening up the post for him; he ingratiated himself with a president of the opposite party who, impatient with regular channels, sent him on important wartime missions.

This is not to say, of course, that his personal ambition was unimportant, for Hurley possessed plenty of drive; he thus made some of his own luck. When Secretary of War James Good died, Hurley contacted every party chairman or other Republican luminary whom he knew who could help him, asking them to write President Hoover in his behalf.[1] These recommendations, and the vigor with which he assumed the interim Secretaryship, convinced the President to name him permanently to the post. In other times, he was not above engineering his own recognition. After completing his wartime assignment in Australia, he wrote to his friend Colonel John Robenson, who was also involved in the mission, urging Robenson to recommend him for the Distinguished Service Cross. General MacArthur, he informed Robenson, was his friend but "had failed to make any kind of recommendation." Colonel Brett wrote a letter for him, he said, which was very "laudatory," but it too "unfortunately does not make any specific recommendation." "I had felt," Hurley continued,

[1] Hurley to George Baird, Nov. 30, 1929, and Hurley to Orville Bullington, Dec. 3, 1929, Hurley Papers.

"that nothing I did while in the combat area, not withstanding all the shooting, justified the award of the Cross, but to fly through the blockade into the combat area when nearly everyone else was leaving does in my opinion justify consideration." [2] During this same mission, he schemed with Colonel Brett to have Nelson T. Johnson fired and himself appointed Minister to Australia; prior to his assignment to China, he made clear to the State Department that he wanted, as a condition of his appointment, to be made ambassador.

If ambition and generous amounts of good fortune contributed much to Hurley's life, so too did the fact that he came from a new state. His return to Oklahoma from Washington, D.C., coincided with statehood. The relatively small population and dearth of professional people normally constituting a governing elite allowed him access to the ground floor, both in business and in political affairs. As he established his law practice, he came to know all the state's important oilmen; he himself ran for the State senate in 1910 and also soon became acquainted with nearly every political figure of any consequence. Moreover, his affiliation with the Republican party in a heavily Democratic state placed him in an advantageous position, especially while the Republican party was the majority party nationally; in part because of the lack of competition, Hurley was a logical choice, if Hoover wanted someone from Oklahoma in his cabinet.

Intellectually, Hurley's credentials were mixed. His formal education was so poor in quality and of such short duration that it is not incorrect to say that he was basically self-educated. Never regularly enrolled in any educational institution until he was sixteen, he completed grade school, high school, and college at Indian University, a rather primitive missionary academy, in a span of five years. Although he later studied at George Washington University, his law degree came from National University Law School in Washington, D.C., not one of the nation's most distinguished.

[2] To John Robenson, Oct. 8, 1943, *ibid.*

His reading was not voluminous nor especially intensive either in his youth or later in life. He read his law books and, of course, briefs and policy memoranda and the periodical press, and he bought and read some Western history, specifically the work of Oklahoma historians Grant Foreman and E. E. Dale; and, after World War II when he had more time, he read and considered outstanding such works as Eisenhower's *Crusade in Europe,* Forrestal's *Diaries,* and Leahy's *I Was There.* While he assembled a fairly sizeable quantity of literature in his personal library, he was never well acquainted with the masters; his favorite book of poetry, for instance, was a collection by Richard Badger entitled *Sun and Saddle Leather.* And with some few exceptions, any knowledge he may have had of the "classics" seldom found its way into his conversation or his prose. As a student at the Indian school he was required to memorize passages from the Bible, particularly from the books of John and Matthew, as well as the Declaration of Independence, the Preamble to the Constitution, and Lincoln's Gettysburg Address; these he never tired of quoting, for he believed they had "a wholesome effect" on his "meager powers of expression." As a consequence, his speech often had a decidedly sententious ring, which to many seemed a front masking extreme intellectual shallowness. Some Foreign Service officers saw him as a man "of little capacity," a "loud talker," a "stuffed shirt," a "Colonel Blimp," and as at least "50 percent bull."

Their evaluation was not wholly incorrect. Certainly Hurley lacked a sophisticated view of China. And in the post-World-War-II era he became a kind of crusading anti-intellectual, who boasted of his primitive educational background and chided American historians for writing so much that was perniciously false, and failing to teach, either in the courses or their books, the fundamental "principles of Americanism."[3]

Yet one can at the same time easily underestimate Hurley's abilities. As his business career and early legal experience as

[3] Hurley to E. Merrill Root, Feb. 11, 1954, *ibid.*

attorney for the Choctaws would indicate, he possessed, if not a creative, at least a solid retentive mind. He proved good at grasping and quickly understanding masses of business data and was, to say the least, a shrewd businessman. Harry Sinclair, who was not accustomed to throwing his money away, placed sincere trust in Hurley's legal abilities, which, in the area of the oil statutes, were considerable; Sinclair paid him a regular retainer and a one million dollar fee for his efforts in negotiating a settlement with the Mexican government in the oil expropriation controversy. In private give and take, as well as in serious diplomatic exchanges, he was not easily buffaloed, nor did he often neglect his homework on important questions with which he was dealing.

On the other hand, his educational deficiencies and narrow intellectual vision imposed a simplistic view of American foreign policy. If the major assignment of the diplomatist is to protect the national interest, he must understand the importance of items related to the nation's territorial integrity or physical intactness as well as to the preservation of its political independence, recognize the need to press the commercial advantage or opportunity of the nation, and be acutely aware of the interests of other states. Perhaps equally important, he should have a highly developed sense of his nation's ideals and goals as inferred from its history, for it is incumbent on the statesman to know what there is about his nation that makes it worth preserving. Hurley's knowledge of American ideals as expressed by the founding fathers, in the Wilsonian peace proposals, and in the Atlantic Charter, was perhaps solid enough. But he seemed unaware of the compromises made with these ideals over the years in pursuance of more mundane matters like American security, commercial advantage, or territorial expansion. An intense nationalist, Hurley believed that, until near the end of World War II, when it began to sacrifice its idealism, the United States had always acted essentially with the right on its side. Further, he demonstrated little knowledge of, or concern for, the national interests of other states.

When one probes beneath the surface it seems apparent that Hurley's ideas on foreign policy reflect the same degree of ambivalence manifested by the American people. James MacGregor Burns in his biography of Franklin Roosevelt sees the former president as "a deeply divided man—divided between the man of principle, of ideals, of faith, crusading for a distant vision, on the one hand; and on the other, the man of Realpolitik, of prudence, of narrow, manageable, short-run goals, intent always on protecting his power and authority in a world of shifting moods and capricious fortune." This same dualism, he avers, "divided the American people themselves, who were vacillating between the evangelical moods of idealism, sentimentalism, and utopianism of one era and older traditions of national self-regard, protectiveness and prudence of another."[4] Burns' assessment, made with reference to Roosevelt's World War II policy, seems accurate indeed, on both counts.

Proponents of *realpolitik* can find plenty in the twentieth-century American experience to support their contention that the United States, because of the wishes of its public, has had an overwhelming weakness for the moralistic-legalistic approach to world politics. The promotion of the arbitration movement and the Bryan "cooling off" treaties, Wilson's "missionary diplomacy" and World War I peace proposals, the "outlawry of war" in the twenties as well as disarmament and the promulgation of the nonrecognition formula in the thirties, reveal little of an American sense of power or affinity for the maintenance of peace through the balance of power.

Yet American policy has had its *realpolitik* face. When the American people have been convinced, as they have often in their history, that the use of power was essential in the advancement of their self-interest, they have warmly counseled its use. Thus the United States did not shrink from employing genocide against the American Indian, nor from using whatever manuever or

---

[4] James MacGregor Burns, *Roosevelt: The Soldier of Freedom, 1940–1945* (New York, 1970), p. vii.

manipulation seemed necessary in gaining access to the continent, nor from using the American Navy to gain an empire from Spain. Though slow to become involved, Americans freely committed their power, moreover, in the winning of their objectives in the wars of the twentieth century. Similarly, early practitioners of American diplomacy recognized the importance of the European balance of power in keeping the peace and safeguarding American security and did not want to risk U.S. interests in the overzealous promotion of an ideal.

Hurley's frequent invoking of the principles of the Atlantic Charter, in which, like Roosevelt, he sincerely believed, his advocacy of postwar anticolonialism, and his support of the United Nations, all constitute his own visionary, principled side. His contempt for Stimson's nonrecognition policy and early advocacy of a stronger stance against Japan, as well as his balance-of-power reasoning regarding the retention of the Philippines, and his pre-World-War-II preparedness views comprise his *realpolitik* side. It is undoubtedly true that all those who deal with the formulation of policy, both in the United States and elsewhere, reflect this same dichotomy. Because of his view of American history, however, Hurley himself did not recognize the dualism, for he naturally identified the ideal with the American position; if the United States used power to promote its own narrow, short-run goals, it did not matter, for, in the process, it also advanced an ideal.

He did, however, make significant contributions to American foreign policy. As Secretary of War and one of President Hoover's advisers, he played a major role in attempting to thwart the drive for Philippine independence in the early thirties. He saw the United States as a benevolent tutor rather than as a colonial master and refused to believe that the independence movement was based on anything other than selfish domestic economic interests and self-aggrandizement among ambitious Filipino leaders. Paradoxically—in view of his strongly anticolonialist post-World-War-II stance—he played the traditional imperialist, yet, because he believed his country acquired the islands largely to "clean them up" and to conduct an experiment in democracy, he did not see the United States as an imperialist power.

As a private envoy for Harry Sinclair, in constant communication with the State Department, he negotiated an agreement with the Cárdenas government of Mexico which broke an economic logjam and cleared the way for settlement of the entire oil expropriation issue. The agreement comprised a healthy recognition of Mexican sovereignty, broke the united front of the oil companies, and was within the context of the Good Neighbor policy as well as in the furtherance of improved Mexican-American relations. But Hurley was in this case not acting on principle, for his early record in the controversy indicates that he deplored the Mexican action and worked to get his government to overturn it. His sensitivity to Mexican nationalism was secondary to his concern for his employers' profits, and he had no qualms about the rectitude of a possible American intervention. When Sinclair saw unilateral negotiations as the only way out, Hurley got him an agreement.

In his assignments to the Southwest Pacific, Russia, and the Middle East, in which he was part military officer (he became, indeed, a "make-believe" general) and part diplomat, he contributed little of much import. His gunrunning mission to Mac-Arthur in the Philippines proved a failure—though he worked at it diligently—because of the intensity of the Japanese blockade. As the first United States Minister to New Zealand, a post he held only briefly and delayed taking as long as possible because he wanted the same job in Australia, he made some rousing speeches but handled no issues important enough to be printed in the Foreign Relations volume. In his trip to Russia, an assignment given him by President Roosevelt so he would quit preaching the merits of defeating Japan first, he served as a superfluous "fact finder," though he was one of the few Western officers actually to witness Soviet troops on the Russian front and appears to have been the first American official to whom Stalin made a promise to enter the Pacific War.

His efforts in the Middle East were largely those of the gadfly, who, often acting on sketchy information, admonished American officials to maintain closer control over Lend Lease, scorned the British for using American materials while at the same time attempting to undermine the economic position of the United States in the region, and worked to reinforce President Roosevelt's dispositions against the creation of a Jewish national state in Palestine; he also played the errand boy for President Roosevelt at the Teheran Conference and helped prick the President's conscience by synthesizing some forward-looking views of the State Department's Middle East Division in drafting the Declaration on Iran. He did not play a major role in shaping American "oil policy." While the President was satisfied with his work, specifically with Hurley's subsequent Iranian Plan, which he praised, Hurley was no specialist in the area, and he flitted in and out of Middle Eastern countries and Washington with such rapidity that he had only a momentary influence on policy at best; he must be seen as only one in a whole congerie of Presidential envoys who swept through the area during the war, mainly because Roosevelt believed the bureaucracy of the State Department too cumbrous to provide him with adequate information.

It was in China, in the most important job of his career, that Hurley made his major wartime mark. With only the limited knowledge of China's history and politics he could assimilate from State Department memoranda and with no knowledge of its language or customs, Hurley arrived in Chungking in early September 1944 as special emissary of the President to mediate the differences between General Stilwell and Chiang Kai-shek. He was unable to soothe feelings that indeed ran deep; and when it appeared to Hurley that only Stilwell stood in the way of the Generalissimo's acceptance of President Roosevelt's proposal to place an American officer in complete charge of Chiang's troops, he recommended Stilwell's recall. Hurley, who was impressed by Chiang and his willingness to cooperate and by Stilwell's abrasiveness, obviously had not perceived the complexity of the reasons behind Chiang's refusal to have Stilwell or that, in fact, firing Stilwell would solve few problems. But it is true that in his position in China, Stilwell's virtues counted for least and his defects for most, and there was ample reason to "sack" him. And General Wedemeyer proved to be a more satisfactory appointment in view of the administration's policy of cooperation with the Generalissimo. One could not, President Roosevelt said of Chiang, "exact commitments from him the way we might do from the Sultan of Morocco." [5] On the related problem of a Kuomintang-Communist agreement, which he worked for nearly a year to achieve, and which, it was hoped, would enable a more effective prosecution of the war against Japan, Hurley similarly failed to perceive the complexities of the problem. In a word, Hurley was ignorant of China, of the Chinese Communists, and of the nature of the struggle. And he arrogantly undertook the negotiating of this extremely complex problem almost singlehandedly. Nevertheless, several points of qualification must be made in evaluating his work there.

The policy set by the Roosevelt administration, predicated as it was on the belief in China as a major power, was to support Chiang Kai-shek as fully as the meager resources allotted to that theater would permit, and to encourage him to wage the war as vigorously as possible against Japan. In China's internal struggle, the United States would seek a compromise between the CCP and the Kuomintang while working to sustain the Generalissimo's government. This was Roosevelt's policy and later Truman's; it was Hurley's only because he agreed with it and was asked to carry it out by both Presidents. While Hurley did become personally close with the Generalissimo, was not prepared to deal with him in the manner suggested by the Foreign Service officers, and was openly hostile to the CCP, many of the concrete manifestations of American support for Chiang originated entirely independent of the Ambassador.

In evaluating this policy, it is important to note that in 1944 and

[5] Memorandum by Roosevelt for General Marshall, Mar. 8, 1943, Roosevelt Papers, Roosevelt Presidential Library, Hyde Park, N.Y.

1945 the United States possessed some influence with Chiang and by threatening to cut off military aid and American dollars could perhaps have pressured him more toward compromise with the Communists. However, the nature of the conflict precluded the success of this approach. The Communists, while they asked for a "coalition" government, and while between 1937 and 1945 they had advocated "cooperation" to fight the Japanese, were interested essentially in destroying the Nationalist government and attaining power. In large part, they viewed the war with Japan as the route to this success, and they never abandoned their goal regardless of the United Front. Chiang Kai-shek had no illusions about the Communist aims and saw them correctly for what they were; thus he had little interest in any compromise solution. In other words, it is difficult to see the situation as anything but an irreconcilable conflict only temporarily soluble. And while the United States may have induced the Generalissimo to "compromise" with the Communists, it had no way of forcing the Communists to compromise with the Kuomintang.

In retrospect it appears that Hurley's was an impossible task; that in fact China's internal problem was beyond the competence of any American to solve. Moreover, the assignment was laden with physical and mental hardships imposed by conditions within China and separation from his family. Hurley was no young man; his eyes bothered him and he needed dental work. "If this letter sounds as if I am tired," he wrote his personal Secretary in August 1945, "you must realize that this is a very difficult climate in which to even exist in summer time. In addition to the effort of mere living I have had a strenuous time. I am worked down." [6]

When viewed in the context of the efforts of both his predecessor as Ambassador and General Marshall's later mission, Hurley's shallowness regarding China may not have been so detrimental. He remained hopeful when greater sophistication of knowledge might well have bred in him the same cynicism and

[6] To Lucille Carter, Aug. 8, 1945, Hurley Papers.

negativism displayed by Ambassador Clarence Gauss; this was not unimportant as long as the United States continued to back Chiang, a course which, in view of the circumstances, was diffi- cult, perhaps impossible, not to follow. Neither Gauss nor Marshall did much better than Hurley in the final analysis. Gauss, resentful of the fact that in 1941 he was asked to exchange his comfortable position as Minister to Australia with Nelson Johnson for the job in Chungking, grew to despise Chinese government officials and virtually gave up hope for the viability of the Na- tionalist government. With all his knowledge garnered in years of experience in China, dating back to 1907, Gauss was not prepared to grapple with the issues of 1944 and 1945. Marshall, with all his prestige, could not bring the CCP and Kuomintang together. General Wedemeyer wrote Hurley in early 1946: "It is my conviction that were it not for the international prestige and the stature of General Marshall, the negotiations between the Chinese Communists and Central Government representatives would break down. In other words, if we removed Marshall in the next year or two, I can foresee no permanence in what he has accomplished so far, for both sides will be at each other's throats again." Marshall, said Wedemeyer, was partially successful only because of his unrestricted powers; these, Marshall himself ad- mitted, Hurley did not have.[7]

Furthermore, if President Roosevelt, who, on the advice of General Marshall and Henry Stimson, was personally responsible for sending Hurley to Chungking, had believed that he was not doing his job as well as possible in the circumstances, or that a new man with a new directive was needed, he had plenty of op- portunity to dismiss him—particularly during Hurley's trip home in March of 1945. The President, however, refused to accept the Foreign Service officers' suggestions as enunciated in the message of February 28 and, instead, returned Hurley to Chungking. There is no evidence to indicate that Roosevelt was unhappy with his

[7] Wedemeyer to Hurley, Mar. 31, 1946, *ibid.*

work. When Truman assumed the presidency, Hurley submitted the customary resignation; not only did the new President refuse at that time to accept it, during their consultations in Washington in the fall of 1945 he pleaded with the Ambassador to return to China.

On some matters, moreover, Hurley demonstrated a degree of perspicacity. He early recognized the necessity of determining Russian intentions in the pursuance of American policy in China; a commitment by Stalin in behalf of Chiang Kai-shek he believed an essential ingredient in the success of the U.S. approach. He erred in placing too much trust in Stalin's word and in assuming that the Soviet dictator would not aid the CCP because it was not truly Communist; he misinterpreted the Chinese Communists and failed to discern the opportunism Stalin was to demonstrate at war's end. Stalin's policy toward the CCP and his aims for the whole of China even now remain unclear; and he apparently would have been willing to work with Chiang when the war was over. Regardless of his pledges, however, once his forces came into contact with the Chinese Communists in the fall of 1945, Stalin would hardly fail to aid the CCP in Manchuria and north China, any more than the United States would fail to assist Chiang Kai-shek. But Hurley was not the only one deceived by the Russians; for, though they were more skeptical than the Ambassador, Harry Hopkins, Averell Harriman, and President Truman adopted a view essentially comparable to Hurley's.

The American Ambassador was also quick to point out the conflict with the ideals of the Atlantic Charter and the possibility of long-term trouble for the United States if it did not prevent the European powers from reacquiring control of their Southeast Asian colonies. The United States, he predicted, would be "sucked in" to a struggle on the side of the colonial powers against Communist imperialism, unless it acted with dispatch to carry out President Roosevelt's suggestions that the colonies be placed beyond the pale of reoccupation. He was impressed with the President's anticolonial ideas. These views Roosevelt confided to him on several occasions; and he was chagrined when the United States did not ultimately implement them; this helped convince him of a conspiracy by the State Department to thwart the President's goals, for he was unaware of the possible postwar consequences of, or difficulty in, an American stand against its wartime allies. He was, moreover, a strong Anglophobe, an attitude which colored his thinking. Our British allies, reported Admiral Leahy, did not like Hurley very much, and that, he said, was "an understatement."

The British were not alone in not liking Hurley very much; and it is partly his personality, and attendant behavior, which obfuscate his work as a diplomatist. Always extremely sharp-tempered, Hurley was drawn into numerous ugly emotional "scenes" throughout his career. As a youth he flew into a rage and nearly beat to death a man who had done him an injustice; he exchanged furious remarks in a congressional hearing with an opposing attorney during his service with the Choctaws; he "blew up" at Senator Harry Hawes in another hearing while Secretary of War, stalked out of another session, and virtually challenged John L. Lewis to a fistfight in still another. In China he threatened to wreck John Davies' career, frequently roared profanely at his staff, and petulantly stopped speaking for several days to General Wedemeyer. When his credentials elevating him to ambassadorial status did not arrive in time for the Teheran Conference, he stormed around like a Cub Scout denied a merit badge. He railed against the State Department, giving full vent to his wrath when he returned to Washington: he performed the recent assignment, he said, with rank which "was just below the Red Cross representative and just above the debutantes." [8]

He also carried on feuds lasting for years, the most notable being with the Foreign Service officers who clashed with him in China; with Dean Acheson, who criticized one of his reports and who represented the Eastern pro-British establishment which

[8] Office Diary, Feb. 17, 1944, *ibid.*

Hurley could not abide; and with Drew Pearson, who attacked Hurley viciously and unfairly in his columns. Pearson jumped on Hurley verbally when the latter was Secretary of War and rode him throughout his public career, falsely accusing him of "crimes" ranging from changing his name to profiteering to anti-Semitism. With the Foreign Service officers and Acheson, Hurley got his own "licks" in over the postwar years; toward Pearson, though he tried to ignore his columns, he harbored a seething hatred fed by a deepening paranoia.[9]

As ambassador, Hurley, perhaps because of an awareness of his own deficiencies regarding China, became deeply sensitive about his role as head of the team. When the Foreign Service officers attempted to advance ideas contrary to his own, he would gather his staff together to lecture them on U.S. policy, often climaxing the sessions with his own remarks, sprinkled with quotations from the Declaration of Independence and the Constitution, about American ideals. As General Wedemeyer indicates, a word of criticism of his efforts was enough to enrage him; and as it became apparent that his mediation was not bringing the desired result, he grew bitter, lashing out at opponents, real or imaginary, who were "sabotaging" his work toward a political settlement, undermining American policy, and attempting to destroy him personally. His apparent insecurity led him to throttle dissent and to insist on limitation of the wide range of reporting on conditions in China so freely carried on under his predecessor and so necessary in the ideal execution of an ambassadorial assignment.

In April 1945, the Deputy Director of the Office of Far Eastern Affairs informed Under Secretary Grew: "During General Hurley's visit here, it was very evident from his remarks that he is extremely suspicious of and entertains a dislike for Foreign Ser-

[9] There was no love lost between Hurley and Harry Hopkins, because the latter erroneously believed Hurley the author of a plan to gather up garbage to feed the poor. The coolness remained until the President forced the two men to make up at Cairo in November, 1943; Elliot Roosevelt to Hurley, Jan. 4, 1950, *ibid.*

vice officers in China. This antipathy has been confirmed by officers returning from Chungking, who have indicated the serious effect it has had upon their morale. . . . In consequence, it is becoming increasingly difficult to persuade Foreign Service officers who have served under General Hurley to return to China. Of equally serious nature are the severe restrictions imposed by General Hurley upon political reporting by officers in China." [10] When John Service tried in October 1944 to offer Hurley some information about the Communist position, he refused even to listen; instead he delivered a "monologue" on his "colorful" past. Later, George Atcheson wired the Secretary of State: "General Hurley began his assignment in Chungking with a strong prejudice against the Department and the Foreign Service and especially officers who had served with his predecessor . . . it was . . . a fixed idea with him that there were officers in the Foreign Service and American military officers who were in opposition to him." [11]

Although it is not my intention to subject Hurley to even a crude psychological analysis, it does appear that the insecurity, even paranoia, which he manifested in greater degree after the war, was an important force in his life. And any explanation of his attacks on the State Department, his impugning of the loyalty of Foreign Service personnel, or his alleging of conspiracies to defeat him in New Mexico seem inadequate unless made partly in these terms. His ego was always tremendous; his appetite for recognition enormous.

An inevitable by-product of this side of Hurley's character is, of course, the prejudice it tends to impose on those who would assess his career; for not only is it difficult to admire him, it is hard to be dispassionate in evaluating his work. Dean Acheson, for instance, in his *Present at the Creation* dismisses him as a cowboy

10 Memorandum by the Deputy Director of the Office of Far Eastern Affairs, Apr. 28, 1945, *F.R., 1945*, VII, 349.

11 The Acting Political Adviser in Japan to the Secretary of State, Dec. 8, 1945, *ibid.*, 733; John S. Service to the author, Mar. 22, 1971.

who struck it rich. While this may be considered a partially accurate characterization, its deprecatory nature is clear, and it is
hardly a satisfactory portrait. He was more than that. He was
ambitious, brash, oversensitive, bombastic, pretentious, in many
ways unprepared for assignments coming his way; he was also, in
sum, a product of the American West where Populist-Progressive
reform sentiment tempered traditional economic and social doctrine, where masculine virtues took precedence over refinement,
and where personality and wealth counted for much and intellectual sophistication for little. A poor boy who made good in the
legendary American tradition and who, through circumstance and
ambition gained some influence and power, he was, in the final
analysis, superficially spectacular but actually rather average,
neither an outstanding statesman nor a great man. He was not the
first American to go far on modest talent, nor the last.

# Bibliography

MANUSCRIPTS

Of the private papers used in this work, by far the most important is the Patrick J. Hurley manuscript collection, Manuscripts Division, Bizzell Library, University of Oklahoma, Norman, Oklahoma; and they deserve special note. Besides the Hurley papers, several other collections proved indispensable in the completion of various parts of the study:

The William E. Borah Papers, Library of Congress

The James Byrnes Papers, Clemson University

The Claire Chennault Papers, Hoover Institution, Stanford University

The William L. Clayton Papers, Truman Presidential Library, Independence, Mo.

The Tom Connally Papers, Library of Congress

The Herbert Hoover Papers, Hoover Presidential Library, West Branch, Iowa

The Harry Hopkins Papers, Roosevelt Presidential Library, Hyde Park, N.Y.

The Stanley K. Hornbeck Papers, Hoover Institution, Stanford University

The Cordell Hull Papers, Library of Congress

The Nelson T. Johnson Papers, Library of Congress

The William Leahy Papers, Library of Congress

The Edwin A. Locke, Jr. Papers, Truman Presidential Library, Independence, Mo.

The Douglas MacArthur Papers, MacArthur Memorial Archives, Norfolk, Va.

Morgenthau Diary (China), Roosevelt Presidential Library, Hyde Park, N.Y.

The George Van Horn Moseley Papers, Library of Congress
The Franklin D. Roosevelt Papers, Roosevelt Presidential Library, Hyde Park, N.Y.
The Edward Stettinius Papers, University of Virginia
The Joseph Stilwell Papers, Hoover Institution, Stanford University
The Henry L. Stimson Papers, Yale University
The Harry S. Truman Papers, Truman Presidential Library, Independence, Mo.

## GOVERNMENT DOCUMENTS

*Unprinted Government Documents*

For unpublished materials relative to the Far Eastern Crisis of 1931–1932, the Mexican Oil Expropriation, Hurley's mission to the Middle East, and especially, his assignment in China, the State Department Archives were used. The records for 1945, when the author researched them, were available, with the usual restrictions, at the Department of State; the earlier documents at the National Archives.

War Department records in the National Archives, especially those of the Bureau of Insular Affairs on the Philippine question, and record group 94 on the Bonus March also proved to be of inestimable value in establishing Hurley's role in each of the above.

*Published Documents*

U.S. Congress, *Congressional Record.*
U.S. Department of State, *Foreign Relations of the United States: Diplomatic Papers,* 1931: Vol. II; and *Japan, 1931–1941* (2 vols.); 1932: Vols. III, IV; 1933: Vol. III; 1938: Vol. V; 1939: Vol. V; 1940: Vol. V; 1941: Vol. VII; 1942: Vol. III; 1943: Vol. IV, and 1943: *China;* 1944: Vols. V, VI; 1945: Vol. VII; 1945: *The Conferences at Malta and Yalta;* 1945: *The Conference of Berlin* (Potsdam), 2 vols.
U.S. Department of State, *United States Relations with China with Special Reference to the Period 1944–1949,* 1949.
U.S. House of Representatives, *Hearings before the Subcommittee on Indian Affairs,* Aug. 11, 1914, 63rd. Cong., 2nd Sess., 1915.
——, *Hearings before the Committee on Insular Affairs on H.R. 7233,* 72nd Cong., 1st Sess., Feb. 10, 1932.

U.S. Senate, Committee on Foreign Relations and Committee on Armed Services, *Military Situation in the Far East*. 82nd Cong., 1st Sess., 1951.

——, *Hearings before the Senate Committee on Territories and Insular Affairs on S. 3377*, 72nd Cong., 1st Sess., Feb. 11 and 13, 1932.

——, *Hearings before the Subcommittee on Privileges and Elections of the Committee on Rules and Administration*, 83rd Cong., 1st Sess., 1954.

——, Committee on Foreign Relations, *State Department Loyalty Investigation*, Senate Report 2108, 81st Cong., 2nd Sess., 1950.

——, Judiciary Committee, *Hearings on The Institute of Pacific Relations*, 82nd Cong., 2nd Sess., 1952.

NEWSPAPERS

The following newspapers are cited in the study: *Akron Beacon Journal, Auckland Star, Boston Herald, Baltimore Sun, Buffalo Evening News*, Cleveland *Plain Dealer*, Cleveland *Press, Detroit Free Press, Detroit News, Indianapolis Times, Milwaukee News*, New York *Herald Tribune*, New York *Times, New York World Telegram, New Zealand Herald*, Oklahoma City *Daily Oklahoman, Philadelphia Evening Bulletin, Philadelphia Record, Richmond News Leader*, San Francisco *Chronicle*, St. *Louis Post Dispatch, Vancouver Sun, Waikato Times, Washington News, Washington Post, Washington Star*.

BOOKS AND ARTICLES

Although the following list is fairly substantial, it is, of course, highly selective. Only those books, articles, and dissertations directly consulted and most pertinent to the study have been included.

*Memoirs, Autobiographies, Published Papers*

Acheson, Dean. *Present at the Creation* (New York, 1969).

Blum, John Morton. *From the Morgenthau Diaries* (Boston, 1967), Vol. III *Years of War*, 1941–1945.

Byrnes, James. *All in One Lifetime* (New York, 1958).

——. *Speaking Frankly* (New York, 1947).

Chennault, Claire L. *Way of a Fighter* (New York, 1949).

Connally, Tom. *My Name is Tom Connally* (New York, 1954).

Daniels, Josephus. *Shirt-Sleeve Diplomat* (Chapel Hill, 1947).

Eisenhower, Dwight D. *At Ease: Stories I Tell to Friends* (New York, 1957).

Forrestal, James. *The Forrestal Diaries*, Walter Millis, ed. (New York, 1951).

Grew, Joseph. *Ten Years in Japan* (New York, 1944).

Grew, Joseph. *Turbulent Era*, 2 Vols. (Boston, 1952).

Hoover, Herbert. *The Memoirs of Herbert Hoover*: Vol. I. *The Great Depression, 1929–1941* (New York, 1952); Vol. II. *The Cabinet and the Presidency* (New York, 1959).

Hull, Cordell. *The Memoirs of Cordell Hull* (New York, 1948).

Ickes, Harold L. *The Secret Diary of Harold Ickes*, Vol. III, *The Lowering Clouds* (New York, 1954).

Kennan, George F. *Memoirs, 1925–1950* (Boston, 1967).

Leahy, William D. *I Was There* (New York, 1950).

Long, Breckinridge. *The War Diary of Breckinridge Long*, Fred L. Israel, ed. (Lincoln, Neb., 1966).

MacArthur, Douglas. *Reminiscences* (New York, 1964).

Murphy, Robert. *Diplomat Among Warriors* (Garden City, N.Y., 1964).

Nelson, Donald M. *Arsenal of Democracy* (New York, 1946).

Richberg, Donald. *My Hero: The Indiscreet Memoirs of an Eventful but Unheroic Life* (New York, 1954).

Roosevelt, Elliott. *As He Saw It* (New York, 1946).

Standley, William H., and Arthur A. Ageton. *Admiral Ambassador to Russia* (Chicago, 1955).

Stettinius, Edward R., Jr. *Roosevelt and the Russians: The Yalta Conference*, Walter Johnson, ed. (Garden City, N.Y., 1949).

Stilwell, Joseph W. *The Stilwell Papers* (New York, 1948).

Stimson, Henry L., and McGeorge Bundy. *On Active Service in Peace and War* (New York, 1948).

Stuart, John Leighton. *Fifty Years in China: The Memoirs of John Leighton Stuart, Missionary and Ambassador* (New York, 1954).

Truman, Harry S. *Memoirs*, Vol. II, *Years of Trial and Hope* (New York, 1958).

Wedemeyer, Albert C. *Wedemeyer Reports!* (New York, 1958).

Welles, Sumner. *Seven Decisions that Shaped History* (New York, 1951).

*Other Books*

Alinsky, Saul. *John L. Lewis* (New York, 1949).

Alsop, Joseph, and Stewart Alsop. *The Reporter's Trade* (New York, 1958).

Ambrose, Stephen E. *The Supreme Commander: The War Years of General Dwight David Eisenhower* (New York, 1970).

Barnett, A. Doak. *China on the Eve of Communist Takeover* (New York, 1963).

Barrett, David D. *Dixie Mission: The United States Army Observer Group in Yenan, 1944* (Berkeley, 1970).

Beal, John Robinson. *Marshall In China* (New York, 1970).

Bemis, Samuel F. *The Latin American Policy of the United States: An Historical Interpretation* (New York, 1943).

Buchanan, A. Russell. *The United States and World War II*, 2 Vols. (New York, 1964).

Buhite, Russell D. *Nelson T. Johnson and American Policy Toward China 1925–1941* (East Lansing, 1968).

Burns, James MacGregor. *Roosevelt: The Soldier of Freedom, 1940–1945* (New York, 1970).

Clemens, Diane Shaver. *Yalta* (New York, 1970).

Cline, Howard F. *The United States and Mexico* (Cambridge, 1953).

Cronon, E. David. *Josephus Daniels in Mexico* (Madison, 1960).

Daniels, Roger. *The Bonus March: An Episode of the Great Depression* (Westport, Conn., 1971).

Davies, John P., Jr. *Foreign and Other Affairs* (New York, 1964).

Debo, Angie. *The Rise and Fall of the Choctaw Republic* (Norman, 1934).

——. *The Road to Disappearance* (Norman, 1941).

DeNovo, John A. *American Interests and Policies in the Middle East, 1900–1939* (Minneapolis, 1963).

Eddy, William A. *F.D.R. Meets Ibn Saud* (New York, 1954).

Engler, Robert. *The Politics of Oil: A Study of Private Power and Democratic Directions* (New York, 1961).

Everest, Alan S. *Morgenthau, The New Deal, and Silver: A Story of Pressure Politics* (New York, 1950).

Fatemi, Nasrollah. *Oil Diplomacy; Powderkeg in Iran* (New York, 1954).

Feis, Herbert. *The Atomic Bomb and the End of World War II* (Princeton, N.J., 1966).

———. *Between War and Peace: The Potsdam Conference* (Princeton, 1960).

———. *The China Tangle* (Princeton, 1953).

———. *Churchill–Roosevelt–Stalin* (Princeton, N.J., 1957).

Ferrell, Robert H. *American Diplomacy in the Great Depression* (New Haven, 1957).

Fink, Reuben. *America and Palestine: The Attitude of Official America and the American People Toward the Rebuilding of Palestine as a Free and Democratic Jewish Commonwealth* (New York, 1944).

Fisher, Sydney N. *The Middle East: A History* (New York, 1959).

Fitzgerald, Charles P. *The Birth of Communist China* (New York, 1966).

Foreman, Grant. *A History of Oklahoma* (Norman, 1942).

Freidel, Frank. *Franklin D. Roosevelt: The Triumph* (Boston, 1956).

Friend, Theodore. *Between Two Empires: The Ordeal of the Philippines, 1929–1946* (New Haven, 1965).

Gardner, Lloyd C. *Economic Aspects of New Deal Diplomacy* (Madison, 1964).

Gibson, Arrell M. *Oklahoma: A History of Five Centuries* (Norman, 1965).

Grunder, Garel, and William Livezey. *The Philippines and the United States* (Norman, 1951).

Hawes, Harry. *Philippine Uncertainty* (New York, 1932).

Heinrichs, Waldo H., Jr. *American Ambassador* (Boston, 1966).

Herzog, Jesús Silva. *Petróleo mexicano: historia de un problema* (Mexico City, 1941).

Hofstadter, Richard. *The Paranoid Style in American Politics and Other Essays* (New York, 1964).

Hoskins, Halford L. *Middle East Oil in United States Foreign Policy* (Washington, 1950).

Hurewitz, J. C. *The Struggle For Palestine* (New York, 1968).

Huthmacher, J. Joseph. *Senator Robert F. Wagner and the Rise of Urban Liberalism* (New York, 1968).

James, D. Clayton. *The Years of MacArthur* (New York, 1970).

Johnson, Claudius. *Borah of Idaho* (New York, 1936).

Johnson, Walter. *1600 Pennsylvania Avenue; Presidents and the People, 1929–1959* (New York, 1960).

Keeley, Joseph Charles. *The China Lobby Man; the Story of Alfred Kohlberg* (New Rochelle, N.Y., 1969).

Kennan, George. *Russia and the West Under Lenin and Stalin* (Boston, 1961).

Kirk, George. *The Middle East in the War* (London, 1952).

Kirk, Grayson V. *Philippine Independence: Motives, Problems, and Prospects* (New York, 1936).

Kolko, Gabriel. *The Politics of War: The World and United States Foreign Policy, 1943–1945* (New York, 1968).

La Moore, Parker. *"Pat" Hurley: The Story of an American* (New York, 1932).

Lohbeck, Don. *Patrick J. Hurley* (Chicago, 1956).

Manuel, Frank E. *The Realities of American-Palestine Relations* (Washington, 1949).

Masterson, V. V. *The Katy Railroad and the Last Frontier* (Norman, 1953).

McKenna, Marian. *Borah* (Ann Arbor, 1961).

McLane, Charles B. *Soviet Policy and the Chinese Communists, 1931–1946* (New York, 1958).

McReynolds, Edwin C. *Oklahoma: A History of the Sooner State* (Norman, 1954).

Morison, Elting E. *Turmoil and Tradition: A Study of the Life and Times of Henry L. Stimson* (Boston, 1960).

Morton, Louis. *Strategy and Command: The First Two Years* (Washington, D.C., 1962).

North, Robert C. *Moscow and the Chinese Communists* (Stanford, 1963).

Payne, Robert. *Chiang Kai-shek* (New York, 1969).

Perkins, Whitney T. *Denial of Empire: The United States and Its Dependencies* (Leiden, 1962).

Pogue, Forrest C. *George Marshall*, Vol. II, *Ordeal and Hope, 1939–1943* (New York, 1966).

Powell, J. Richard. *The Mexican Petroleum Industry 1938–1950* (Berkeley and Los Angeles, 1956).

Pratt, Julius. *Cordell Hull*, 2 Vols. (New York, 1964).

Richberg, Donald. *The Mexican Oil Seizure* (New York, 1940).

Rogow, Arnold A. *James Forrestal* (New York, 1963).

Romanus, Charles F., and Riley Sunderland. *Stilwell's Command Problems* (Washington, D.C., 1956).

———. *Stilwell's Mission to China* (Washington, D.C., 1953).

———. *Time Runs Out in C.B.I.* (Washington, D.C., 1959).

Rosinger, Lawrence. *China's War Time Politics, 1937–1944* (Princeton, N.J., 1945).

Rothstein, Andrew. *Soviet Foreign Policy During the Patriotic War*, Vol. I, June 22, 1941–Dec. 31, 1943 (London, n.d.).

———. *Soviet Policy During the Patriotic War: Documents and Materials*, Vol. II, Jan. 1, 1944–Dec. 31, 1944 (London, 1946).

Rovere, Richard H. *Senator Joe McCarthy* (Cleveland, 1960).

Rovere, Richard, and Arthur Schlesinger, Jr. *The MacArthur Controversy* (New York, 1965).

Sakran, Frank C. *Palestine Dilemma: Arab Rights Versus Zionist Aspirations* (Washington, 1948).

Schlesinger, Arthur M., Jr. *The Crisis of the Old Order, 1919–1933* (Boston, 1957).

Service, John S. *The Amerasia Papers: Some Problems in the History of U.S.–China Relations* (Berkeley, 1971).

Sherwood, Robert E. *Roosevelt and Hopkins* (New York, 1948).

Shewmaker, Kenneth E. *Americans and Chinese Communists, 1927–1945: A Persuading Encounter* (Ithaca, 1971).

Smith, Gaddis. *American Diplomacy During the Second World War* (New York, 1965).

Snell, John L. *Illusion and Necessity* (Boston, 1963).

Snell, John L., ed. *The Meaning of Yalta* (Baton Rouge, 1956).

Tang Tsou. *America's Failure in China, 1941–1950* (Chicago, 1963).

Taylor, Allan. *Prelude to Israel: An Analysis of Zionist Diplomacy, 1827–1947* (New York, 1959).

Taylor, George E. *The Philippines and the United States: Problems of Partnership* (New York, 1964).

Theoharis, Athan G. *The Yalta Myths: An Issue in U.S. Politics 1945–1955* (Columbia, Mo., 1970).

Tuchman, Barbara. *Stilwell and the American Experience in China* (New York, 1970).

Turner, Katharine C. *Red Men Calling on the Great White Father* (Norman, 1951).

Wardell, Morris. *A Political History of the Cherokee Nation* (Norman, 1938).

Warren, Harris G. *Herbert Hoover and the Great Depression* (New York, 1959).

Westerfield, H. Bradford. *Foreign Policy and Party Politics: Pearl Harbor to Korea* (New Haven, 1955).

Weyl, Nathaniel and Sylvia. *The Reconquest of Mexico: The Years of Lázaro Cardenas* (New York, 1939).

White, Theodore H., and Annalee Jacoby. *Thunder Out of China* (New York, 1946).

Wood, Bryce. *The Making of the Good Neighbor Policy* (New York, 1961).

Wright, Gordon. *The Ordeal of Total War* (New York, 1968).

Young, Arthur N. *China and the Helping Hand, 1937–1945* (Cambridge, 1963).

*Articles*

Anderson, Paul Y. "Tear Gas, Bayonets and Votes: The President Opens His Reelection Campaign," *Nation*, CXXV (Aug. 17, 1932), 138.

Bastert, Russell H. "The Two American Diplomacies," *Yale Review* (Summer 1960), 518–538.

Bateman, Herman E. "Observations on President Roosevelt's Health During World War II," *Mississippi Valley Historical Review* (June, 1956), 82–102.

Chennault, Claire L. "The Chinese Civil War," *Vital Speeches*, XV (May 15, 1949), 468–474.

"China Yahoo!" *Time*, XLV (January 1, 1945), 28–29.

Cohen, Warren I. "American Observers and the Sino-Soviet Friendship Treaty of August, 1945," *Pacific Historical Review*, XXV (Aug., 1966), 347–349.

——. "The Development of Chinese Communist Policy Toward the United States, 1922–1933," *Orbis* (Spring, 1967), 219–237.

——. "The Development of Chinese Communist Policy Toward the United States, 1934–1945," *Orbis* (Summer, 1967), 551–569.

Dulles, Foster Rhea, and Gerald E. Ridinger. "The Anti-Colonial Policies of Franklin D. Roosevelt," *Political Science Quarterly* (March, 1955), 1–18.

Feis, Herbert. "The Anglo-American Oil Agreement," *Yale Law Journal* LV (Aug., 1946), 1174–1190.

Friend, Theodore. "American Interests and Philippine Independence, 1929–1933," *Philippine Studies,* Vol. 11 (1963), 505–523.

——. "Philippine Independence and the Last Lame-Duck Congress," *Philippine Studies,* Vol. 12 (1964), 260–274.

——. "Philippine Interests and the Mission for Independence, 1929–1932," *Philippine Studies,* Vol. 12 (1964), 63–82.

Halperin, Samuel, and Irvin Oden. "The United States in Search of a Policy: Franklin D. Roosevelt and Palestine," *Review of Politics,* XXIV (July, 1962), 320–41.

"Hurley-Burley," *Time,* XLVI (Dec. 17, 1945), 18–19.

"Hurley Burly," *Newsweek,* XXVI (Dec. 10, 1945), 34–35.

Killigrew, John W. "The Army and the Bonus Incident," *Military Affairs,* XXVI (Summer, 1962), 59–65.

Leahy, William D. "Notes on the Yalta Conference," *Wisconsin Magazine of History,* XXXVIII (Winter, 1954), 67–72, 110–113.

Lisio, Donald J. "A Blunder Becomes Catastrophe: Hoover, the Legion, and the Bonus Army," *Wisconsin Magazine of History,* 51 (Autumn, 1967), 37–50.

Morton, Louis. "Soviet Intervention in the War with Japan," *Foreign Affairs* (July, 1962), 653–662.

"Our Choice in China," *New Republic,* CXIII (Dec. 10, 1945), 781–782.

"Out Swinging," *Time,* XLVI (Dec. 10, 1945), 18–19.

Shewmaker, Kenneth E. "The 'Agrarian Reformer' Myth," *China Quarterly* (April–June 1968), 66–81.

——. "The Mandate of Heavan vs. U.S. Newsmen in China," *Journalism Quarterly,* Vol. 46, No. 2 (Summer, 1969), 274–280.

Stewart, Maxwell S. "Exit Pat Hurley," *Nation,* CLXI (Dec. 8, 1945), 614–615.

——. "The Myth of Patrick J. Hurley," *Nation,* CLXI (Nov. 10, 1945), 489–491.

Vivian, James F., and Jean H. "The Bonus March of 1932: The Role of General George Van Horn Moseley," *Wisconsin Magazine of History,* 51 (Autumn, 1967), 26–36.

Wertenbaker, Charles. "The China Lobby," *Reporter,* VI (April 15 and 29, 1952).

*Dissertations*

Smith, Thomas. "Alone in China: Patrick J. Hurley's Attempt to Unify China, 1944–1945," unpublished doctoral dissertation, University of Oklahoma, 1966.

Sneller, Maurice P., Jr. "The Bonus March of 1932: A Study of Depression Leadership and its Legacy," unpublished doctoral dissertation, University of Virginia, 1960.

# Index

Acheson, Dean, 130-131, 260, 290-293, 296, 320, 322
Aguinaldo, Emilio, 63
Amerasia, 268, 283, 293
American China Policy Association, 286
American League for a Free Palestine, 112
American Legion, 58
American Military Observer Section, 188
American Palestine Committee, 112
Anderson, Clinton, 272, 299
Anderson, Paul Y., 57
As-Said, Nuri, 113
Atcheson, George, 188, 190, 237, 261, 273, 322
Atlantic Charter, 118, 126, 238, 243, 248, 291
*Atlantic Monthly*, 302, 303
Atlee, Clement, 251

Bacone College, 10
Balfour, Arthur J., 111
Balfour Declaration, 111
Ballantine, Joseph, 147
Ballinger, Webster, 20, 22
Barrett, David, 167, 180
Barrett, Frank, 301
Ben-Gurion, David, 110-111
Ben Youssef, Sidi Mohammed, 110
Berle, Adolf A., 97
Bertram, James, 200
Bingham, Hiram, 69, 74
Bird, Willis, 180
Bohlen, Charles E., 128

Bonus Expeditionary Force, 47-48, 54-57, 61
Borah, William E., 41-43, 74
Brandeis, Louis, 112
Brett, Col. George, 104, 308-309
Bridges, Styles, 278
British Army Aid Group, 240
Byrnes, James, 229, 232, 257, 260, 266, 271, 275

Cairo Conference, 123, 144
Caldwell, Roy, 28
Camacho, Manuel, 98
Cardenas, Lázaro, 83, 88, 93, 314; approaches Sinclair Company for settlement, 91-92; nationalizes U.S. oil property, 85; proposal for settling oil controversy, 89-90
Celler, Emanuel, 114
Chambers, Whittaker, 283
Chapin, Roy, 79
Chavez, Dennis, 298, 300
Chen Cheng, 177
Chennault, Claire, 124, 139, 143, 240
Chiang Ching-kuo, 228
Chiang Kai-shek, 122, 185, 315; asks U.S. to join in agreement with U.S.S.R., 227; conflict with Stilwell, 146; desire for U.S. aid and military mission, 253; desires U.S. as advisor in relations with U.S.S.R., 220; problems in government of China, 138; rejects Communist proposals, 172-173; reluctance to reform his army, 142;

337

Library of Congress Cataloging in Publication Data
(For library cataloging purposes only)

Buhite, Russell D.
    Patrick J. Hurley and American foreign policy.

    Bibliography: p.
    1. Hurley, Patrick Jay, 1883–1963.   2. United
States—Foreign relations—1933–1945.
E748.H96B83        327'.2'0924 [B]        72-10917
ISBN 0-8014-0751-6

*Patrick J. Hurley and*
*American Foreign Policy*

Designed by R. E. Rosenbaum.
Composed by Vail-Ballou Press, Inc.,
in 10 point linotype Caledonia, 3 points leaded,
with display lines in monotype Deepdene
Printed letterpress from type by Vail-Ballou Press
on Warren's 1854 text, 60 pound basis,
with the Cornell University Press watermark.
Bound by Vail-Ballou Press
in Columbia book cloth
and stamped in All Purpose foil.